BRIGHTER
THAN THE
BAGHDAD
SUN

BRIGHTER THAN THE BAGHDAD SUN

Saddam Hussein's Nuclear Threat to the United States

Shyam Bhatia and
Daniel McGrory

Since 1947
REGNERY
PUBLISHING, INC.
An Eagle Publishing Company • Washington, DC

Library of Congress Cataloging-in-Publication Data

Bhatia, Shyam, 1950-
Brighter than the Baghdad sun : Saddam Hussein's nuclear threat to the United States / Shyam Bhatia, Daniel McGrory.
p. cm.
Includes index.
ISBN 0-89526-251-7
1. Nuclear weapons—Iraq. 2. Iraq—Military policy. 3. Hussein, Saddam, 1937-
4. Persian Gulf War, 1991. 5. Nuclear arms control—Iraq. 6. United Nations. Special Commission on Iraq. 7. United States—Military policy.
I. Title: Saddam Hussein's nuclear threat to the United States. II. McGrory, Daniel. III. Title.

UA853.I72 B43 2000
327.1'747'09567—dc21   00-021944

Published in the United States by
Regnery Publishing, Inc.
An Eagle Publishing Company
One Massachusetts Avenue, NW
Washington, DC 20001
www.regnery.com

First published in Great Britain in 1999
by Little, Brown and Company

Distributed to the trade by
National Book Network
4720-A Boston Way
Lanham, MD 20706

Printed on acid-free paper
Manufactured in the United States of America

10 9 8 7 6 5 4 3 2 1

Books are available in quantity for promotional or premium use. Write to Director of Special Sales, Regnery Publishing, Inc., One Massachusetts Avenue, NW, Washington, DC 20001, for information on discounts and terms or call (202) 216-0600.

For Crispin, Rupert, Anna and James

CONTENTS

ACKNOWLEDGEMENTS

A brave band of Iraqi men and women helped us with our research. Some still live in Iraq and others are in exile abroad until such time as it is safe for them to return. We have not named them at their own request and for their own security, but they know who they are and we salute them for their courage in sharing their insights with us.

Foremost among those we can name are Hussein and Berniece Shahristani. Their idealism and selfless dedication to improving the welfare of their people is an inspiring reminder of a decent Iraq that has somehow managed to survive the monstrous regime of Saddam Hussein.

In London, Sahib Al Hakim, of Iraqi Human Rights, and Zaab Sethna from the Iraqi National Congress cheerfully allowed us to tap their resources, as did Mark Gutteridge in Coventry and Tim Trevan and Terry Taylor at the International Institute of Strategic Studies in London.

In the United States we were fortunate to have access to Rolf Ekeus, David Kay, Bob Galluci, Dave Dorn and Scott Ritter. We also acknowledge with gratitude the scholarship of Marvin Miller at MIT in Boston and that of Paul Leventhal and Steve Dolley at the Nuclear Control Institute in Washington, DC.

Last but not least we thank Faith Evans, Alan Samson and Caroline North for their patience and encouragement throughout the preparation of this book.

PROLOGUE

Zakho, northern Iraq, March 1991

Nobody gets a second chance to escape from Saddam Hussein.

Hassan was working for the Iraqi president's most cherished secret project and knew what happened to defectors who were caught.

With every step on the narrow mountain pass Hassan sank ankle deep in the mud and snow. Driven by fear, he never noticed his hands and feet were cut and bleeding. He trudged on, wondering whether anyone would believe his story of what Saddam was planning to do to his enemies. Shielding his eyes against the driving blizzard he could just make out the shape of four American Marines, about a hundred yards ahead of him, who were offering bread to the outstretched hands of a thousand Iraqi refugees.

Hassan barely had strength enough to shove himself through the heaving line of bodies, always careful to hide his face in case Saddam had sent someone after him. He had to shout to make himself heard. It was his perfect English accent that caught the attention of the Marine captain.

'Please, please take me to your commanding officer,' Hassan pleaded. 'I'm a nuclear engineer. I have information you must know about.'

The swarms of refugees pressing against him were too concerned with grabbing food to bother listening to what this bedraggled figure was trying to say. The American captain wasn't sure if he believed Hassan's story, but for some reason he reached into the crowd and, grabbing the collar of his suit, dragged the scientist toward him. The other Marines edged closer together as some in the crowd took violent exception to what they saw as Hassan's rescue. The captain bundled Hassan towards the Humvee parked on a narrow plateau. It was only then that Hassan realised he was crying.

The captain offered him a cigarette and said, 'You better have a tale worth telling.' Hassan simply nodded.

The Gulf War had just ended and revolts by Saddam's long-suffering people had erupted on Iraq's borders. Without Allied help the rebellion had no chance of succeeding. In the violent confusion all that Saddam's enemies could do was run. Friend and foe were indistinguishable, so the Americans had to be cautious about who they welcomed into their safe haven. The Marine captain had seen a number of military and political defectors escape across the mountains of Kurdistan to Turkey. Hassan was the first scientist to make a run for it.

Hassan tugged his suit jacket around his face as the Humvee bumped down the mountain towards the Iraqi border town of Zakho. He was surprised to see American patrols at every major crossroads. Soldiers were handing out cartons of cigarettes to groups of old Kurdish men who stood on street corners saluting the Americans as their liberators. Children chased after every military vehicle, knowing the drivers would always throw them chocolate bars from their ration packs. The sounds of Bruce Springsteen, Bon Jovi and other rock bands pounded from the army trucks that choked Zakho. The Stars and Stripes and the colours of a dozen army units tugged at the flagpoles of every building the military had commandeered. The retreating Iraqi army had picked clean most buildings and so American engineers cannibalised what they could to provide the most rudimentary comforts. Hassan shook his head in disbelief. His country was being occupied by Western troops and Saddam had made sure the Iraqi people didn't know about it. He asked the Marine captain if the Americans were to march on Baghdad. There was no reply.

The Humvee headed for what the troops had nicknamed 'Spookville', the high school that had been occupied by the Central Intelligence Agency (CIA).

The captain left Hassan at the front door. The scientist was told to wait. Glancing down at his torn and filthy blue pinstripe suit and the handmade shoes that had split open at the toes, Hassan smiled, thinking to himself he hardly looked the prize defector who had evaded Saddam's clutches. If his interrogators thought the same they were soon to realise his worth.

On President George Bush's orders, teams of nuclear, chemical and biological warfare experts had been dispatched to Spookville. Three of them invited Hassan into a sparsely furnished office.

They never introduced themselves, but simply motioned for him to speak first. Hassan asked, 'Do you know Oak Ridge?' The three Americans glanced across at each other. Hassan drew himself up in his chair and said, 'We have built an exact replica of your Oak Ridge nuclear facility in Iraq.' Staring at the disbelief in their faces, Hassan spent the next half-hour explaining how far Saddam's scientists had progressed in building a nuclear bomb. One of the Americans left the room to make a telephone call. Within the hour Hassan found himself strapped into an air force helicopter heading for the Incirlik air base in Turkey. From there he was put on a military transport plane for Andrews Air Force Base near Washington, DC.

He was the first of a half-dozen key defectors who would help unlock the secrets of Saddam's nuclear ambitions. What these highly trained scientists disclosed would change the way

America and its allies looked at Saddam. Their most terrifying revelation was that just before the Allied coalition launched its ground war in Operation Desert Storm, Saddam was going to detonate a nuclear bomb on the outskirts of Kuwait City. He didn't care how many of his own conscripts he killed, knowing the nuclear fallout would envelop tens of thousands of Allied servicemen and women who were dug in along Kuwait's desert borders.

It made the CIA and others realise just how little they still knew about their enemy.

Washington, 2 January 1991

The largest invasion force for nearly a half-century was about to go to war in the Arabian desert and none of the Allied coalition knew what Saddam was going to do.

Deep inside the Pentagon yet another planning meeting was groping for answers.

It was the CIA's delegate who was the first to speak.

'Only dead men tell tales about Saddam Hussein,' he growled. 'Informers in Iraq don't stay alive for long.'

His audience stared at him in silence.

The agent cleared his throat when he was asked to describe Saddam.

'Mad, bad and dangerous,' he said. 'The trouble is we don't know how mad, bad and dangerous he can be.'

The nervous laughter among some of those around the oval table in the Pentagon stopped abruptly as the intelligence officer passed around a reminder of Saddam's cruelty.

'I told you the dead can tell tales,' the agent repeated.

The victims in the colour photographs looked more like statues carved in yellow stone. In one, a mother had her baby clasped to her chest. The woman's eyes stared out with a look of bewilderment. Those who saw it could only wonder what she was thinking when the waves of sarin gas washed over her and a thousand others in the Kurdish mountain village in northern Iraq.

'He could do the same to us,' the CIA veteran said.

According to the latest intelligence, Saddam Hussein had sarin and mustard gas at his disposal as well as a dozen other toxins, including anthrax. Those at the table were then invited to pick up a neatly bound folder that contained what Pentagon planners liked to call a 'worst-case scenario'. The document explained that if Saddam was cornered he would likely retaliate by launching a chemical attack against the half-million men and women camped out in the desert of Saudi Arabia beside their tanks and armoured personnel carriers. A hundred thousand body bags had been quietly shipped to the Gulf just in case.

Despite constant satellite surveillance of Iraq since the August morning in 1990 when Saddam's troops had overrun Kuwait, nobody realised that he could do much worse. At more than twenty secret installations around the Republic of Iraq, in buildings disguised as schools and factories and in laboratories underneath some of Saddam's favourite palaces, was a scientific staff that approached twenty thousand. All of them were working on building the bomb.

The most vital installation was also the most inconspicuous. Saddam had designed it that way. The Al Atheer complex was a low-lying jumble of buildings, shorn up by scaffolding that looked as if it had been dumped in the desert, forty kilometres southeast of Baghdad.

Al Atheer was the key to Saddam's nuclear operation and proof that he had the facility to design a nuclear warhead.

Its existence was of supreme importance to the Iraqi leader, and yet the CIA and other Western intelligence agencies didn't even know it existed. Instead their assessments, computer models and war games mocked as 'fanciful' the idea that Saddam posed any credible nuclear threat.

Geneva, 9 January 1991

In a hotel suite, Secretary of State James Baker handed a letter to Iraq's envoy, Tariq Aziz, when the futile last effort at brokering a diplomatic compromise floundered. Aziz pushed the letter back across the table. Baker, in his slow drawl, insisted that Aziz read it.

'So there can be no misunderstanding.'

Aziz unfolded the paper, read it, looked up at his adversary and then studied the contents again, this time with a perceptible shake in the hand holding the typewritten sheet.

In it George Bush warned the Iraqi president that if he dared use any chemical or biological weapons on Allied troops or any neighbouring countries, 'We will send you back to the pre-industrial age and it will take centuries for Iraq to recover from America's response.'

Aziz struggled to maintain his composure, mumbling he was not some messenger boy and that if Bush wanted to say anything to Saddam Hussein, he should do it himself. Baker stood up to leave. Resting both hands on the table, he leaned towards the Iraqi envoy and said, 'We are clear, aren't we?'

Aziz had no doubt that the United States was prepared to use nuclear weapons. Deep beneath the warm waters of the Persian Gulf two American submarines were already on station. Each possessed the capacity to deliver nuclear retribution.

Baker, like United Nations Secretary-General Javier Pérez de Cuéllar, French President Francois Mitterrand, Soviet President Mikhail Gorbachev and all the other emissaries who sought to broker a deal with Saddam Hussein to obtain Iraq's withdrawal from Kuwait, was left with the conviction that Saddam didn't want a compromise. Baker couldn't fathom why. Iraq's armies were no match for what the Allies had assembled on Iraq's borders. So why was Saddam still marching towards certain defeat?

As he left the failed peace talks an exasperated Baker turned to an aide and asked, 'Are we missing something?'

Baghdad, 15 January 1991

The Volvo bus with blacked-out windows made a sharp turn into el Nassr Street. Its headlights were dimmed as it raced through the dark and silent streets. Baghdad was practising another civil defence emergency drill. The few old men who sat grilling carp and warming themselves over a wood fire at the café beside the River Tigris did not bother to look up as the white bus ghosted past them for the second time in as many hours.

Locked inside were three members of Saddam Hussein's Revolutionary Command Council: Izzat Ibrahim, Iraq's ailing vice-president; General Hamid Mahmoud, Saddam's long-serving private secretary; and Hussein Kamil, Saddam's ambitious son-in-law. Kamil, a former motorcycle outrider and presidential bodyguard, had risen to power through marriage to Saddam's eldest daughter, Raghad, and was now one of the most powerful men in Iraq.

It was a little before midnight, barely thirty-six hours before expiration of the UN's ultimatum for Iraq to pull all its troops out of Kuwait. There was little conversation. Those on board prudently assumed that their vehicle was bugged. They were well used to being driven around Baghdad in darkness so that they would have no idea where they were to rendezvous with their president.

The automatic gears whined as the bus groaned down the slopes of an underground car park. The vehicle disgorged its nervous cargo beside an elevator door that was guarded by eight soldiers from Saddam's personal bodyguard, the Amn Al Khass. After the usual exhaustive search by those charged with protecting their leader, the three men were marched into that night's subterranean command post somewhere in the suburbs of Baghdad.

These places all looked alike. It could have been the same room every night for all they knew – though it was generally believed that Saddam randomly swapped his meeting places to stay a step ahead of would-be assassins. Staff at a dozen of his residences routinely prepared three different dishes for dinner, never knowing where Saddam would dine.

The metal doors swung open. Inside, four places were set at the dark oak table, each with a water decanter, crystal glasses, a bowl of grapes and a fresh notepad. A spotlight picked out a life-size portrait of Saddam, his scimitar drawn, dressed in flowing white Bedouin robes and seated astride a stallion.

At the end of the room Saddam sat in a high-backed black leather chair, the receding crown of hair just visible through a fog of cigar smoke. A manila folder marked 'PC3' in Saddam's own handwriting – his code for 'Petro Chemical 3' – rested on the desk in front of him. This uninspiring title betrayed the lingering influence of Soviet scientists who used to work for Saddam, and revealed nothing of its true significance.

All present knew that inside the folder were details of Iraq's Manhattan Project, an $18 billion, nineteen-year attempt to build a nuclear bomb that had been mired in secrecy, deceit and murder. Saddam had shown his willingness to sacrifice millions of Iraqis to pursue his ultimate obsession of joining the nuclear club. Hospitals were left short of equipment, factories laboured with outdated technology and debts to his neighbours of $60 billion were left outstanding while Iraq's oil money was squandered on building the bomb.

Izzat Ibrahim broke the tense silence. This Saddam loyalist was dying of lung cancer and had the least to fear from antagonising the leader. 'Your Excellency's suggestions for defending our missile batteries have been implemented and all that remains . . .' He did not get a chance to finish the sentence.

Saddam stood up and shouted, 'I want no more excuses. No more apologies. We haven't any more time.'

The president fixed his stare on his son-in-law, Kamil, who among his many titles and responsibilities had the task of delivering the bomb.

'Our enemies will not wait much longer to attack us from the skies, but they are not ready for all-out war. Give me the bomb and we will avenge the centuries of wrong. Grab every ounce of uranium we have, from every facility we built, from what we have hidden and what we can still steal. Tell every scientist they are ordered never to sleep until they have our means of deliverance.'

Saddam had no way of knowing when – or if – the multinational coalition would send its armies across Iraq's borders. But he was relying on diplomatic initiatives by the French and Russians and others who fancied themselves peacemakers to gain him time to build his bomb.

Those present knew the consequences of contradicting such an order. Hussein Kamil pointed to the one telephone on the desk. Saddam nodded and Kamil immediately called the scientist Jaffar Dhia Jaffar, regarded by many as the father of Iraq's atomic bomb.

No pleasantries were exchanged, no explanations offered for this late-night interruption as Kamil spat out Saddam's orders, mimicking the president's insults and threats. Saddam smiled. His son-in-law was once more demonstrating his suitability for this job. Kamil was there not for his grasp of nuclear fission but for his willingness to make anyone's life a misery to continually prove his loyalty.

Jaffar said little, knowing it was pointless in such circumstances to debate the well-rehearsed technical arguments. He doodled on a piece of paper beside the telephone, his pencil always trailing back to the point where it began. Saddam's plan, first dictated in August 1990, was to loot the highly enriched uranium imported from France and the Soviet Union, melt it down and fabricate a crude device that would be as powerful as the bomb dropped on Hiroshima.

Until now Jaffar had never asked the obvious question: If he did deliver the bomb, would Saddam use it? The physicist shivered, preferring not to dwell on the implications for his countrymen. He was too honourable a man not to have questioned the morality of what Saddam was asking him to do, but Jaffar had suffered for asking questions once before. He had been locked up and tortured in the Abu Ghraib prison and his best friend, the nuclear chemist Hussein Shahristani, was still there.

When George Bush ordered military action against Iraq in the early hours of 17 January 1991, he hoped for a swift victory, with a minimum of casualties. He did not know that Operation Desert Storm would simply be a prelude to yet another conflict, or that it would reveal the degree to which the West had underestimated the ambition of Saddam Hussein and the strength and near-readiness of Iraq's nuclear capabilities.

In Baghdad, men like Jaffar had correctly calculated that, short of having the evidence stare them in the face, few Western experts were likely to surmise that Iraq was so close to realising its nuclear ambition.

Jaffar would say: 'They think we've gone from camels to Cadillacs in fifty years. We'll show them what we can do.'

In January 1991, it was Iraq's accumulation of chemical weapons and its willingness to use them that struck fear into all those who committed troops to fight in the Gulf War.

Every day Allied troops would fumble through practise drills in the desert, trying to wriggle into chemical warfare suits in the few seconds they would get to save their lives. They were taught to inject themselves with an antidote, and lectured time and again never to use it even on your best friend. The order was, save it for yourself. Out there nobody else can help you. Their recurring nightmare was of choking to death as clouds of poison gas drifted across their frontlines. Such was the dread of a chemical attack that it would be years before the West realised Saddam possessed an even greater threat – the atomic bomb.

The story of how Saddam got the bomb, and how close he came to using it, can now be told.

The testimony of the defectors proved crucial. They were indistinguishable from the thousands of other refugees in filthy clothes who walked for miles across the jagged peaks of Kurdistan or through the marshlands of southern Iraq to escape Saddam's reach.

None of them knew the whole story, but each provided a piece of the jigsaw that over the next nine years helped slowly unravel Saddam's nuclear ambitions. The defectors identified secret laboratories. They listed Western companies that supplied them. They reproduced rough diagrams of blueprints they had seen.

A few did exaggerate. One defector, who had been an engineer at the Tuwaitha complex near Baghdad, claimed that Saddam had actually tested a small nuclear device. Inquiries with the Turkish government and checks of seismograph tests disproved this claim. But there was enough compelling evidence for the West to realise that Iraq's nuclear programme had progressed much further than they had assumed.

What sealed the West's conviction was the escape of one of Saddam's own family – the man he had trusted to deliver him the bomb.

In 1995 Hussein Kamil, Saddam's son-in-law and second in command, escaped across the desert to Jordan with his wife and children to save his own skin. Kamil relished the look on the faces of the American debriefing team as they listened in incredulous silence to his detailed account of one night in October 1990 – three months after the invasion of Kuwait – during which Saddam had calmly weighed the options of where to detonate his nuclear bomb.

During one private session, Kamil claimed that Saddam had said he would like to pack the bomb onto a boat and detonate it in Israel's deep-water harbour of Haifa. Saddam gave up the idea only because he recognised his doomsday boat could never have eluded the coalition's fleet of ships enforcing the UN's trade and weapons embargo.

Intelligence agencies and UN weapons inspectors suspected Kamil was exaggerating to earn himself political asylum in a safe house in Virginia. Kamil was not without personal ambition, but the evidence he produced next proved beyond doubt that he was telling the truth.

Among the documents Kamil had stuffed into the trunk of his armour-plated black Mercedes as he fled Baghdad were pictures of the black box that scientists call a neutron generator. This was the size of a shoebox and looked innocent enough. American scientific experts taking part in Kamil's debriefing knew differently. This is the device that starts the chain reaction leading to an explosion.

Hidden under a wedge of $100 bills in Kamil's tan leather holdall were the blueprints for explosive lenses, an intricate pattern of thirty-two shaped charges arranged like the petals of a tulip. Kamil described to his debriefers how in underground bunkers at a military testing range near Al Atheer, technicians had successfully carried out twenty tests on the lenses. With precision timing measured in millionths of a second, these lenses focus shock waves to ignite the explosive charge wrapped around the nuclear core.

'Make no mistake about it, my friends,' Kamil said. 'He meant to do it. He was going to detonate a bomb before your forces had time to invade our 19th Province. Kuwait, as you call it.'

Saddam's response to the accusations he had a bomb was to dismiss them as 'a cocktail of CIA propaganda and the self-serving ramblings of United Nations weapons inspectors'.

For years Western agents and the weapons teams would joust with Saddam to uncover the secrecy and subterfuge shrouding Iraq's nuclear programme.

It is true that few live to tell tales on Saddam Hussein, especially if they have the misfortune to stumble upon his secrets, or to be privy to them. Saddam's memory is long and so is the arm of his security forces. The execution of his vengeance is brutal and absolute.

For that reason, most of the real heroes of this book must remain faceless. Many have been the victims of Saddam's cruelty. None is completely safe even though these people may now live abroad in relative freedom. Some of their stories are extraordinary. This book could not have been written without their trust and the credible information which they generously and bravely entrusted to us. Through their individual and accumulated stories, compiled over a period of eight years, we have been able to construct what we are confident is an accurate account of Saddam's steady acquisition of nuclear technology.

We are also able to draw portraits of the individuals who have been instrumental in forging the weapons of ultimate destruction upon which the President for Life of Iraq – or his successors – may yet depend to retain absolute power.

Most alarmingly, the testimony of those charged with uncovering Saddam's secrets reveals how the West and its leaders have failed to grasp the full extent of the Iraqi dictator's menace.

1

MONICA'S WAR

Washington, December 1998

President Clinton had stayed up late into the night talking to his lawyers. They had become something of a permanent fixture wandering the White House corridors as Clinton struggled to explain why he had been caught lying about his relationship with a young intern named Monica Lewinsky.

His aides were at pains to insist during their daily press briefings that the president was not neglecting his duties. They deliberately leaked how after spending six hours with his lawyers he had walked into a meeting with his national security advisers over Iraq and took up where he had left off at their previous get-together. Some of the military aides in the room were not so convinced. They thought the president seemed preoccupied.

He had good reason to be. It was 15 December 1998, and his critics in the House of Representatives were moving to impeach him. But the White House had a diversion planned. Clinton's team already knew that Richard Butler, the head of the United Nations Special Commission (UNSCOM) – the

group responsible for inspecting Iraq's stockpile of weapons –
was poised to deliver a damning report revealing that Saddam
Hussein's deceptions had continually thwarted UN inspectors, and that as a result UNSCOM was all but finished.
Clinton was aware that, once Butler's report was in hand, he
would have little option but to launch air strikes against Iraq,
in what would become known as Operation Desert Fox. For
Clinton, the timing couldn't have been more fortuitous.

In fact, the targets had been picked weeks before. The Joint
Chiefs and the CIA told the president he should have attacked
the previous month when Iraqi generals in the south signalled
they were ready to stage a coup against Saddam. But Bill
Clinton had been sceptical. He had heard such stories before.
He had even secretly bankrolled other Iraqi officers only to
find that they had been working for Saddam and were being
used by Baghdad to flush out traitors in an operation sub-
sidised by America. This time the officers and men of Iraq's
XI Mechanised Division, based in Al Amarah in southern
Iraq, did make their move, but Clinton turned his back on
them and the coup was extinguished with predictable ferocity.
The reports of mass executions that filtered through never
caused much of a stir in Washington, which was far too
absorbed with the Lewinsky affair to notice.

The strain was showing in Clinton's physical appearance.
Staff had to apply more than a light touch of make-up before
his public appearances to camouflage the bags under his eyes
and the sallow complexion. White House sources told how
aides were sworn to secrecy about the screaming matches
between the president and his wife, Hillary.

Reports had reached State Department diplomats of how
one morning she had burst into the room while members of
President Clinton's security team were briefing him about
Saddam's efforts to redeploy some of his Republican Guard
units. Throwing a newspaper at her husband that contained
some new humiliating revelation about his sexual adventures
with the plump White House intern, the first lady slapped

him across the face. Embarrassed at what they were witnessing, the security team did not know whether to leave. They had no need. After a barrage of insults Mrs Clinton stormed out, threatening to end their sham marriage. Clinton stood stunned. He tried to make light of Hillary's tantrum and quickly returned to the agenda in front of him. To those in the room it was clear the president was no longer concentrating.

CIA sources told how, when intelligence officers first tried to explain how this winter coup in Al Amarah could succeed if it had American firepower to support it, they noticed that Clinton was gazing down at a copy of Independent Counsel Kenneth Starr's report detailing the president's alleged impeachable offenses. His complexion was florid. Many noticed that he was more short-tempered than usual, and visitors to the Oval Office were given only a few minutes to make their pitch, whatever the subject.

There was festering discontent that his lawyers had a free run of the Oval Office and enjoyed more access to the president than his national security advisers. Aides would apologise that his door was closed again and gently explain that to Clinton, Kenneth Starr was a bigger menace than Saddam.

He and his lawyers were so engrossed in preparing detailed responses to Starr's accusations of perjury, witness tampering and obstruction of evidence that the president was oblivious to the opportunity he was being given to rid himself of Saddam.

The coup plotters told the CIA they had sympathisers in place across Iraq. They claimed to have on their side one of Saddam's most trusted lieutenants, who would murder the Iraqi leader once the Mechanised Division moved out of its barracks. Clinton seemed to ignore the evidence that up to 15 per cent of the Republican Guard, along with tens of thousands of regular soldiers, had deserted. All they needed from the White House was a promise to use America's air force to strike Iraqi armour as it moved south to take on this uprising. Try as they might through the late autumn months they could not get Clinton to listen.

By December – with the impeachment hearings in the House drawing nearer – Clinton switched tack. Senior White House aides told how the president needed a diversion from the endless diet of headlines about Monica. He also needed to distract America's attention.

He had, however, sharply admonished one of his staff who dared joke that they needed a war like in *Wag the Dog*, the film in which a president mired by scandal launches an imaginary attack against Albania to distract attention from problems at home and secure his reelection. The parallel was obvious.

Clinton was preoccupied with his own political survival, not Saddam's. He never considered resigning but was haunted by the thought that he would end his presidency as a laughingstock. An arrogant man, Clinton needed to restore his personal credibility, and how better than by going to war against America's bogeyman?

Certainly the timing of this latest crisis in Baghdad was propitious. On the morning of 16 December, at 7 AM Eastern Time, Clinton walked into the Oval Office and pointedly ignored the press clippings about the latest episode of 'Interngate'. His national security advisers fanned out around him as the president ordered that 200 aircraft, 20 warships, and 15 B52 long-range bombers should unload 400 cruise missiles on Iraq that afternoon. The UN Security Council was not even due to meet to discuss Richard Butler's UNSCOM report until later that morning.

Yet Clinton had already locked in the orders to fire at 3:10 that same afternoon. The first Tomahawk missiles were in the air when Clinton contacted Congress. His speechwriters were busy working on his address to the nation in which Saddam would be warned, 'If you act recklessly, you will pay a heavy price.'

The irony was not lost on Congress. They were about to deal with a president who behaved recklessly in love and who many now believed was behaving recklessly at war. But with American pilots and sailors in action in the Persian Gulf, the

House of Representatives had no choice but to delay its impeachment proceedings.

Many congressmen did so reluctantly, breaking with the tradition of offering bipartisan support when American forces are at war. This time his critics openly accused the president of using American servicemen and women for his own selfish needs to deflect the headlines away from Monica.

Ninety minutes before the announcement from Capitol Hill, Clinton had gone on television to explain why after months of prevaricating he was ordering air strikes.

Monica intruded even at this moment of international high drama. Looking straight into the camera Clinton said, 'Let me close by addressing one other issue. Saddam Hussein and the other enemies of peace may have thought that the serious debate currently before the House of Representatives would distract Americans or weaken our resolve to face him down. But once more, the United States has proven that although we are never eager to use force, when we must act in America's vital interests, we will do so.'

Clinton had won breathing space, and his aides naively expected that Congress would be loath to censure the commander-in-chief during armed conflict, particularly as they were sure he would win this final battle with Saddam.

What nobody outside the Oval Office knew that morning was that the only real target was the Iraqi desert fox himself. This operation was all about killing Saddam.

For months the CIA had been using spies insinuated among the weapons inspectors to monitor Saddam Hussein's movements. Senior intelligence officers believed they had tracked the Iraqi leader to two hideouts – the first, a capacious villa on the outskirts of Baghdad and the other, an undistinguished army barracks in the capital which had one of the deepest bunkers in Iraq. Both sites were bombed in the first salvo of missiles.

But American officials didn't know that the Iraqis had discovered the eavesdropping operation and that Saddam had moved elsewhere. The missiles missed their target again.

To taunt his attackers, Saddam appeared on the Al Jazira television satellite channel, even as Baghdad was being bombarded, as evidence of his continued survival. Clinton's despair was obvious only to those closest to him. He had never let on that killing Saddam was the true purpose of this mission. That, after all, was against the law. Clinton was in enough trouble with Congress without having to explain why for the past four years he was in breach of Executive Order 12333, which forbids a president to plot the assassination of a foreign leader.

The evidence for this intended coup is hidden in the secret files of the CIA, which list in minute detail the Agency's various spectacular failures. In the summer of 1996 an Iraqi intelligence officer impudently contacted the CIA station chief in Amman, on captured CIA communications equipment, to boast that Baghdad knew of the plot to use a former army chief of staff to shoot Saddam. Before ending the one-way conversation the Iraqi told the American how all plotters had been rounded up and executed, 'so pack your bags and go home.'

Throughout his presidency, yearning for the 'silver bullet' has been at the heart of Clinton's flawed strategy for dealing with Saddam. The most difficult decisions had been taken before Clinton's inauguration in January 1993. Under President George Bush the Allies had expelled Saddam from Kuwait but were divided about what to do with him. Electioneering interrupted Bush's efforts to forge an effective opposition to Saddam that would replace the Ba'athist totalitarian regime with a democratic alternative.

Clinton didn't care about such strategies. He came to power criticising Bush for spending too much time on Iraq and not enough on the economy, health care and education. It was no accident that his first overseas trip as president was to the Far East, which is where Clinton thought America's long-term economic future lay. In the early days of his administration

Clinton did not believe that Saddam posed much of a threat to Iraq's neighbours or to American forces still in the Gulf.

He was swiftly reminded of Saddam's menace with the discovery of a crude plot to blow up George Bush's motorcade when the former president arrived in Kuwait to receive the thanks of its grateful government and people. Clinton's retaliation was immediate but meek. He ordered the bombing of the intelligence headquarters building in Baghdad.

This was the kind of 'quick fix' that appealed to Clinton. There were no US casualties, no Iraqi civilian was injured or killed and American laser-guided weapons looked impressive on the early evening bulletins. The editorial writers were generous in their praise of the youthful and apparently resolute new president. But none of this solved the problem of what to do with a Saddam hell-bent on rearming his country with nuclear, chemical and biological weapons.

Clinton's short attention span, and his hopes that an assassin could neatly do the job for him, meant that the president could not be bothered to nurture the fledgling Iraqi opposition. By the same token the UNSCOM weapons inspectors who uncovered evidence that Saddam was cheating would find that long-promised American support was missing when it was needed most.

Former inspectors revealed that UNSCOM would plead with the White House to back an intricate six-month plan to ensnare Saddam once and for all. The Clinton administration wanted results faster than that and so would lose interest after a matter of weeks. Privately Clinton would offer American military support for the UNSCOM operation only to change his mind.

It was a dishonest policy that would sacrifice the lives of innocent people to mask the single aim of killing Saddam.

The Clinton administration had no interest in getting embroiled with Iraqi insurgents who wanted to supplant the apparatus of the entire Ba'athist state. The Clinton philosophy was far simpler – cut the head off the beast and the beast dies.

He would brush aside those analysts in the National Security Council who warned that simply replacing Saddam was not the answer.

Clinton's greatest betrayal came in the spring of 1995. Leaders of the Iraqi National Congress (INC), which George Bush had helped create as his final legacy, told CIA agents in the region that they had collected enough men and weapons to start an uprising in the mountain villages of northern Iraq. They were sure that once they started shooting, thousands of Iraqi conscripts would desert and join them in what was a declared United Nations safe haven.

CIA agents who had spent months in Iraqi towns like Zakho believed that at long last their chance had come and even alerted their old enemy, Iran, to move some of its troops to the border. The State Department wanted Tehran to know that since Saddam's end was in sight this was an ideal time for the mullahs to settle scores with local adversaries like the left-wing terrorists from the Mujahedeen Khalq, which had enjoyed Saddam's protection for so long. What the CIA hoped was that Saddam in turn would have to shunt troops to the Iranian border and divert them away from the incipient uprising.

The Iranians wanted proof of what the CIA was offering them. Because US diplomats were not meant to be in direct contact with the Iranians, the INC had to act as go-between in a near farcical operation. INC officials invited US and Iranian diplomats to the Khadra hotel in Salahadin in northern Iraq; once there, the rival diplomats stood at opposite ends of a long corridor while an INC representative carried written details of the plan to the Iranians.

Several Iraqi commanders did take the bait and defected with their army units – only to find the White House had abandoned them.

Many of the young advisers whom Clinton had brought with him from Arkansas panicked. They were scared that Iraq would fragment. They frightened their president with visions of the Kurds in the north extending their fight to the foothills of Turkey. They would sit for hours with Clinton, worrying that the Shiite groups in the south would side with Iran and that this was a war they couldn't control.

Iraq's opposition was never given a chance to prove it could replace the Baghdad dictatorship. The CIA agent who encouraged the uprising was suddenly told to inform the Kurdish leaders in the INC coalition that 'all bets were off'. That message came even as Saddam's tanks closed in on their strongholds.

In his book *Tyranny's Ally*, David Wurmser describes how, in order to save themselves, the Kurdish factions, including the powerful Kurdish Democratic Party (KDP), gave up the fight and pledged their loyalty to Saddam, insisting they had never been part of the plot. The Iraqi president didn't believe them and slaughtered tens of thousands of them as a warning to others.

This betrayal never featured on American television. Clinton's slick information machine made sure of that. Months later, when anguished survivors of this bloody episode complained of the White House's treachery, Clinton's team retaliated by getting American diplomats in Amman to dismiss the INC in the *Los Angeles Times* as 'a feckless bunch who couldn't hold up a 7-Eleven'. Later these same diplomats would claim that this insurrection was sponsored by 'maverick CIA operatives' acting on their own in northern Iraq. It would take several more months before former CIA Director John Deutch confessed to ABC anchorman Peter Jennings that the White House had indeed promised air support to the Kurds and that none of his agents had ever acted on his own.

A letter emerged, written by Vice-President Al Gore in August 1993 and sent in Clinton's name, promising INC President Ahmed Chalabi that the United States 'affirms its solid commitment to your struggle' and swearing that Americans 'will not turn our backs'.

Clinton's betrayal of the INC meant that a tribal uprising

that erupted immediately afterwards on the outskirts of the capital had even less of a chance succeeding.

Strangely, this uprising had begun as a family affair. In a typical display of monstrous behaviour Saddam's eldest son, Uday, had raped the teenage daughter of a high-ranking air force officer from the Dulayami tribe, who were among the regime's most loyal followers.

Iraqi opposition leaders described how the aggrieved father, accompanied by a close friend of Saddam, General Muhammad Madhlum al-Dulayami, went to see the Iraqi leader to demand he punish his son. Instead the two officers found themselves in prison. After weeks of torture they were released, but the general wanted revenge and persuaded several leading air force and Republican Guard officers to join in a coup. He even sought the support of the INC and was secretly taken to meet CIA agents in northern Iraq.

America had yet to realise that Saddam had his spies inside the INC, and within days of this covert meeting the general and other ringleaders were arrested. When their families asked for their return, Saddam promised he would send them home. The following day their dismembered bodies were shipped back to their tribal stronghold at Ramadi.

In the riots that followed, Saddam's handpicked governor of the region was murdered. Thousands took to the streets. The Dulayami, the INC and others radioed the CIA, pleading for the American jets that were patrolling the no-fly zone above them to turn their rockets on the approaching Iraqi tank divisions. The United States never responded.

Still the rebellion grew, with more tribes joining the insurrection that Saddam's special forces, led by his younger son, Qusay, could not quell. Elite Republican Guard units changed sides and supported an attack on the notorious Abu Ghraib prison in the western outskirts of Baghdad, certain of finding more recruits for the uprising. They also tried to seize a radio station to broadcast a call to arms to other dissident army units. They again begged the Americans for help, but it never came. Without the critical American support, the rebellion could not sustain itself once Saddam was given time to mobilise his forces. This uprising, like all the others, was eventually crushed.

The Clinton administration made sure this terrible failure was never broadcast to the American people.

Whatever it may say, the White House has never wanted a revolution in Iraq. It has sought to persuade its supporters that Saddam alone is to blame. Get rid of him and relations with America and the rest of the world could be dramatically repaired.

Consistent with this simplistic policy that demanded a 'quick kill', the Clinton administration switched its support to a group of disaffected army officers who they thought could deliver the silver bullet. They were known as the Wifaq movement. CIA officers who for years had been working with the INC and other Iraqi dissident groups were kept in the dark about this plot.

Asked two years later, in 1997, what exactly Clinton's policy was in those days, Assistant Secretary of State Robert Pelletreau admitted on American television, 'The only way we were going to succeed in unseating the existing regime was through an internal military coup against it.'

This was further proof, if it was needed, why the White House had so cynically deserted the earlier uprisings. Rather than risk US troops, the Clinton administration found it much more convenient to try to co-opt one of a half-dozen generals who could get close enough to Saddam to murder him. When in the summer of 1995 Saddam's son-in-law, Hussein Kamil, defected to Jordan, the CIA was as interested in extracting the names of any other would-be assassins among the army's high command as in the nuclear secrets he was carrying with him.

Among the few privy to the White House's obsession with finding someone to fire the silver bullet was Washington's long-term ally King Hussein of Jordan, who was alarmed by this secret change in US policy. According to a senior Jordanian diplomat, King Hussein flew to London in September 1995 to warn INC President Ahmed Chalabi that all Clinton was really looking for was an assassin. The warning came too late.

By then Clinton had approved $6 million for Wifaq. He made sure the money could not be traced back to the White House and didn't want to know how Wifaq intended to dispatch Saddam. The first installment was used to open a Wifaq office in Amman and a radio station.

Privately, King Hussein pleaded with Clinton not to trust these people. He told the president how George Bush had shunned such contacts, realising they were riddled with Saddam's double agents. Clinton ignored the king – with fatal consequences. Weeks later, in October 1995, a bomb destroyed the INC headquarters in northern Iraq, killing twenty-nine people. The INC would prove that Wifaq agents planted the device. The CIA ignored that evidence even after one of the bomb-makers admitted in a videotaped message sent in March 1996 to the Arab press that Saddam had ordered him to kill the INC president, Chalabi.

The CIA was under pressure from President Clinton to deliver and was struggling to explain how they could be spending so much money on assassination plots and yet their target was still breathing.

Clinton was far too cunning ever to publicly admit his game plan was to assassinate Saddam. The reasons were obvious. Of course, he knew any such public admission would be a flagrant violation of Executive Order 12333. But even beyond that, every day that Saddam stayed alive was evidence of Clinton's failure. It was better to hide true policy objectives with sound bites like 'keeping Saddam contained in his box' and 'degrading' his weapons of mass destruction.

The White House used to talk about destroying these weapons, but Clinton recognised this was impossible and subtly shifted ground. His critics felt the president enjoyed a sympathetic press and were frustrated when Clinton was allowed to claim that sanctions and his so-called 'aggressive containment' policy meant Saddam was no longer a threat to Iraq's neighbours or the minorities within Iraqi borders. Clinton was concerned about preserving his own image and credibility. Word had filtered back to him that allies, particularly those in the Gulf, were wondering whether he was fit to lead the international coalition. This was also a question being asked by millions of Americans. Behind the scenes at the United Nations, diplomats doubted Clinton's leadership credentials. At an impromptu drinks party given by a European ambassador, one senior western diplomat was heard asking, 'Can a man who can't control himself, control the alliance?'

The United Nations and its weapons inspectors posed the same question. Clinton had wrapped himself in the UN flag from the first days of his presidency. He could not conceive that America would ever need to go to war again to defend itself. The United States would instead use its position as the only superpower to support peacekeeping missions abroad. Nevertheless, while professing his faith in multilateralism, Clinton would all too often act unilaterally when it suited his own opinion poll ratings. The United Nations could do little but complain in private. No intervention force was possible without American involvement, so peacekeeping missions began only when the White House said, and ended when Clinton lost interest.

His early experiences in Bosnia, Haiti and Somalia were policy follies and reinforced his personal conviction not to use foot soldiers. In the spring of 1994 Clinton had his aides rethink America's peacekeeping role. The basic conclusion of Presidential Decision Directive 25 was that the United States could not extinguish every bush fire. It was also contemptuous of the UN's ability to resolve conflicts. The directive laid down strict conditions before America would commit troops to any future peacekeeping mission. The first rule was that any such operation had to advance America's interests. To

Clinton that meant his approval ratings. Most importantly, there had to be an assured early exit for American troops.

It did suit Clinton to allow the United Nations to lead the fight against Saddam. This absolved him of responsibility and let Saddam know the entire world, not just America, was against him.

In February 1998, the president ducked the weapons inspectors' pleas for armed intervention when Saddam stopped them from searching his palaces, where the UN team knew vital equipment was hidden. This time UN Secretary-General Kofi Annan said he would go to Baghdad. Clinton expected the world's most senior diplomat to wave the big stick, which would save the American president from having to take a strong stand against the Iraqis. Instead, Annan struck a deal with Saddam, agreeing that the UN teams could launch no surprise inspections of Saddam's palaces and that their mission would be finished within four months. Television reports showed Annan smiling and shaking hands with Saddam, and remarking, 'I think we can do business together.'

The arms inspectors complained about Annan's deal, particularly his concession that UNSCOM teams would have to give advance written warning of their inspections. The agreement also troubled many Pentagon officials, and American critics railed against the UN's appeasement policy. In answer to this criticism, Clinton condemned Annan in private meetings with officials.

But, tellingly, the president told the State Department to back the UN's stance. Just weeks later Saddam predictably reneged on his deal with the UN.

In truth, President Clinton didn't want surprise raids any more than Annan did. Congress had voted for the UNSCOM weapons inspectors' mandate to disarm Iraq, but all Clinton really wanted from UNSCOM was for them to harass Saddam and keep him preoccupied. That was why Clinton's spin doctors invented a sound bite for this, calling it 'aggressive containment'.

The Clinton administration never wanted UNSCOM's inspectors to publicise the most flagrant examples of Saddam's deceit. If they had, the insult to America would have demanded an air strike at the very least. Yet the White House also wanted to keep the squeeze on Saddam to limit his room for manoeuvre. Inevitably, Washington's tactics ended up as a mass of contradictions.

Presidential aides deliberately leaked wildly exaggerated claims about what Saddam was still hiding. By doing so they guaranteed there would never be an end to the searches in the Iraqi desert. The White House insisted Saddam was hiding 200 Scud missiles. UNSCOM inspectors were sure only a dozen Scuds were unaccounted for. If they found the missing dozen the UN teams could say their job was done. But since Washington had set an impossible target of locating 200 missiles, there was no chance that UNSCOM's role would end. This was Clinton's game. He needed UNSCOM to keep up the harassment of Saddam and let the inspectors do the dirty work for him.

The muddle of Clinton's thinking was that he boasted Saddam was no threat and 'safely in his box'. And yet in the next breath Clinton claimed the Iraqi dictator was sitting on 200 deadly rockets that could easily reach Israel, as well as American troops in Saudi Arabia and Kuwait.

When the UNSCOM inspectors tried to call Clinton's bluff by asking for help in tracing the missing missiles, they were rebuffed. Inspectors wanted to launch surprise raids to uncover the dozen Scuds they knew were hidden under Saddam's palaces and the homes of other Iraqi VIPs. The State Department sided with others in the UN Security Council who thought that to be an unwarranted intrusion on the privacy of the Iraqi leader. Heartened by this reluctance to offend diplomatic protocol, Saddam promptly gave the UN a list of his 'private leadership sites' that were off-limits to sneak inspections. It numbered over a thousand.

At times the inspectors felt the White House was sabotaging

their operations. Using its own spies, UNSCOM discovered that a shipment of gyroscopes vital for guidance systems was on its way from Russia to Baghdad. The consignment was found in a warehouse in Jordan, and in August 1995 UNSCOM inspector Scott Ritter asked his go-betweens in the CIA to track the ultimate destination of the gyroscopes. By November the CIA had done nothing. Some of the gyroscopes had by that time been moved into Iraq. Ritter decided UNSCOM's only option was to take the initiative and seize the cargo by themselves. The CIA was embarrassed, but Ritter and his colleagues were not allowed to publicise their find so once again the Americans were not required to punish this flagrant sanctions-busting by a dictator clearly rebuilding his war machine.

The already sour relationship between UNSCOM and the White House deteriorated further with every discovery the inspectors made. Whenever the Clinton administration was reluctantly goaded into taking action, it would launch a few cruise missiles but would refuse to contemplate sending in ground forces to back up the inspectors.

Saddam watched Clinton's lame explanations on the Cable News Network (CNN) and sensed the president's reluctance to engage him in battle. Typically, he began to prod at what he believed was a wounded president to see how he would respond. The Iraqi leader began in April 1997 by flagrantly challenging the no-fly zone. Saddam sent helicopters to Iraq's border with Saudi Arabia, saying they were to fly home pilgrims returning from Mecca. Clinton did nothing, so Saddam got bolder still. That summer he threatened to shoot down the U2 spy planes that America had loaned UNSCOM for surveillance work. Clinton gave orders to ground the flights. Saddam then accused the UN inspectors of being spies. Clinton said nothing to defend them, because he was not about to admit that the CIA had infiltrated a United Nations operation. As a result, the UNSCOM teams – full of genuine inspectors who were not intelligence agents – were abandoned.

Saddam felt confident enough by that October to ban the weapons teams from inspecting sites. Remarkably Clinton then went on television to claim Saddam had never been weaker since the end of the Gulf War and congratulated himself for 'standing strong against a rogue regime.' Embarrassingly, it would take Russia's intervention this time to get Saddam to relent over the UNSCOM teams. America's allies were asking out loud where all this was going to end.

Clinton's failure to eliminate Saddam, and the White House's refusal to back any revolutionary change in Iraqi society, left very few policy choices. National Security Adviser Sandy Berger admitted as much in a late night telephone call to a senior official, Richard Clarke. A National Security Council source revealed that an exasperated Berger told Clarke, 'Face it, we have no strategy on Iraq.'

White House aides conceded they dare not admit that the administration had wasted millions of dollars, and cost countless lives, trying to find an assassin. The best that Clinton and his staff could offer was to support sanctions, which the president told the American people would ultimately bring down Saddam. He knew otherwise, but he had no alternative. This is why he needed UNSCOM: As long as the inspectors suspected Saddam was still hiding weapons of mass destruction, sanctions would remain.

When three members of the UN Security Council – Russia, France and China – proposed easing sanctions, Clinton let slip his personal vindictiveness: 'Sanctions will stay until the end of time or as long as he [Saddam] lasts.' Once again it was plain that Clinton had no intention of supporting UN resolutions, but was determined to follow his own low-risk, low-cost agenda.

The contradictions of US policy came to a head at a public meeting in Dayton, Ohio. Secretary of State Madeleine Albright took the podium with her televised road show and found herself heckled when she described Saddam as the most dangerous man since Hitler. Her audience, unaware of the many botched attempts to assassinate him, asked why the United States in the seven years since the Gulf War had failed to disarm and overthrow the Iraqi dictator. In essence, the question was, If Saddam is such a menace, then why hasn't America done everything in its power to neutralise him? The normally forthright Albright fumbled for a reply, exposing the moral and intellectual bankruptcy of the Clinton administration's arguments.

With his formidable instincts for gauging the public mood, Clinton sensed the American people had no more stomach for another Gulf War than he did. Why should they when he had been telling them that Saddam was safely in his box? In the reelection campaign nobody had questioned his strategy over Iraq. Pundits could not remember his challenger, Bob Dole, mentioning the subject, and with the economy strong, the president had won reelection easily. It did not, however, remove the Iraqi problem, or bring Clinton any closer to a solution.

In all this, Clinton rarely thought to ask the advice of his vice-president, Al Gore. When he did it was a fig leaf, in order to have Gore sign his name on letters to Iraqi opposition leaders. Thus if something went wrong the smoking gun was for once not in Clinton's hands.

Gore was seldom present at meetings with national security advisers, or when the CIA produced its latest intelligence on Saddam. This snub made a mockery of Clinton's election promise to make his vice-president a vital player in the administration. Clinton, it seems, had little regard for Gore's judgement on foreign affairs. Sources reveal that the vice-president moaned to his staff about being excluded, but he did not air his grievances in public, since he was more concerned with protecting his own ambitions to succeed Clinton.

By the time of Operation Desert Fox in late 1998, Gore was content to give the White House a wide berth, thus allowing him to keep his distance from the Lewinsky affair.

Clinton's Iraq policy was, in short, simplistic. The president and his team clung to the belief that removing the tyrant of Baghdad was all that was required to solve the Iraqi situation, but the roots of the Ba'athist regime go deep. Ba'athist policy holds that the individual is subservient to the state. Saddam is at the apex of this system that envisages a Pan-Arab socialist state stretching from the shores of the Atlantic to the Red Sea. This vision, borrowing from a mixture of National Socialism and Marxist-Leninist doctrine, is used to excuse all the human rights abuses done in its name.

This was as totalitarian a system as that run by the Communists in the Soviet Union and Eastern Europe, which America had earlier helped dismantle by supporting the democratic and entrepreneurial forces inside those states. Clinton had neither the vision nor the courage to realise he needed to do the same in Iraq by nurturing similar, broad-based democratic reform movements. Success in Iraq would generate a domino effect throughout the region, smashing the impact of Ba'athism and opening the door to a new era of democracy that the major Arab states have never enjoyed.

Congressional leaders of both parties have never been given a convincing explanation as to why the president waited so long to disburse the $97 million authorised for the Iraqi opposition. Critics accuse Clinton of talking tough, doing little and achieving nothing. Indeed, gesture politics has been the hallmark of Clinton's foreign policy.

When nineteen American servicemen were killed in a terrorist attack on their base in Dhahran, Saudi Arabia, in 1996, Clinton vowed, 'We will not rest in our efforts to find who is responsible for this outrage, to pursue them and to punish them.' In fact the investigation of the Khobar Towers bombing fizzled out within weeks because the Saudi government would not cooperate in confirming America's suspicion that Iran was to blame. Bereaved families characterised the president's handling of the case as 'weak'.

Clinton was to use the same familiar threats to avenge the

car bombing of the US embassies in Kenya and Tanzania. The White House blamed the Saudi billionaire turned terrorist Osama Bin Ladin, but Clinton's response was an ineffectual missile strike on Sudan and Afghanistan, where intelligence experts say Bin Ladin and his followers have their bases.

Operation Desert Fox, the December 1998 bombardment of Iraq, was the grandest gesture of them all. It suited Clinton for his own narrow reasons to authorise the attack, but little was achieved in the seventy-hour air raid on Saddam Hussein's suspected hiding places. The proof of that was the near-clandestine war that the Allies continued to wage through most of 1999.

Throughout that year American and British pilots bombed Iraq almost daily, flying approximately a thousand sorties a month, though these raids received scant media attention in the United States. Friendly Arab governments repeatedly expressed their concern that this kind of low-intensity warfare in which innocent civilians suffered and were sometimes killed was winning sympathy for Saddam.

The State Department has offered no consolation to these valid concerns. Unlike Ronald Reagan or George Bush, Clinton has never had a coherent philosophy at the heart of his foreign policy. When he does try to explain what he is doing he is muddled and contradictory. In justifying Desert Fox, Clinton told his fellow Americans in a televised address how he had to bomb to ensure that the weapons inspectors could keep policing Saddam. But the American president did not use the bombing to force Saddam to let UNSCOM return and continue its job. Quite the contrary. UN surveillance teams were banned from Iraq, and Saddam has had months to rebuild his deadly arsenal away from the prying eyes of international weapons inspectors.

Such attention to detail was hardly to be expected from a man who, when he should have been planning the precise objectives of Desert Fox, was engrossed in answering the eighty-one detailed questions that the House Judiciary Committee had sent him about the Monica Lewinsky scandal.

Ironically, the Desert Fox bombing campaign did not earn Clinton the reprieve he had hoped for. Four days after the bombardment began, the House voted to begin impeachment proceedings. Determined to deny his congressional critics their moment of glory, Clinton trumped them with an extraordinary public relations coup. Desert Fox was ended as mysteriously as it began. Military commanders in the Gulf were not briefed in advance of the president's decision to call off the operation.

Gathering his speechwriters around him, Clinton told them his television address should not last long. He did not want to have to justify in detail what the past seventy hours had been about. The last American pilots were still flying back to their bases as he rehearsed his lines twice while technicians set up their camera in the Oval Office. Clinton scored out a line or two as a make-up artist dabbed at the perspiration glistening on his forehead. For the first time in weeks his aides seemed relaxed as they moved around the office, confident that Clinton would as always deliver a faultless public performance. The president asked for quiet, gulped a glass of water and began to read the twenty-seven paragraphs to explain why he was calling off Desert Fox. A few seconds into his speech, Clinton stumbled over his lines and apologised for it. The strain of Monica was beginning to tell.

What he had to say would have surprised the UNSCOM teams, the Iraqi opposition, the Security Council and his allies. To all of them he promised unswerving support they knew from experience he would never deliver. He swore to defend the Kurds if they were attacked again. Yet on 29 July 1999, his close friend and assistant secretary of state, Strobe Talbott, would write the Kurds to tell them that Washington could not provide any protection for a promised meeting of the opposition national assembly. Patrick Clawson of the Washington-based Centre for Near East Policy tells how the

Kurds had to ask the Iranians to keep a watchful eye on them after the Americans had again let them down. Weapons inspectors were led to believe Clinton would make sure they went back, but by the beginning of the year 2000 they still had not returned. He pledged to work with Radio Free Iraq to counter Saddam's propaganda, but broadcasting equipment was never sent to the opposition groups.

The greatest betrayal has yet to come. Throughout the Free World the American president is justly perceived as the custodian of peace and democratic values. Clinton is unique among international leaders in having the greatest possible access to privileged information and intelligence about the potent threat that Saddam remains. Narrow self-interest and lack of personal political courage are the reasons why Clinton has ducked the fight. The legacy he hands over to his successor is far more dangerous than the one he inherited.

Given the significant threat Saddam posed to the United States before Bill Clinton gained the White House, that is a frightening thought.

2

THE BEACH BALL

Baghdad, October 1990

Saddam Hussein stared at his reflection in the shining metallic ball that his son-in-law had awkwardly manoeuvred alongside the president's desk. Slowly tracing his finger along the polished surface of the silver globe, Saddam said, 'So this is what it will look like?'

Hussein Kamil nodded and reached out with his right hand to steady the scale model of the first Arab nuclear bomb that Iraqi weapons experts had spent most of the past year designing.

'Yes, Saidi,' Kamil said in the reverential way he always addressed his father-in-law. 'Our people say it will weigh one tonne, with an explosive force of over 20,000 tonnes of TNT, and they promise it will be twice as powerful as the bomb dropped on Hiroshima.'

Kamil glanced across at the only other person in the room, Dr Jaffar Dhia Jaffar, expecting him to endorse the destructive powers of the device that shimmered in front of them, but Saddam's senior scientist said nothing. He was distracted, trying to calculate in his own mind how quickly this bomb could be tested.

Dr Jaffar watched Saddam gently rolling what looked like a shimmering beach ball across the floor of the mobile trailer home that the president had taken to using to get around Baghdad by night. Jaffar realised this was how their quest to be the first Arab nation to possess a nuclear bomb would end.

Saddam's original order had been for his scientists to create a stockpile of fifty nuclear bombs, which was what he expected from his $18 billion investment.

Seeing the Allied coalition forces tipping into the region in what President Bush was calling Operation Desert Shield, Saddam had first told Dr Jaffar in August of that year to accelerate the process to give him a device, no matter how crude or imperfect – the key was to deliver a bomb to confound his enemies. Two months on, Saddam was anxious to know how this crash programme was progressing.

Anxious to ingratiate himself still further, Kamil snatched a page of calculations from Jaffar's hand and thrust it at the president. For a moment Saddam looked bewildered at the jumble of equations on the typewritten sheet, until Kamil pointed to the last line that confirmed Iraq possessed a stockpile of thirty kilograms of weapons-grade uranium – far, far more than the international community believed.

Saddam knew enough of the physics to appreciate that ten kilograms was sufficient for a bomb and a smile formed at the edges of his mouth. Reassured by this evidence, Saddam looked at the two men standing in front of him and said, 'So I have your word that this mechanism will burn brighter than the Baghdad sun?'

Kamil responded: 'Saidi, under your glorious leadership our scientists have created the most powerful weapon for our Arab nation and our brothers. With this, Excellency, our country will be impregnable.'

The president eased himself awkwardly out of his chair and tapped the sheet of Jaffar's equations on the map that covered an entire wall of his trailer home. Jaffar noticed that Iraq's neighbour, Kuwait, had been erased from the chart and was now called the 19th Province. The air conditioning in the trailer caught a tiny red flag that was pinned on the outer ring road that encircled Kuwait City, pointing to one of the test sites Saddam was considering for what United Nations weapons inspectors were to dub the 'beach ball' bomb.

For the first time Jaffar had no doubts that Saddam meant to detonate this device. The scientist suddenly thought of how many would die. He pictured the hundreds of Iraqi conscripts at checkpoints around the city and the thousands of Kuwaitis trapped in their capital who would be killed in the initial blast. He thought about the Western hostages being held in the city's hotels and at some military installations as human shields who would be consumed in the fireball. He imagined the radiation cloud drifting over the coalition forces digging themselves into the desert along the Saudi border and the warships anchored in the Gulf.

Jaffar shivered and went back to his mental arithmetic, calculating how many more weeks his scientists would need before Saddam could realise his ultimate ambition.

Two more flags were stuck on desert scrubland that was closest to Israel and where Saddam had already positioned most of his Scud missile batteries. Kamil handed him another file. This was one from the weapons-design team working at the top-secret research facility at Al Atheer. Kamil scored his pen along the paragraph that predicted the team could deliver the real 'beach ball' by April 1991 at the latest.

Jaffar coughed nervously and interrupted, 'Your Excellency, this device is too heavy to be delivered by our missiles.'

Saddam held up his hand. 'Why does that matter? Surely it can be moved on one of our tank transporters?' he said, running the sheaf of papers along the straight lines of the highway that connects Baghdad to its neighbours in the Gulf. 'It takes only eight hours to drive to Kuwait City.'

This was not the bomb that Saddam craved. The 'beach

ball' he was pushing back and forth across the ice-blue carpet of his trailer home was the bastard offspring of a much more sophisticated programme. Before he had run out of money in 1990, the first bomb had been scheduled to roll off the assembly line at Al Atheer the following year. It should have been the first of several dozen much more compact devices that Saddam intended to slot into the nosecones of his Badr 2000 missiles.

The crash programme he ordered that night was as much a gamble as his desperate plan of five years before. Back then he had told his scientists to plunder long strips of radioactive metal from his two functioning nuclear reactors and drop them on the tens of thousands of young Iranians forced to advance in suicidal human waves across the Iraqi front lines.

He cursed under his breath at how much his murderous eight-year war with his neighbour, Iran, had cost him and how his treacherous Arab brothers Kuwait and Saudi Arabia had welched on their promise to pay $40 billion each for him to do their dirty work against the ayatollahs in Tehran.

'I will teach them to deceive me,' he said, touching the polished surface of the 'beach ball' that had come to rest at his feet. He never called it a bomb, preferring to talk about 'the mechanism'.

'There are to be no more delays. The mechanism will be ready by February.'

That deadline would be impossible to meet, but Dr Jaffar sensed from the edge in Saddam's voice that this was not the occasion to argue about the delivery date. He always knew Saddam intended to test the mechanism not just once but several times, just as the Great Powers had done after the Second World War.

The physicist was momentarily distracted, imagining the gaseous mushroom cloud erupting from the test site Saddam had called Al Sahara, a vast fenced-off patch of desert scrub in the southwest, one of the possible nuclear proving grounds, close to the borders of Israel and Jordan.

Saddam was breathless now as he paced around his desk, jabbing the air with a Havana cigar to emphasise the urgency of every word. His orders were to scrape up every particle of highly enriched uranium fuel (HEU) given to Baghdad by France and the Soviet Union, chop it into pieces, dissolve it in acid and then reforge it like the segments of an orange that would come together with the greatest force mankind had ever created.

What nobody outside this room realised was the sheer quantity of HEU Saddam had managed to stockpile. Thirteen kilograms had been bought from France for the experimental nuclear reactor that the Israelis had bombed a decade earlier, in 1981. Another seventeen kilograms of weapons-grade-quality uranium had arrived in fits and starts from the Soviet Union for the even smaller experimental reactor gifted to Iraq's pro-communist regime in 1959.

Saddam had entrusted the protection of this uranium to a team picked from his Amn Al Khass bodyguards. They maintained a constant vigil outside the sealed laboratory where the thirty kilograms of weapons-grade fuel was secreted at the country's national nuclear research centre at Tuwaitha, eighteen kilometres south of Baghdad.

Every six months a team of inspectors from the Vienna headquarters of the International Atomic Energy Agency (IAEA) would pitch up in Baghdad to certify that Saddam was using this fuel for peaceful experiments and not siphoning it off for any nefarious purpose, like making a bomb.

One night during a formal dinner being given in the IAEA's honour, when one of the inspectors joked about Iraq's experimenting with a bomb, Kamil had nearly choked. As his bodyguard pummelled him on the back, the head of Iraq's Ministry of Industry and Military Industrialisation made his apologies and left the room.

The courtesy of these inspectors always amused Saddam. The IAEA team was on its honour never to let on to inquisitive outsiders like the CIA how much uranium the members of the nuclear club possessed. Signatories like Iraq gave their word they were telling the truth and, in the spirit of such exercises, this was always accepted without question.

Jaffar had to pretend to laugh as Saddam repeated for what the physicist thought must be the hundredth time the story of how he had let Iraq join this club only so that he could learn how to cheat the IAEA's rules. The deception was made easier by the fact Iraq was allowed to pick the nationalities of the inspectors. Saddam chose teams from Russia and Hungary. That was because these were friendly governments, and the inspectors they sent were so enthralled by the hospitality they received that they spent as little time as possible touring nuclear sites. The IAEA rule book also said that the inspectors could go only where Saddam let them.

Just months after Saddam ordered his crash bomb-making programme at this late-night summit in his trailer home, the IAEA's safeguards director, Jon Jennekens, praised Iraq's cooperation with his agency as exemplary. Saddam cherished the director's report that read: 'The IAEA is not concerned that if Iraq is to be put under great military or diplomatic pressure, the Iraqi leadership would seize its store of HEU and build a nuclear device.'

Saddam did not need to labour the point to his three aides that night about what the consequences would be if the IAEA discovered his intended sleight of hand. If word slipped out that his scientists were working with enriched uranium it could provoke another air strike by the Israelis, and this time there were hundreds of American and British jets in the region that would join in.

'Once the inspectors are gone, Saidi,' Kamil told Saddam, 'we will have time to do as you order and seize the uranium. Jaffar will make sure we have the mechanism ready before the inspectors return in six months.' Jaffar scowled, knowing that the detestable Kamil had as usual passed the buck.

As Kamil blurted out another tiresome stream of flattery, Jaffar pretended to look out of the trailer window, though he knew he could not see anything through the thick, bullet-proof, blacked-out glass.

Saddam had bought twelve of these identical outsized motor homes which had been customised for his own comfort and security. Each was equipped with a computer console on his desk that would put him in touch with any number of his personnel. He stabbed at one of the buttons and told his secretary to call one of his mistresses. Saddam dismissed his visitors with a wave and swivelled around in his chair.

While Jaffar struggled to remove the cumbersome silver 'beach ball', Kamil bowed, kissed his father-in-law's shoulder and hurried from the trailer. Jaffar had barely got out of the door before the trailer slipped into gear and accelerated away. Both Jaffar and Kamil's cars were left locked and watched over by some of Saddam's bodyguards until the president's vehicle disappeared from view.

Kamil didn't bother with pleasantries as he walked away from Jaffar, who was trying to manhandle the scale model of the 'beach ball' bomb into the back of his Japanese car. Kamil drove straight to Al Atheer, rebuking a drowsy security guard at the main gate for not showing the appropriate servility at his arrival and then threatening to have him shot for not putting him through a more rigorous search.

The scientists working the night shift were startled to see the stocky figure of Kamil bustle through the door even though this was his third visit to the site in as many days. He usually kept more civilised hours, but most of the staff dropped what they were doing to gather around him. Kamil had set up rival teams of weapons designers to compete against each other to produce the blueprints for the 'beach ball' bomb that he had displayed in Saddam's trailer home.

He mimicked his father-in-law's bullying histrionics and told the weary technicians they had to increase their efforts to meet Saddam's new ultimatum, adding, 'Al Atheer is like my child and no father likes to see his child fail.'

Al Atheer had been built to escape the scrutiny of any

passing satellite. The electrified fencing was erected so far from the complex that spy cameras missed it in their vague sweep over the area. They also missed the cleverly disguised tank traps and look-out posts surrounding the site. When the CIA saw scaffolding that Kamil had ordered deliberately left clinging to the chimney of the main building, the agents presumed it was still under construction and so didn't warrant further detailed discussion until it was nearer completion. Half the buildings stood purposely empty, but in the occupied cluster where technicians worked around the clock Kamil had procured the most sophisticated lathes, presses and other equipment needed to design and manufacture 'the mechanism'.

Kamil ended his visit that night by slowly repeating the date by which Saddam had to have his bomb. 'There will be no more excuses. You do not have long, so stop standing around staring at me. Get back to work and work harder than you ever have before.'

The only clue the CIA had about Iraq's nuclear progress came by accident when Saddam agreed to let US and British hostages return home a month before the start of the Gulf War. Those who were held in or near the nuclear research centre at Tuwaitha were routinely screened for any evidence of radioactive contamination. Although they were all pronounced fit and healthy, uranium carbide particles were discovered on their clothing. These particles were analysed at the Lawrence Livermore laboratory in California, located in the Livermore Valley eighty kilometres inland from Berkeley. It was only then that American scientists realised the uranium specks had been enriched way beyond the 20 per cent purity needed for routine experiments.

General Colin Powell, the first black officer to head the Joint Chiefs of Staff, vowed to ensure America's intelligence-gathering apparatus would never be left so naked again. He was about to ask a half-million combat personnel to risk their lives against what could be a rainstorm of chemical weapons and he didn't know what to expect from Saddam. This was because some faceless accountants in Washington thought it a waste of money to pay for spies in places like Baghdad.

As a consequence the West had missed Saddam's most precious secret, the existence of Al Atheer. The site remained undiscovered for months after the Gulf War was over. Indeed, its true significance was never fully understood until Kamil's defection in 1995.

The West should have realised Al Atheer's worth when, eleven months before the invasion of Kuwait, a foreign newspaper reporter using bogus credentials tried to gain access to the facility. He almost succeeded, a fact that triggered a frenzied alarm among Iraq's security officials responsible for the nuclear programme.

Farzad Bazoft, a freelance reporter working for the London *Observer*, was shadowed by Iraqi intelligence agents as he drove to within a kilometre of Al Atheer. Thirty-four-year-old Bazoft had arrived in Baghdad to cover local elections in Iraqi Kurdistan. Within days of his arrival, reports started to filter out of Baghdad about an explosion at an ammunition centre south of the capital. Posing as an Indian doctor, he decided to investigate, unaware that he was about to peer through the doorway of the most jealously guarded military site in the whole of Iraq.

Al Qa Qaa, where the explosion happened, spreads for twenty square kilometres. This is where the Iraqis were testing the lenses for a nuclear bomb. North of it was the Balad Al Shuhada factory making solid fuels for rockets. Due south and sandwiched between Al Qa Qaa and the other high-explosives testing centre of Al Hatteen were the low-slung buildings of Al Atheer, built for Saddam's bomb designers, who were known as 'Group 4'.

Bazoft drove his hired ambulance south from Baghdad and turned right off the main highway until he came to the main entrance of Al Qa Qaa. From there he turned left along the boundary fence, stopping every few hundred metres to take soil samples. Less than a kilometre from where he was observed making sketches of the Al Qa Qaa area, Al Atheer's elite workforce was working flat out on Japanese computers to round off the first in a series of five blueprints for a home-produced nuclear bomb.

Fearful that Bazoft might have stumbled upon the secret of the weapons-design centre, Saddam ordered him arrested and held in solitary confinement in Abu Ghraib prison.

From the time of his arrest in September 1989 until his execution the following March, Bazoft was questioned daily and tortured by the Mukhabarat secret police. Foreign diplomats who protested when Bazoft was sentenced to death never believed that Saddam would dare carry out the execution. But the Iraqi leader was convinced that Bazoft was a spy, and signed the order for him to be hanged. The journalist was taken from his cell and dressed in a white shift. When he asked his captors why, Bazoft was told nothing. After being forced to write a letter to his parents, his hands were tied behind his back. Minutes later he was dead.

Bazoft's arrest generated panic among the Group 4 workforce. Convinced that their secret research centre had been uncovered, the scientists feared they could be the victims of another Israeli military strike. They were sent home until the Iraqis were sure that the secrets of Al Atheer were safe.

When the design teams returned, Hussein Kamil was there to meet them. Gathering them together in the administration building, he warned them that the Bazoft affair was proof that Iraq's enemies were forever conspiring against the Motherland. His voice dropped as he announced that a number of their colleagues had been 'disciplined' for the security lapse and would not be returning to Al Atheer. Nobody asked what had become of them. Work and rapid progress towards the bomb were their only insurance policy.

Kamil's protégé and director of Al Atheer was a Scottish-university-trained physicist, Khalid Al Sa'id, whose loyalty to the Ba'ath Party was second to none. He was among the first batch of Iraqi scientists sent to Moscow in 1959, along with others like Hussein Shahristani, a brilliant chemist who would become one of the few who ever tried to thwart Saddam's ambition of acquiring the bomb. Sa'id had no such qualms and, starting at Tuwaitha, where he worked directly under Jaffar, he had been closely associated with Al Atheer since construction started in 1987.

The others in the design teams were an assorted mixture of chemists, metallurgists, computer analysts, engineers of varying descriptions and physicists. Most had been groomed in the secret laboratories at Tuwaitha. The workshops there were numbered, giving no hint to visitors about what was going on inside. In buildings number twenty-three and ninety were the laboratories for perfecting gas diffusion and laser enrichment. The numbers of the buildings were deliberately jumbled so that the teams working on the same projects were dispersed around the complex.

From Tuwaitha the scientists were moved on to other research and development centres. Some joined Dr Jaffar's teams at Tarmiya and Ash Sharqat. These were exact replicas of the American nuclear centre at Oak Ridge, Tennessee, where scientists had designed the bomb dropped on Hiroshima.

In May 1990 all 300 members of the Al Atheer workforce had jammed inside the largest laboratory to witness Kamil presiding over a ribbon-cutting ceremony. Few of the scientists had any respect for him, believing that his authority derived solely from his marriage to Saddam's daughter. But all were afraid of him.

Kamil's speech, parroting Saddam's key phrases, reinforced their sense of insecurity. 'You are the cream of our scientific elite,' he told them. 'The country expects much from you. Those who work hard will be rewarded; those who fail to match up to the country's expectations . . .' He did not complete his sentence. He had no need to.

The fear every scientist had to live with intensified after the invasion of Kuwait and Saddam's decision to go for a crash nuclear development programme. Worst affected were the specialists in charge of chopping up the radioactive HEU before it was sent for dissolving in the nitric acid vats of the LAMA hot metallurgy testing laboratory in Tuwaitha.

Work started immediately after the IAEA inspectors left Tuwaitha at the end of November. Because the fuel was radioactive, it could be handled only through lead-shielded glove boxes, slowing down the process and provoking fresh rounds of abuse from Kamil. The first sample of chopped fuel was due at the LAMA lab on 17 January when fate intervened.

Operation Desert Storm had been launched the night before when Tuwaitha, like other strategic targets, had been heavily bombed. Among the pre-selected targets were the physics and chemical research laboratories in buildings eighty and eighty-five. A thick cloud cover obscured the complex as a squadron of American F117 Stealth bombers closed in on Tuwaitha. The poor weather had diverted them from their original target and on their way back to the US base at Khamis Msheit the pilots were ordered to drop their payloads on what the military planners regarded as a consolation prize – Tuwaitha. As Iraqi surface-to-air missiles streaked up towards him, one pilot misjudged his timing and released his bombs a fraction of a second late. The LAMA lab, his unintended target, went up in smoke.

With it went Saddam's dream of deploying the 'beach ball' bomb before the Allied armies could push him out of Kuwait.

What it did not destroy was his ambition to make Iraq a nuclear power. His pursuit of the bomb had begun in 1972, when few outside Iraq had ever heard his name.

3

GENESIS

Baghdad, spring 1972

The invitation to the new recruits of Department 3000 came in an unexpected telephone call at the end of their first week on the payroll of Saddam's secret nuclear project. It was late in the evening and they argued among themselves about whether to bother answering the white phone, as none could remember it ringing before and, besides, they had just settled an hour-long squabble about where they should go to eat.

Curiosity persuaded Ahmed Hassan to pick up the receiver. There were no pleasantries. Instead the caller berated Hassan for keeping him waiting so long and demanded to know his name. Hassan stuttered as he repeated it twice and then began nodding furiously as though trying to absorb some complicated instruction. Even after the caller had obviously delivered his brusque message Hassan stared at the silent receiver for a minute or more, ignoring the other scientists in the room who sensed his anxiety. 'That was Saddam Hussein's office,' he said finally. 'We have to go to the Al Haitham building at 10 PM, all of us.'

As his colleagues began peppering him with questions,

Hassan held up his hand and said, 'Someone will come to collect us. Before then we mustn't make any calls or tell anyone where we are going.'

They all knew of the Al Haitham complex, a stark eight-storey building on the banks of the Tigris that looked across the river to Saddam's presidential palace. The villas adjoining it on Korneesh Street had been among the most coveted during the days of King Faisal, but most residents had moved out amid rumours that Al Haitham had become a head-quarters of the Mukhabarat secret police.

Forty minutes after the telephone call, six guards in olive green fatigues pushed their way into the laboratory and gestured for the sixteen scientists to follow them. They were ushered on to a minibus which took them on a meandering route around the capital before the vehicle was swallowed up by the electronically controlled metal gates that masked the entrance to the complex.

Without speaking, the men walked in single file along a gravel path, careful to sidestep the sprinklers that were irrigating the lawns. Hassan glanced up and noticed that every light in the building had been turned off.

It was April 1972 and Saddam was beginning to flex his muscles inside the ruling Ba'ath Party. The scientists had heard stories about what Vice-President Saddam did to those who displeased him and had no desire to test such rumours. If they were to be punished the scientists could not understand why, because it was at Saddam's request that they had turned their backs on coveted research posts in foreign universities and returned home to pioneer Iraq's quest for nuclear energy.

Saddam had made his name in the party as an assassin, but within seven years he would become his country's undisputed leader. He admired dictators like Stalin and Hitler. For years he carried a copy of Hitler's *Mein Kampf* around with him, and, like the Nazi Führer, Saddam understood the nature of power. He was convinced that possessing a nuclear bomb would make him unassailable in the region. To do this he

needed to nurture the best minds in Iraq. Saddam would
make it his business to siphon off as much money as the technicians needed to realise his ambition. They didn't know it,
but these scientists were about to become the first of his
nuclear mercenaries.

None that night fancied being the first to reach the enormous smoked glass doors which opened automatically at their
approach. Just inside stood a welcoming committee comprised
of the Institute's Palestinian director, Marwan Nakshbandi,
and two of his deputies, who grinned conspiratorially at their
nervous guests.

'Welcome, my dear friends and colleagues, welcome to the
Al Haitham Institute,' Nakshbandi said as he grasped the
hand of each of his guests in turn. 'Please don't be alarmed,
we are all friends here. You must be in need of refreshment,'
he continued in a lisping, almost effeminate voice and clapped
his hands to summon a dozen half-naked girls who sashayed
barefoot into the room carrying silver trays of canapes and
drinks.

The scientists glanced at each other, unsure if this was some
kind of trap, and stood transfixed as the women eased olives
from under the waistbands of their bikini briefs and into the
chilled glasses of martini.

Hassan thought this choreographed gesture so absurd he
suppressed the urge to laugh, and was glad that he did as the
director announced to the astonished company that the girls
were there to do a great deal more than just serve cocktails.

The women were all Iraqis, all in their twenties, and,
thought Hassan, they all looked curiously similar, as if they
had been cloned by the director. His partner for the evening
gave her name as Mina, but she was clearly uncomfortable in
such a gathering. As the two sat together on a settee, Mina
whispered that she had joined the Institute as a research assistant, but once there was given little choice except to do as she
was told.

Before she could say any more the director reappeared, his

complexion now flushed with drink. It was the signal for the girls to melt away and only when they were safely out of earshot did the director begin to explain that Al Haitham was the heart of Iraq's secret project to build the nuclear bomb. These men were now part of that secret whether they liked it or not. They had been seduced and compromised.

The director warned, 'All of you must ensure that anyone outside this circle remains convinced you are only working on our civil nuclear research programme.'

The rewards for the men of Department 3000 were immediate. Each of them was given a set of car keys for a new Toyota. As he handed the keys around, the director said, 'I hope none of you have any problems about working on our new project.' If they did, no one was brave enough to say so.

Hassan was troubled by what he was being asked to do and six months later confessed as much to one of his superiors whom he thought he could trust. The official told him not to worry and that he would arrange for Hassan to be transferred to other duties. Before that could happen Hassan died in a car crash. His family was told that he was involved in an accident after he had been drinking.

For the scientists who stayed, the job was to divert the uranium fuel from the French reactor that Vice-President Saddam was negotiating to buy from French Premier Jacques Chirac. Saddam promised them riches and privilege beyond the scope of their imagination if they succeeded, but he jailed and executed enough of them in the next twenty-five years to remind them of the price of failure. Al Haitham was his creation, the refinement of his experiences from childhood that sex, money and above all fear could get you anything you desired.

Tikrit, 1943

He always had the same dream as a child. He saw himself running along the unpaved streets of his birthplace, away from the dirt, the cloying heat and the stench of animals roaming through the mud-and-wattle shack that was his first home.

The family's goatherd was often housed in more comfort than the young Saddam, an indignity he would not forget. There was no running water, no electricity and seldom enough space for him to find shelter.

A castle ruin looks down on Tikrit, a disapproving reminder of grander times. This was the birthplace of Saladin, the most revered Muslim fighter who liberated Jerusalem from the Crusaders. Eight hundred years on, this town by the Tigris had little to recommend it to travellers. Saddam was miserable here as a child, though this was conveniently forgotten in later years when he became president and began rewriting his own and Tikrit's history. He lavished money on the town, a good deal of it on monuments to himself, as if to erase the scars of those wretched early years.

His mother, Sabha Tulfah, was a heavy-set woman with broad shoulders and narrow, piercing eyes. Her prominent, angular nose dominated a round face that was seldom creased by a smile. Local gossip had it that Sabha was never granted the dignity of a proper wedding to Saddam's father, Hussein Abdel Majeed. It was said she was abandoned days after discovering she was pregnant and before her marriage vows could be formalised. The official version that Saddam insisted on was that Majeed tragically died before seeing his first son.

Saddam was born on 28 April 1937 at the home of his uncle, Khairallah Tulfah, Sabha's brother. Sabha had to virtually abandon the child to his uncle's care while she went to find work and in his early years Saddam was to endure the taunts of other children over his illegitimacy. But his uncle taught the athletically built boy how to fight and use his physical strength to have his revenge on his enemies. This lesson served Saddam well.

In Europe the drumbeat of war was getting louder and his uncle, a staunch supporter of Iraq's pro-Nazi prime minister,

Rashid Ali Al Kailani, lectured the young Saddam about the evils of British colonial occupation. Khairallah joined in a hopeless military assault on a British airbase. He was dismissed from the army and jailed.

Saddam's loathing of the British was compounded by whispers in the town that his father had once worked as a night-watchman at a base used by British forces and, worse, that his mother was forced into prostitution with some members of the garrison. Whatever the veracity of such stories, Saddam would in later years execute anyone he heard spreading such gossip.

After he was freed from jail Khairallah suggested that Saddam and his mother might do better in Baghdad. Sabha was reluctant to leave, and her son's initial enthusiasm for the idea waned once they were there and the only work she could find was as a chambermaid and waitress in a rundown hotel patronised by labourers and farm workers.

He saw little of his mother in those first days as she was made to work punishing hours, scavenging what food she could from the hotel kitchens for her nine-year-old son. Saddam never allows anyone to refer to those days and was enraged when he realised there was a popular nursery rhyme which began 'Sabha, clear the plates'. It was banned by presidential decree.

A month after arriving in Baghdad, Saddam was to suffer the cruellest indignity of his life.

On an August night he was sitting half hidden in the corner of his mother's room when three men hammered on the door. They had obviously been drinking for hours and proferred money to Sabha. She knew her son was there and tried to push the men away. 'Gahba,' they laughed – the Arabic slang for prostitute – as they roughly twisted her around the room, grabbing at her clothes.

She could smell the alcohol on their breath as each in turn forced her to have sex with them on the thin, straw mattress they had tossed on to the floor. One of the men noticed the muscularly built boy cowering in the shadows and grabbed at his hair, forcing him down to his knees. Saddam was raped, his mother trying to reach out to protect him, calling for him not to cry out or he would be killed.

After the assault Saddam became a sullen and withdrawn child. His moods worsened when his mother married Hasan Ibrahim, a brother of Saddam's late father. Ibrahim had little affection for the boy, and to amuse himself when he was drunk he would make Saddam dance by thrashing at his feet with a cane. This and the searing memory of what had happened to him in the hotel room persuaded Saddam he would never again be a victim.

It was while he was at secondary school in Baghdad in 1955 that he joined the emerging Ba'ath Party, comprised of socialists who were committed to the idea of a single Arab nation and who despised the old colonial powers. He volunteered his services as hired muscle, roaming the streets in search of his party's political enemies. At the age of twenty-one he was implicated in the murder of a local government official and was jailed. Thugs from the Ba'ath Party made sure there were no witnesses willing to testify against him and he was freed from prison.

Saddam was rewarded with 'a glorious mission'. In October 1959 he was picked as one of the hit team to assassinate President Abdul Karim Kassem as he drove through Baghdad. Saddam was only supposed to be a lookout, but as the cavalcade approached he lost his nerve and began firing indiscriminately at the president's motorcycle outriders. In the chaos that followed Saddam was shot in the thigh by one of his own comrades as they fled.

Typically, Saddam gave a very different account of the ambush which had him heroically holding off General Kassem's bodyguards until his ammunition ran out and then escaping first by horseback across the desert and then by swimming the freezing and swollen waters of the Tigris with a dagger clutched between his teeth. This he used to gouge the bullet out of his thigh before continuing his journey to Damascus and then to Cairo.

Iraq's introduction to the nuclear fraternity began innocently with King Faisal II, who in 1954 embraced the fashionable desire in the developing world to reap the benefits of harnessing the atom to provide cheap energy and medical research. These were simple times. The king, together with his allies in Turkey and Pakistan, funded a research centre in Baghdad which was really no more than a spartan collection of laboratories.

Faisal showed little interest in or appreciation of the fledgling programme and this weak and ineffectual man was overthrown in 1958, to be succeeded by the pro-communist regime of General Kassem. One of Kassem's first acts as president was to seize on a deal with Moscow for forty industrial projects, the centrepiece being a small two-megawatt research reactor built at Tuwaitha, sixteen kilometres southeast of the capital.

More importantly, the general decided to send forty of Iraq's most gifted scientists to Moscow for training, among them an impressionable seventeen-year-old aspiring chemist, Hussein Shahristani, whose protests that he would rather be taught in England were ignored.

Born into a respectable Shia Muslim family, the majority community in Iraq, the young Shahristani came first in the 1958 baccalaureate examinations that test every high-school student. The rule was that the top hundred students were given a generous grant of $750 a month to study abroad. Like Shahristani, most of the students wanted to go to Britain, the old colonial power, but General Kassem wanted to change that, for his government wanted closer links with the Kremlin.

So it was that the slightly built and shy Shahristani found himself in Moscow in 1959, billeted with two other students in a cramped room with cracked window panes that did little to insulate them from the ferocious Russian winters. His natural diffidence stopped him from complaining. Instead he taught himself Russian and studied harder than anyone, though he continued to pester the Iraqi Ministry of Higher Education to let him go to England.

After two years in Moscow Shahristani was in 1961 transferred to Ipswich Civic College, where the nineteen-year-old took three science 'A' levels in record time. His prodigious talents were nurtured further at Imperial College, London, where he impressed staff with his grasp of chemical engineering. Aware of his ever-increasing value to them, Iraqi officials moved him on to Toronto for his doctorate.

Unbeknownst to Shahristani, another brilliant young Iraqi scientist had arrived in London to absorb all he could about nuclear physics. Like Shahristani, Jaffar Dhia Jaffar ended up at Imperial College. These two were destined to become the architects of Iraq's fledgling nuclear programme. But Saddam Hussein was to expect more from them: these were to be the scientists he chose to deliver him the bomb. One would do as Saddam demanded; the other would suffer years of persecution for refusing.

As students, both found their academic tasks easy, but the obvious social disparity between them meant the young men enjoyed very different responses to what London had on offer in the so-called Swinging Sixties. Jaffar had an affection for velvet suits in bilious shades, but Shahristani had neither the money nor the inclination to bother with the more ludicrous fashions on offer in Carnaby Street.

Shahristani found the music of groups like the Beatles and the Rolling Stones jarring and was more interested in the technological advances being made in Harold Wilson's Britain than the debate over free contraception. It wasn't just his shyness or his strict adherence to Islam that prevented him from behaving like other students. Shahristani felt an obligation to his country, which was paying for him to be educated, and so was driven by a desire to do better than the best.

Jaffar did not share his countryman's obsession with academia and he more than made up for Shahristani's abstemiousness. A handsome man with unkempt hair and an engaging smile, Jaffar boasted to anyone who would listen how his father was a man of considerable private means. His father had served as a minister in the royal court, maintained a flat in London and had more than enough money to fund the foreign education of all three of his sons.

Those who knew the young Jaffar noticed how he spent much of his time trying to affect the manners and speech of the British upper classes. He worked hard at improving his accent, and once claimed that the most precious legacy from his time at Imperial College was the taste he acquired for vintage claret. Inevitably, Jaffar was also to acquire an English wife, though his marriage to Phyllis Brock was always a doomed affair.

While Shahristani went to Canada to develop his nuclear expertise Jaffar moved to various institutes around Europe. This included a stint at the prestigious International Centre for Theoretical Physics, funded by the shah of Iran and built on a bluff above the Adriatic Sea near Trieste. His research also allowed him access to the European Community's main nuclear research facility in Geneva. Twenty years later, as weapons inspectors toured Iraq searching for evidence of Jaffar's nuclear handiwork, there was acute embarrassment amongst officials at CERN – the European Centre for Nuclear Research – when they realised that they had unwittingly helped Saddam's top scientist build his bomb.

The English connection cemented the friendship of the two scientists years later when they were both appointed advisers to the Atomic Energy Commission in Tuwaitha. Powerful forces were reshaping Iraq at that time that would greatly affect the lives of both men.

When Shahristani left for Moscow in 1959, General Kassem was in power. By the time the young chemist graduated from Imperial College with a first-class honours degree in 1965, Kassem had been overthrown and replaced by General Abdul Salem Arif.

The task of formally inaugurating the Tuwaitha campus in 1965 was given to Arif's prime minister, Taher Yahya, for whom nuclear energy was as alien as the solar system. The star attraction at Tuwaitha was the experimental reactor – IR2 – that Prime Minister Taher was escorted around before the ribbon was cut. He seemed puzzled as the Soviet scientist, speaking through a translator, tried to explain the mysteries of the atom. The problem lay with the Arabic word 'furin', which translates as either reactor or oven – the clay contraption that some Iraqi families still use to bake their bread. After listening to a half-hour of explanations, the exasperated Taher stopped and turned to one of his advisers. 'Ask him,' he said, pointing to the Russian, 'how long will it take before we can taste the bread from the oven?'

The two men, Shahristani and Jaffar, had adjacent offices at Tuwaitha. They were relaxed in each other's company and would socialise with each other. When they were alone they would speculate about what their country was intending to do with its nuclear know-how. Until the Ba'athists assumed complete power in 1968 dabbling in nuclear research was a symbol of statehood, as much as membership in the United Nations or running a state airline.

Meanwhile, frustrated by his exile in Cairo after the botched assassination mission, Saddam had returned to Iraq in 1963 and was fortunate to find that his kinsman from Tikrit, Hassan Al Bakr, was party leader. Saddam soon impressed cousin Hassan by his seemingly infinite capacity to inflict cruelty. Soon after the Ba'ath Party consolidated its exclusive grip on power in 1968, Saddam was appointed vice-president.

Saddam exploited the few friendships he made in the party, none more so than that with Adnan Hussein Hamdani. It was Hamdani who had hidden Saddam in his house in the hours after the bungled assassination attempt. Years earlier, Saddam had been rescued by Hamdani's father after being severely beaten by one of his mother's lovers.

When Hamdani became minister of planning, Saddam knew his schoolboy friend could be useful to him. Saddam needed help to pay for the equipment and machine tools to build up his secret nuclear network and Hamdani was able to skim funds from the national budget.

Hamdani was therefore close enough to Saddam to know some of his secrets. One was that on an official trip to Cuba, Vice-President Saddam Hussein underwent surgery for a back complaint. Saddam didn't want anyone to know about this, believing it could be interpreted as a sign of weakness. The only evidence Saddam ever showed of his back problem was his preference for a high-backed wooden chair.

Saddam was confident that his secret was safe. But at a social gathering where Saddam was sitting on this same high wooden chair, he teased Hamdani, saying, 'Look, Adnan, how I am sitting much higher than you.'

The men had been drinking and Hamdani forgot himself for a moment, replying, 'Yes, but look how much more comfortable I am.' Enraged by this allusion to his secret back operation Saddam shot back, 'I will gouge out the eyes of anyone who thinks they are better than me.'

Soon after he came to power in 1979 Saddam had twenty-three party elders executed – and Hamdani was among them. When his family came to collect his body for burial Saddam's bodyguards were waiting. 'Take off the sheet covering the traitor's body,' they insisted. 'Saddam Hussein instructs you to look at the face.' When they peeled back the bloodstained sheet they found Hamdani's eyes had been gouged out.

4

FINDING THE EXPERTS

On 18 May 1974, Saddam Hussein was chairing a meeting of
the Revolutionary Command Council in his vice-presidential
office when a nervous aide slipped a single sheet of paper in
front of him. It was a copy of a news story from Reuters that
morning, confirming that India had successfully tested a
nuclear bomb in the remote Thar desert of Rajasthan.
Saddam was impressed, but not amused.

'If the Hindis [Indians] can do it, why can't we?' he asked
those at the table.

He had already secretly spent millions on his bomb project
and had precious little to show for it. And yet here was starv-
ing India, an inferior third world country that had dragged its
bomb to the test site on the back of an ox cart, banging on the
doors of the exclusive nuclear club.

The Ba'ath Party had been trying to recruit nuclear experts
from all across the Arab world since 1971. There was no
reason for any sleight of hand as Iraq had signed the Nuclear
Non-Proliferation Treaty in 1969. Saddam's mission was to
get hold of the technology he needed without showing his
true intent. He had two options: he could acquire uranium or
he could acquire plutonium.

The plutonium option was seen as the more attractive but risky choice by most of the experts that Saddam drafted into Department 3000. They included men like Dr Muyesser Al Mallah, a US-educated engineer and the first director of Tuwaitha; Dr Humam Abdul Khaliq, his successor and secretary-general of the evolving Iraqi Atomic Energy Agency; and young physicists like Dr Khidr Hamza who escaped to the West after the Gulf War.

Hamza, who was a $150-a-month physicist at Tuwaitha in 1971, remembers being approached in that year by Al Mallah, who told him that the only way to obtain more funding was to get ministers to see the value of a military programme. The fifty-page report drawn up by Hamza and others in 1972 examined both options. It emphasised above all that Iraq should build its nuclear infrastructure by training its own scientists and importing key technologies from the West. Hamza's report stressed that the ultimate objective was for Iraq to have mastery of its own nuclear fuel cycle, from mining uranium and fabricating fuel up to the final stage of its enrichment or reprocessing.

Department 3000 studied how other nations had developed their bomb. The existing nuclear powers built devices based both on plutonium and on enriched uranium. To get either type of explosive material, bomb-makers start with the raw material of natural uranium which is mined in South Africa, Brazil, Canada, Australia and the United States.

This uranium is made up of two parts or isotopes. Most of it – 99.3 per cent of it, in fact – is made up of the comparatively harmless uranium 238. The rest of it – the other 0.7 per cent – is made up of lighter uranium 235. It is the uranium 235 atoms that split in an uncontrolled chain reaction leading to an explosion: the world's modern big bang.

The scientists' job is to find a way of separating these two isotopes, by assembling or 'enriching' a sufficient proportion of the scarce uranium 235 to more than 90 per cent. This weapons-grade or highly enriched uranium – also known as

HEU – was the type used in the bomb the Americans dropped on Hiroshima in 1945. It was also the sort of bomb that Saddam cherished from the start of his programme.

The other way to make a bomb – the plutonium route – also starts with natural uranium. Instead of being enriched, however, the isotopes are separated. Scientists fabricate the uranium into fuel rods inside a reactor. Once the chain reaction starts, millions of newly liberated neutrons begin to change the atoms of uranium 238 into an artificially created element called plutonium.

The next stage involves the hazardous step of removing the used and radioactive fuel rods from the reactor. This is the start of what is known as reprocessing. The fuel rods are required to cool before they are chopped up and dissolved in an acid solution to separate the plutonium from the remaining uranium. Because of the high levels of radioactivity this work can be done only with the protection of lead-shielded 'hot cells' or reprocessing plants.

In the early days Iraq had neither. What Hamza and most of the other scientists were unaware of was that Saddam, along with his handful of most trusted advisers, had already picked the uranium route as the one to follow.

In 1974, the Iraqis would begin negotiations with the French to buy a powerful seventy-megawatt experimental reactor. All reactors have dual use possibilities. They can be run for scientific experiments and, suitably adapted, they can also be used for the production of weapons-grade material. However, the proposed acquisition of the reactor was perfectly consistent with Baghdad's stated intention of harnessing the atom to produce cheap energy.

Vice-President Saddam's plan depended on Iraq's being able to loot enough enriched uranium fuel from the reactor he was hoping to buy from France. This would be melted down and reshaped to make a bomb. To throw everyone off the scent, he decided on an expensive ruse of spending millions of dollars on projects to supposedly get hold of plutonium. He never had any intention of doing so, but his enemies wasted months trying to thwart his bogus plan.

Outsiders who inquired why Iraq was so interested in nuclear technology were told that its scientists recognised that oil would not last forever. Iraq might have the world's second largest reserves of black gold after Saudi Arabia, but in Baghdad the scientists were playing their part in Saddam's subterfuge by asserting the need to find environmentally sound energy alternatives for the future.

Saddam's preoccupation throughout the early years of his nuclear power programme was to find enough trained staff to work in the laboratories he wished to create. The job of finding the best minds was taken over by the Strategic Planning Committee that Saddam established in 1974 with his cousin, Adnan Khairallah, later minister of defence, and his old friend Adnan Hamdani, the minister of planning. All three recognised that to run such a programme they needed money, and so they figured out a way to siphon off 5 per cent of Iraq's fast-growing oil revenue. This is what paid for the building of Tuwaitha and the recruitment drive of scientists.

The trouble was that Saddam was so paralysed by distrust that the majority of scientists allowed to study abroad were either Ba'ath Party loyalists or cronies who were Sunni Muslims like him from his own Tikrit heartland, and these were not necessarily the best candidates. Those who were picked had their monthly grants increased and were promised well-paid jobs when they returned. Hundreds of Iraqis were being trained in Russia and the West, but that was still not enough. Saddam was persuaded he had to widen his net and recruit foreign technicians, boasting that Iraq was the best paymaster in the Arab world, better even than Saudi Arabia. Among those applying for a teaching job in Iraq was an Egyptian reactor engineer, Yehiya El Meshed. When he turned up in Baghdad he was sent straight to the headquarters of the Atomic Energy Commission, where the Iraqis told him his talents would be better appreciated.

Recruits soon discovered the personal cost of signing up with Saddam. For example, several of the Iraqi scientists sent abroad to acquire the necessary technical skills returned home with American and British wives, much to the envy of their colleagues. Hussein Shahristani remembers the day when they were summoned to a meeting by their departmental head, a fierce and humourless Ba'ath Party appointee, who read from a piece of paper: 'By decree of the vice-president, his excellency Saddam Hussein, you are ordered to divorce all foreign wives.' Protests fell on deaf ears. Most complied, fearful of losing their privileges or their lives. Shahristani was among the handful who refused.

There was no question in the minds of those working for Department 3000 who was orchestrating the show. Saddam Hussein was in fact making most of his country's key decisions by the early 1970s. At home he had masterminded the nationalisation of the oil industry and took credit for suppressing a rebellion of the Kurds in northern Iraq with his customary brutality. Abroad he brokered the Treaty of Friendship and Cooperation with the old Soviet Union in 1972, and appeased their troublesome neighbour, Iran. For the moment Saddam preferred to adopt the profile of the humble and loyal vice-president. He realised that President Bakr still enjoyed the affection of the army, as befits one of the veterans of the 1958 revolution who fought and overthrew the monarchy.

The majority of Iraqis obviously knew nothing of the after-hours antics at Al Haitham or about Department 3000. Indeed, in the coffee shops and bazaars most had never heard of Saddam Hussein until 1973 when he played the role of the loyal deputy on a heroic scale in the almost farcical attempt to kill President Bakr at Baghdad airport on his return from a state visit to Poland.

The plot was devised by Nadhim Kazzar, the head of the secret service and a Saddam appointee. The attempted coup was foiled when Bakr's plane was delayed for four hours. The assassins at the airport presumed their plot must have been discovered and fled.

Kazzar thought the same. In a desperate bid to escape he took two ministers hostage and drove maniacally towards the Iranian border, threatening to kill his captives if anyone tried to stop him. The president ordered Kazzar arrested and Saddam took command of the airborne posse who captured the fugitive, though not before he had shot one of his hostages and wounded another. Revenge was swift. Within a week Kazzar had been tried and executed. Saddam was again eager to take the credit; nevertheless, there were murmurs inside the party that he might have had a hand in the plot.

Bakr did not believe the allegation, though by now he had little affection for Mr Deputy. What he recognised was that it was Saddam who had helped him purge any potential rivals, as his ever-resourceful vice-president was happy to betray and dispose of anyone, even those who had regarded themselves as allies. Saddam always ensured there were those around him who would watch his back.

He was adept at mobilising his own staff, siphoning government money to pay for their services and careful not to attract the jealousy or curiosity of others in the Revolutionary Command Council. He saw conspiracies everywhere, and was obsessed with his personal safety.

The obvious place to find bodyguards was the army, but Saddam did not trust the military high command. He had not forgiven the insult he was given at age twenty, when his application to join the Baghdad Military Academy was refused. As he gained in influence, he was determined to have his revenge on the generals who had spurned him.

So it was that one night at Abu Ghraib, the prison guards slumped in the watchtower heard the powerful car engine gunning towards them long before they could make out its shape through the gloom of the yellow arc lights. Leaping to their feet, they twisted the beam of the spotlight along the perimeter fence until it picked up the Mercedes which was closing fast on the main gates.

No one had told the night shift to expect visitors. One of the guards squinted through his binoculars and could make out the prison governor shuffling uneasily from foot to foot and nervously tugging at the seams of his suit trousers. When he looked up, the Mercedes had squealed to a stop and from the back seat emerged a barrel-chested figure swathed in a black astrakhan overcoat against the desert night. The guards watched the governor salute and then kiss the vice-president on both cheeks. Saddam had come on a grotesque recruiting drive.

Inside the prison gates Saddam and his entourage swept towards the governor's office while warders moved through the sleeping prison, rousing handpicked inmates from their narrow metal bunk beds. Earlier that evening the vice-president had sent a message to the governor that said: 'Bring me your cruellest people.'

Saddam had a fascination with those who had killed with their bare hands and for those on Death Row who had dismembered bodies in their efforts to disguise their crime. The governor wasn't sure what Saddam wanted with these creatures, and Saddam was not inclined to explain himself. He was known to deliver lectures to prisoners before signing their death warrants in front of them, then watching them plead for mercy as they were shot in the back of the neck. Tonight, the vice-president threw off his coat, settled into a chair and nodded for the first candidate to be brought before him.

Outside the door the shaven-haired prisoner, who was serving a life sentence for strangling a neighbour over a land dispute, strained to hear what was being discussed. A midnight summons was hardly routine even by the cruel standards of Abu Ghraib.

The prisoner, still handcuffed and manacled at the ankles, was shoved into the office with such force that the effort of trying to stay on his feet nearly propelled him into Saddam's lap. He looked into the prisoner's eyes.

'Do you know me?' Saddam asked.

The prisoner, a heavily built man with a prominent scar on his nose, glanced around the room anxious to know what response was expected of him.

Saddam waved the convict away, and a guard grabbed at the collar of the man's prison uniform. The convict dropped to his knees.

'What is it that you could want of someone as unworthy as me?'

Saddam jabbed a finger in his chest. 'What would you do for me if I did a favour for you? Remember I can reprieve you, but I could also have you shot this instant.'

'Ask anything, sir, it shall be yours,' he said.

Saddam toyed with him, wondering out loud whether to commute his death sentence to ten years, and then asked what he would do if he was freed.

Aware he had to keep raising the emotional stakes, the prisoner was almost shouting as he pledged: 'I would give up my life for you, my children's lives.'

Saddam was laughing now, a cue for those around him to do likewise.

'I will not only release you, I will give you a thousand dinars.' The vice-president then turned to his bodyguard, saying, 'Give this man *ten* thousand dinars [$30,000].'

The expression on the prisoner's face changed. He was now sure that this was a cruel burlesque and that he would be shot. He tried to stand, desperate to regain some dignity if these were to be his last few minutes. 'Don't mock me, sir. I am a poor man. I beg you not to laugh at me.'

Those around the governor's office fell silent, fearful of Saddam's reaction to this insolence. The vice-president raised himself awkwardly out of his chair, his recurrent back problem paining him, and stood over the prisoner.

'You are mine now. You are released and you will have a car, your own house and more money, but you will serve me and only me and do so without question.'

The prisoner's handcuffs rattled as he reached out to kiss Saddam's hand. He had joined the vice-president's private army. By the end of the night Saddam had selected another seven men to be part of his shadow force. None of them were allowed to return to their cells and were instead taken to a barracks in the northern suburbs of the capital where they were issued new identities and assigned to one of six close protection units who would shield Saddam at all times.

His philosophy of survival was brutally simple: trust nobody.

He once explained to Prince Bandr, the Saudi ambassador to Washington, about his method of governing: 'I look into a person's eyes and if I have suspicions then I get rid of them.'

'But what if you are wrong about them plotting against you?' the prince enquired.

Saddam laughed. 'I would rather be wrong and eliminate them than leave them. I would rather find out later I was mistaken than let them kill me.'

He had an uncanny foresight in anticipating what his opponents were up to and always seemed to be one step ahead. He also ascertained that obedience was taught early to the young in Iraq. Each morning lessons began with teachers' asking children what their parents were saying about the government.

The Ba'ath Party had informers in every factory, university, hospital and military unit, and in this climate of distrust Saddam thrived. Long before he became president he had his own loyalists in place, not least in his nuclear programme.

Shahristani admits he frequently drove past Al Haitham, not knowing what was going on inside until a chance encounter with a laboratory technician who let slip that one entire floor was dedicated to experiments involving uranium enrichment using lasers. Shahristani guessed what that meant and began asking questions. He was made to suffer for this perceived treachery, astonished to be told one day in 1973 that his services were no longer needed at Tuwaitha and that he was being reassigned with fifty others to teaching duties in different parts of the country.

It was noticeable that the suave and urbane Dr Jaffar somehow managed to avoid this government diktat and stayed in the capital. Shahristani had his passport confiscated and was sent to Mosul University in the north of the country, though this enforced exile lasted just over a year until he was recalled to Tuwaitha in 1974. The party had been weeding out those it regarded as unreliable without thinking of their scientific value. It took Saddam's apparatchiks a year to realise their mistake and for Shahristani and others to be reprieved.

The day he got back to Baghdad Shahristani was summoned to a meeting at the presidential palace with Humam Abdul Khaliq, the incoming secretary-general of the Iraqi Atomic Energy Commission. His host embraced him with fulsome apologies, offering him tea and assuring him he could have his passport back. It took Shahristani an hour to drive from the palace to the necessary office to retrieve his travel documents, but by the time he arrived his name had been removed from the banned list and he was handed back his green Iraqi passport.

A week later he was called to a second meeting in Saddam's spacious office in the presidential palace. This time the mood had changed. Saddam was sitting at the head of the table, ignoring all those fanned out around him and running his finger up and down a balance sheet.

During the year Shahristani and others had been exiled, money from the vice-president's covert programme had gone missing in the amount of $350,000. (It had been skimmed off by party loyalists to build themselves a fun palace complete with bars and swimming pools in an orchard on the banks of the Tigris. This was to replace Al Haitham, which had returned to its drabber incarnation as a think tank.)

Each scientist was now handed a blank piece of paper.

'If you truly know nothing about this,' Saddam said, 'then sign your name. But be warned. If we later discover that you do know something you will be in trouble.'

With a clear conscience Shahristani scribbled on his paper, 'I know nothing.'

Shahristani noticed that at their next meeting some of his colleagues were missing. Nobody dared ask what had become of them. Saddam couldn't care less about how his scientists indulged themselves, but he didn't like being cheated.

Some of the scientists were moved in 1974 to new offices in underground facilities in the Qasr-Al-Nihayyah, the Palace of the End, where Vice-President Hussein had an office. Buried elsewhere in its many rooms was a torture chamber that the Ba'athists had set up immediately after first taking power.

Saddam was a frequent visitor to this corner of the palace, where he refined the instruments of torture, including a device that resembled an office guillotine which was used to chop off the tips of suspects' fingers. Evidence of this handiwork was strewn on the floor along with bloodstained clothes torn from victims who seldom left alive.

The scientists knew nothing about what went on inside this so-called interrogation centre, but then how could they as secrecy was paramount? Inside the Workers' Union, the palace and the Al Haitham Institute brilliant young scientists were caressed and bullied into working for Saddam's secret bomb-making programme.

On the other side of Baghdad in the laboratories at Tuwaitha, Iraqi and foreign scientists freely mingled and opened their doors to inspectors from the International Atomic Energy Agency, confident that what they were doing was for peaceful purposes. This twin-track nuclear policy, one peaceful and the other lethal, was the key to Saddam's thinking.

For the next five years Shahristani and Jaffar were the respectable face of the Iraqi Atomic Energy Commission. They would be very much in evidence in 1975 when Baghdad hosted a conference on Peaceful Use of Atomic Energy for Scientific and Economic Development. When negotiations started that year to purchase the $80 million French Osirak reactor, Shahristani and Jaffar were the key scientific members of the delegation that travelled between Baghdad and Paris to hammer out the details.

The attraction of the French deal on Osirak was the type of fuel it used – weapons-grade uranium enriched to 93 per cent and ideal for building a bomb. France was so desperate to endear itself to Saddam that it happily committed itself to selling six fuel bundles of ten kilograms each, easily enough for half-a-dozen nuclear bombs.

For Shahristani and Jaffar the type of fuel they bought was irrelevant. For them the advantage of the powerful French reactor was like acquiring a new generation of computer. Experiments that would take twenty days to conduct in the older and smaller Russian reactor, which the hapless Prime Minister Yahya had mistaken for a bread oven, could be concluded in one day using Osirak.

Meanwhile, Vice-President Saddam thought it time that his country should have a seat among the ruling elite of nuclear powers. He wanted Iraq to be on the Board of Governors of the International Atomic Energy Agency at its glass and chrome tower block headquarters close to the Ferris wheel made famous by Harry Lime, the spy from Graham Greene's novel *The Third Man*.

To the outside world this was still more evidence of Iraq's peaceful intentions. In truth it was to facilitate his infiltration of the IAEA's inspection regime so that when the time came for Iraq to be investigated, he would know how to cover his tracks. Unfortunately, his diplomats in Vienna had made no efforts to lobby the other IAEA members and when the delegation from Baghdad turned up in Vienna in July 1974, nobody knew about Iraq's candidacy.

When told about this, Saddam flew into a murderous rage, hurling furniture about his office and ordering the entire embassy purged. The more fortunate diplomats were demoted and sent to disagreeable postings. The more senior figures were executed.

To win a seat on the IAEA board Saddam created the post of scientific attaché at the Vienna embassy, a job given to Suroor Mahmoud Mirza, who happened to be the brother of his most senior bodyguard. Mahmoud was an engaging figure and, aided by a generous entertainment allowance, he persuaded the IAEA to embrace Iraq.

Mahmoud passed on to Baghdad priceless intelligence such as how the West was enjoying unprecedented success in using satellites to uncover secret nuclear activities, including those conducted underground. Iraq therefore discovered how to build installations that would not be spotted from the skies. In Vienna, the IAEA members complimented the Iraqis on their exemplary behaviour.

Not every nation was so convinced. The Israelis were suspicious about Iraq's real intentions for the French reactor. The Israeli secret service, Mossad, had long been watching Vice-President Saddam Hussein. It had at first dismissed him as just another Arab thug trying to boost his standing with rabid street corner speeches against the Jews – until oil prices boomed in 1973, making Iraq super-rich.

When it got a copy of the Osirak deal from its agents in Paris the secret service sent an urgent warning to Israel's prime minister, Yitzhak Rabin, about what the Iraqis had really gone shopping for in France. Mossad turned for advice to its own nuclear expert, Professor Yuval Ne'eman. At a hastily arranged meeting the professor pored over the design details of the Iraqi order.

'Why on earth do they want a seventy-megawatt reactor? For the kind of experiments they say they are doing they could get away with their old Russian two-megawatt reactor. That could keep them going for twenty years, unless this new one is for manufacturing plutonium.'

Rabin understood what this meant. Mossad was ordered to

shadow Saddam's efforts and to watch every nuclear scientist with any connection to Iraq. The agency was told it could spend what it needed either to turn these scientists into defectors or to eliminate them. At all costs Mossad was told to stop Iraq from getting even close to owning the bomb.

The French prime minister, Jacques Chirac, had visited Baghdad in December 1974 amid much pomp. The French, like other Western industrialised powers, were suffering from the fall out of the OPEC-driven oil price rises and were hustling for new contracts for their weaponry and other exports.

Vice-President Saddam offered to take care of Chirac's visit and in their several meetings the two men enjoyed an unexpected rapport, much to the surprise of the travelling French entourage. At the end of the visit the French prime minister warmly embraced Saddam, calling him 'a personal friend', and returned home with a sheaf of lucrative contracts worth over 15 billion francs. One of them was the deal to supply the brand new reactor.

To cement this marriage of convenience Saddam made one of his rare forays abroad, travelling to Paris the following year. The Iraqi vice-president enjoyed inspecting the honour guard, taking the salute and being received as a de facto head of state. To express his gratitude, he decided on a culinary treat for his French hosts. He ordered the Iraqi Airways presidential jumbo jet to collect all available supplies of Nile perch from Baghdad's fish markets and fly them to Paris.

The stinking cargo of fish was deposited in the grounds of the Parisian palace where Saddam and his entourage were being accommodated. Exasperated French chefs watched open-mouthed as the Iraqi cooks flown in by Saddam slowly roasted the fish over smoking fires that defaced the ornamental gardens.

This assault on his palate did not diminish Chirac's appetite for finalising the contract for the reactor in 1975.

Saddam's unrealised childhood ambition had been to follow his beloved uncle, Khairallah Tulfah, into the Iraqi army, but his compensation came in January 1976 when he persuaded President Bakr to appoint him lieutenant-general, the army's chief of staff. He insisted the appointment should be back-dated to the summer of 1973, which was of enormous help in later years when it came to embellishing his career. Indeed, in 1976 he commissioned a film that was shown in every Iraqi cinema eulogising his long and distinguished military career. Those who knew the truth did not point out the obvious inaccuracies.

Strangling dissent among the military was Saddam's first priority as its new chief of staff, and to do this he installed his Tikriti relatives in key positions. His favourite cousin with whom he had played as a child, Adnan Khairallah, was already a colonel – a rank that reflected his family connec-tions, not his abilities. Saddam now had him appointed defence minister.

Once again Bakr agreed, but palace aides noticed that Saddam Hussein's ideas of grandeur were beginning to show in their dealings with him. Saddam took to calling himself 'Mr Deputy', and he insisted that even the president address him as such. If Bakr sent for him, Saddam would refuse to leave his office on the other side of the presidential com-pound until a formal request was delivered by an equerry. He would not enter the president's room until announced by his aide-de-camp.

At this stage there were no streets named after him, no public buildings dedicated in his honour, and the huge murals of Saddam in various garb had yet to appear. Instead, in public he played the loyal subordinate and the devoted family man. He let it be known that there was no matter so important that he would not interrupt a meeting to sew a button on his daughter's coat before she went to school. To prove it, he had the state-run newspapers show photographs of him darning Raghad's coat while his staff were left waiting.

There were press reports of how the vice-president would disguise himself so that he could drop into factories and schools to ask what Iraqis really thought. Of course, when they discovered his real identity those he met would fall at his feet and salute a true man of the people.

The other great myth was Saddam as the loyal, loving husband. He cleverly censored all but the barest details of his marriage to Sajidah Tulfah, the daughter of his favourite uncle, whom he says he was betrothed to at the age of eight. Sajidah has never been permitted to give her version of their courtship and photographs of the couple are rare. One of these is a formal and rather stiff portrait taken on the wedding day in 1963. She was more handsome than beautiful, with a moon face framed by a short bob of lustrous black hair. Her large brown eyes are heavily shaded with black mascara and her lips are tightly pursed. He is standing beside her, a tall slender figure with an open, almost pleasing face dominated by soft brown eyes. He had yet to acquire the trademark moustache.

Sajidah was the better educated and more socially adept of the two, but she knew never to question the rising star of the Ba'ath Party about his political machinations. Many families did approach her for help in placing their children in privileged positions. Others, less fortunate, pleaded with her to use her influence with Saddam to spare loved ones who faced execution.

One of Saddam's more enduring affairs was with the daughter of a prominent cleric; he became obsessed with her. For a time, he visited her regularly for sex. While lying in her bed one afternoon, he complained that the decor was hardly fit for someone of his eminence and told her to have it refurbished before his next visit. The woman, who was trying to caress and coax Saddam into further sexual arousal, bravely suggested that their relationship had become a scandal because of her father's position and so he should marry her. Saddam came up with an ingenious solution before his next encounter with the woman. He forced her into marriage with one of his supine bodyguards, and ordered her bedroom redecorated to his own personal taste.

Saddam's dishonest approach to marital fidelity paralleled the conduct of his nuclear programme, saying one thing and doing another. He engaged in countless affairs – most were just dalliances with socialites who had taken his fancy. At nights when Saddam was holed up in his office watching television he would order his guards to go and find a woman he had seen on the screen. The woman's assent was never sought in these liaisons. Saddam took vindictive pleasure in humiliating married women, a legacy perhaps from his own troubled childhood and his shame about his mother's sexual behaviour.

Meanwhile, there were some in the Elysée who had second thoughts about the Iraqi purchase of Osirak. In 1977, prompted by screams of protest from the Israeli ambassador and more subtle diplomatic prodding from the White House, the French government abruptly tried to change the type of fuel it had promised. Instead of weapons-grade uranium, the French told an Iraqi delegation, they had developed a new fuel suitable for Osirak. It was called caramel and was only enriched to 20 per cent, good enough for scientific research but hopeless for the bomb.

Shahristani said he had no objection. He was stunned at the outraged reaction of his fellow delegates. Abdul Khaliq shouted at their French hosts that this was a question of principle and existing contracts could not be broken. After some hesitation the French agreed.

Because Saddam wanted the bomb and because India had succeeded in building and testing one, Saddam swallowed his contempt for the Indians and took a personal interest in the career of their chief nuclear physicist, Raja Ramanna. Four years after seeing the Reuters report, Saddam invited Ramanna to visit Iraq as his personal guest.

The Indian scientist spent just under a week in the Iraqi capital, touring Tuwaitha and meeting dozens of his Iraqi contemporaries. At the end of his visit, Saddam invited him to his office.

'You have done enough for your country,' he told the bemused Ramanna. 'Don't go back. Stay here and take over our nuclear programme. I will pay you whatever you want.' Saddam reached over to the tall, broad-shouldered physicist and said, 'I expect you to honour this offer.'

Ramanna stayed awake all that night, fearful Saddam would prevent him from catching his flight home. He never went back to Iraq.

Saddam's nuclear programme was growing, but at Al Haitham the members of what was surely the world's only nuclear brothel were drawing unwelcome attention to themselves. Some of the younger recruits, faced with such obvious temptations, found it hard to contain their exuberance. This was already a city where neighbours knew better than to criticise the louche behaviour of what were obviously favoured sons of the regime, so complaints were few.

Nevertheless, the gossip about Al Haitham and the late-night car crashes on the wide boulevards adjacent to Korneesh Street with the drivers the worse for drink eventually reached the austere president, Hassan Al Bakr. There was an almost puritanical streak in the president, who felt that the country should not be cheated by these highly qualified, well-paid experts.

Over the next few weeks Bakr made it his business to discover just what it was the scientists were doing at Al Haitham after dark. When told about half-naked women carousing about a top-secret building that he believed was Iraq's prize academic powerhouse, he was incandescent.

On an October night he ordered two truckloads of police and soldiers to invade Al Haitham. The hit squad knew enough about the Institute's layout to begin their attack through the same smoked glass doors at the back of the building used by the evening revellers.

The assault, led by Saddam's half-brother Barzan Tikriti, was over in a matter of minutes. Marwan Nakshbandi, the

Institute's director, was last seen being dragged from his office, screaming his innocence. His pleas for clemency were ignored: he was hanged within forty-eight hours.

Almost all the young women were executed by firing squad. Bakr signed their death warrants – ignoring the fact that most had been forced into prostitution. Only two of the women were spared, both of whom had influential family connections. Bakr agreed they could return to their previous jobs as secretaries at the Tuwaitha Nuclear Research Centre, where stifling security meant their silence was assured.

Saddam purposely looked the other way during this purge. The vice-president did nothing to save any lives, regarding the victims as frankly irrelevant. Besides, he had anticipated that there would be setbacks and was just relieved that none of his senior scientists were punished.

Some time later Vice-President Saddam would move some of his staff in Department 3000 to the Workers' Union building, which is opposite what was to become Baghdad's most prestigious hotel for foreign visitors, the Al Rashid. Saddam gave two floors of the building to Department 3000 and ensured that enough of his own party henchmen were there to monitor the scientists' progress and, more important, their loyalty.

On their flight home from their trip in 1977 for the final negotiations for Osirak, Shahristani and Jaffar sat side by side. Shahristani wanted to ask his colleague what the wrangling was about over the fuel they had just bought. The stern faces of others in the delegation in the first-class section of the Iraqi Airways jumbo jet persuaded him to do otherwise. Instead he buried his head in a newspaper. He laughed when he turned the page.

Jaffar asked what was so amusing. Shahristani pointed to an article.

'Can you believe that when the newly installed president of the Comoros Islands first realised he had become leader, he excitedly ran to tell his mother? She slapped her son hard across the face and said, "Don't be so stupid." Can you imagine how fabulous to live in a regime that is as mad as that?' Shahristani asked.

Jaffar looked down at his magazine. 'We do,' he said.

5

PALACE COUP

It was well after midnight when the Revolutionary Command Council assembled at the presidential palace on 11 July 1979. The men could not help glancing at President Bakr's empty chair. All of them knew why they were there, but Saddam was determined to extract all the melodrama he could.

The vice-president kept them waiting for an hour before the door was flung open and he marched in. Saddam had chosen yet another absurd new military uniform for the occasion. The rest of the table stood to attention, scraping their chairs across the marble floor as they leaped to their feet.

'Comrades, I regret to inform you that our beloved president . . .' Saddam's voice trailed away. He dug a handkerchief from his trouser pocket and dabbed at his eyes.

'Comrades, it is time the heroic founder of our glorious republic was allowed to rest. He is an old man now. He has confided in me, his loyal and obedient deputy, that since his wife's death his dearest wish is to spend his last days in his garden surrounded by his grandchildren.'

From the far side of the room came an interruption. 'Brother leader!' the voice called out.

Saddam ignored it, preparing to plough on with his stage-managed performance.

'Brother leader, I must insist as a fraternal comrade that I speak.' The square figure of the Council's secretary-general, Muhie Abd Al Hussein Mashhadi, eased back in his chair and took a deep breath.

'Comrade chairman, surely after so many years of glorious service to our revolution it is unthinkable that our president should stand down. If he is ill, then let him rest until he is better and he can return to his rightful position.'

Slowly and deliberately Saddam reached inside his military tunic and extracted a sheet of paper. He held it up to the delegates though all of them were too far away to make out what was typed on it. 'Comrades, these are the words of our beloved Hassan Al Bakr.' Saddam paused and began to read:

Dear Comrades,
   My health has recently reached the stage where I can no longer assume responsibility in a manner that satisfies my conscience and is commensurate with the magnitude of the missions with which the Command has entrusted me. Therefore, I insist that comrade Saddam Hussein and my comrades in the party leadership and in the Revolutionary Command Council respond to my request to be relieved of my responsibilities in the Party and the State.

Saddam had staged his palace coup.

The elderly Bakr had no choice but to do as he was told by his former vice-president. Humiliatingly, he was forced to go on television and ask the country to accept his deputy as its new president. Saddam did not wait for the broadcast to finish to begin his own inauguration. The grey-haired Bakr was still on screen when his forty-two-year-old deputy was taking an oath of allegiance as the fifth president of the Republic of Iraq.

Saddam had copied the tactics of one of his political heroes – Joseph Stalin – biding his time until he was ready to ease aside the old guard. Like Stalin, Saddam lost no time in purging any and every possible threat.

He began with the outspoken Mashhadi, who had recklessly questioned his right to remove President Bakr. Mashhadi was relieved of his duties and accused of being behind 'a Zionist plot' to take over the country. This invention gave the new president the excuse for a round-up of friend and foe that would once and for all stamp his authority over the Iraqi people. When an extraordinary meeting of senior party figures was convened on 22 July, Saddam listened to one of his stooges present fabricated evidence against Mashhadi and twenty-two others from the Command Council.

As Saddam listened to the names being read out, he began to weep. Around him the people were on their feet chanting, 'Hail Saddam,' and 'Death to the traitors.'

Then Saddam raised a hand and they fell silent. With a dramatic flourish he produced from his trouser pocket his own list of suspects which he began to read slowly and deliberately while the entire spectacle was filmed. All around the hall bodyguards led away the sixty-six people whom he named. Within days all would face a firing squad made up of party comrades summoned from all parts of Iraq to 'share the responsibility of saving the glorious revolution'.

The ministers of petroleum, education and industry were among those who were shot after being sentenced by a kangaroo court. Not all comrades were dignified with a show trial. A number were simply gunned down in the streets.

Saddam's ruthlessness was beyond doubt, but civil servants who had worked with him as vice-president admired his ability to swiftly master detailed briefs. What fascinated him most was anything to do with new technology and Saddam made sure his staff got hold of the latest issues of Western magazines that kept up with the latest developments.

During his time as vice-president Saddam preached the

need for economic restraint, but as president he betrayed that ideal. In his first ten years as president he wasted $326 billion in oil revenues on wars and on the development of a 'super-gun' to launch a nuclear warhead. He built more than thirty private palaces, and spent millions on terrorist groups like Abu Nidal. Above all, he spent money on his nuclear obsession.

The first beneficiaries of his early days as president were the few members of his family from Tikrit who had shown him kindness as a boy. He built a palace for his mother – and made sure she was never seen in public, to avoid the risk of provoking cruel jibes about her past. His beloved uncle, Khairallah, was appointed mayor of Baghdad and proceeded to loot the city's treasury with impunity. The corruption was so shameless under his governorship that Saddam was eventually forced to shut down a number of his uncle's companies and execute several of the mayor's subordinates, but the old man survived.

Saddam was so devoted to Khairallah that he ordered the state press to publish his uncle's so-called philosophy of life, a treatise entitled 'Three Whom God Should Not Have Created: Persians, Jews and Flies'. (Khairallah apparently regarded flies as the least of these evils.) Saddam was to borrow phrases from this tract for some of his own speeches.

His half-brother Barzan was confirmed as head of security and his cousin Adnan, Khairallah's son, was promoted to deputy commander-in-chief of the armed forces. Saddam added to his own long list of titles the rank of field marshal. The new leader wasted no time in indulging himself. A French fashion house was ordered to design and produce more than 250 identical suits. Saddam also had other uniforms and tribal costumes made for every occasion. It was said he never wore the same shirt twice. And a Danish shipyard received a commission to build a presidential yacht.

While the American president is shadowed at all times by a military aide carrying a briefcase handcuffed to his wrist, containing the nuclear launch codes, Saddam was followed by a flunkey bearing an engraved box full of Havana cigars – a gift from his old friend Fidel Castro. Every few steps the president would wheel around and hold out his hand for a fresh cigar, which was clipped and lit by another trailing servant. After a few puffs the cigar was discarded and Saddam would reach for another one.

In the immediate aftermath of Saddam's takeover, the nuclear fraternity did not know what to expect. Veterans of the nuclear programme who had been there since it started in 1958 were now serving under their fifth leader and this one was by far the most capricious and violent. Senior scientists, like the rest of the Baghdad elite, had heard the stories of party stalwarts and their family and friends simply disappearing in the first weeks of his reign and wondered if their community would be the next to suffer.

In one of the compounds of identical white villas built to house the scientists, the only obvious change was the increase in plain-clothes police who tailed them everywhere they went. Their telephones were routinely tapped. Two weeks after Saddam's takeover, a young metallurgist employed at the Tuwaitha complex telephoned his mother in Basra to report what life was like in Baghdad. The fifteen-minute call was not indiscreet; however, before the young man replaced the receiver in its cradle he heard the entire conversation played back to him. Surveillance cameras started appearing in every laboratory, compound and home, and there were rumours of secretly placed microphones to record conversations even within the privacy of family bedrooms.

So great was the fear of Big Brother Saddam watching over them that when the telephone rang in the office of Abdel Razak Al Hashemi, the second in command of Iraq's Atomic Energy Commission, the usually placid geologist literally jumped to his feet.

Sitting across the desk from him was a quizzical Hussein Shahristani, who had dropped in for a chat about some new laboratory equipment required for Tuwaitha. Shahristani knew from Hashemi's expression that the caller was someone important. When his boss started to mutter 'Yes, Saidi' every few seconds, he realised it was Saddam.

Hashemi was using the ultimate expression of subservience, meaning 'my lord', and was bobbing up and down in the privacy of his own office, furiously nodding his head in case he was being secretly filmed. He also motioned for Shahristani to stand up. Instead, the thirty-seven-year-old chemist was barely able to control his laughter. 'Sit down, you fool. Have you no self-respect?'

The perspiring Hashemi was becoming ever more hysterical. Sweat patches started to stain his armpits. To his visitor he mouthed a desperate plea: 'Stand up, for God's sake, or we'll both be killed!'

By the time the conversation ended, Hashemi was so afraid that Saddam would overhear Shahristani's disrespectful comments that he did not know whether to obey his visitor's demand to sit down, or remain standing for the sake of his leader. He stood contorted and hovered above his chair unable to do either.

The telephone call from Saddam summoned Hashemi and his boss at the Iraqi Atomic Energy Commission, Abdul Khaliq, to come and see him immediately. Fortunately both men were in their offices within the palace compound and together they walked across the courtyard to Saddam's private quarters. Too terrified to speak and unsure of what to expect, they waited in an anteroom and were served sweet tea while the president attended to other business.

When they were finally allowed in on the heels of a bodyguard, they found Saddam engrossed in the contents of a thick, black file. After a further few minutes, Saddam looked up at them and motioned for them to sit down before launching into a monologue about the need to accelerate the nuclear programme.

'Our enemies are strong, but we will be stronger,' Saddam told them. 'I am now the head of the Iraqi family and it is my decision that our beloved country needs the nuclear shield before the Zionists and their American friends attack us. For such a glorious cause, let me assure you there is no shortage of resources. If we all do our duty, Iraq will become the greatest power of the Middle East.'

Saddam lectured them for another hour in his flat, deliberate and monotonous style. He measured every word and paused before every new sentence. The president cautioned them there could be no mistakes at this delicate stage in the country's history as he had yet to consolidate his revolution.

When the new president made his first state visit to Tuwaitha, accompanied by his personal photographer to record his triumph, millions had already been invested in the building programme and billions more were still to come. In keeping with Saddam's directives to preserve secrecy at all costs, the architects tried to disguise the extra power lines and ventilation shafts needed for the future development of the bomb. Saddam was appalled at what he found.

Instead of being shown what he presumed would be a heavily defended complex of white-tiled laboratories humming with activity, he was escorted around what looked like a series of senior common rooms replicated from the Ivy League campuses of America.

'The Iraqi people have been spending their money on this?' an enraged Saddam screamed at Abdul Khaliq.

Khaliq tried to splutter some justification of the infant project. The president held up his hand.

'This is too important to be left like this,' Saddam said, pointing to his army chief of staff. 'It must be sealed off and hidden.'

In the following weeks Saddam had his troops move more sand to buttress Tuwaitha than the pharaohs used to build the pyramids of Egypt. Thirty-five-metre-high barricades were flung around the complex. The camouflage of the most sensitive installations was so successful that when international inspectors later walked around the site, they were in total ignorance of what the scientists there called 'the invisible buildings'.

Saddam had always despised intellectuals, the more so because he needed them if he was to get his bomb. He was convinced that behind his back the scientists were mocking him for his own lack of education – he had lasted barely a year at the University of Cairo, where he studied law during his enforced exile from Iraq in 1962. Saddam found more novel ways to acquire his degree. In 1972 he enrolled at Baghdad University, though his career there consisted of him showing up on graduation day with a pistol around his waist and accompanied by half-a-dozen heavily armed minders. It was no surprise therefore when the dean of studies invited Saddam to come up first to receive his honours degree. Four years later, in 1976, he turned up again with even more bodyguards to get his master's degree.

University records show that his academic prowess was exceeded only by that of his eldest son Uday, who in 1984 graduated from the engineering department with a pass mark in his final exams of 99.6 per cent, the best result ever achieved by any student. It was all the more remarkable because of the fact that Uday had never bothered to attend a lecture. In 1998, Uday excelled himself academically by suddenly revealing himself as the author of a 400-page PhD dissertation, entitled 'The Post Cold War World', which was printed and distributed free to the citizens of Baghdad.

Such was his insecurity from childhood that Saddam believed bestowing a degree on himself would make scientists see him with renewed respect, just as he thought that senior army officers would take more notice of what he had to say because he wore the insignia of a field marshal on his uniform. The real reason they all followed orders was fear. Saddam excelled at that discipline and seldom missed an opportunity to repeat the lesson whenever the opportunity arose.

A progress report from Tuwaitha delivered to his office made dull reading and Saddam was tempted to ignore its contents until his eye caught the last few lines. The author was blaming lack of proper equipment for the longer than expected delay in completing an experiment that his atomic advisers told him had been finished months before. The scientist responsible for that document was in Abu Ghraib prison by nightfall.

When his wife heard about his detention, she used a friend who was a relative of the president to ask for a meeting with Saddam so she might plead his case. A week later, with still no word of her husband, she was ordered to go to an address in one of the more affluent suburbs of Baghdad. She was not told why.

On her arrival, the woman, who ran her own successful clothing business in the capital, was roughly searched by two bodyguards who made lewd comments about her figure. She was slim and small with blue eyes and shoulder-length streaked blonde hair. She was so nervous that she was biting her long red fingernails.

After a two-hour wait she was pushed into a large drawing room. Every wall was decorated with gilt mirrors. Pendulous chandeliers threw shadows across a thick pink carpet. The woman immediately recognised the figure of Saddam Hussein. His head was bent over a file resting on the knees of his fawn suit. To disguise her nervousness, the woman tried to concentrate on the ornate plaster carvings on the high ceilings.

'You do not feel shame for what your husband has done?' Saddam said suddenly as he waved the file at her. 'He has been a very bad boy.'

Before the woman could ask of what her husband was accused, Saddam said, 'I should punish you, bitch. I will fuck you and climb over his dead body to get to you.'

Saddam lunged at the woman, pushing her back on to a settee and tearing at her grey pleated skirt and silk blouse. The woman begged him to stop. He pushed his hands roughly under the cotton skirt and made a grab at her underwear.

She remembers screaming instinctively, reaching up and

scratching her long nails down Saddam's face, drawing blood which dripped on to his white shirt. The president reeled back, lashing out at her and trying to staunch his wound with a handkerchief. His bodyguards had by now rushed into the room and Saddam ordered them to take the woman away. Once they had her outside, the guards beat her nearly senseless and ripped out several of her nails. Though she escaped with her life, her husband was not so fortunate.

The following evening Saddam arranged for the wife of a jailed Iraqi diplomat to be brought to him. Her husband had been arrested for an alleged currency fraud and she knew that such a crime was punishable by death. The woman guessed instantly what was expected of her. She dropped to her knees, eulogising the president who sat in front of her and begging for clemency for her husband, who was, she swore, a loyal and devoted servant.

Saddam reached down and lifted the woman on to his lap, unbuttoning her dress as he did so. Without a word being said he raped her from behind, pushing her back on to the floor when he had finished with her. That same night her husband was released from Abu Ghraib, though his captors made sure he knew the graphic details of his wife's performance.

Such savage assaults on respectable married women were by no means a rarity. Saddam saw each one as his way of avenging the assaults on his mother by those who had bought her sexual favours. He never blamed Sabha for what she had been obliged to do for their survival. She was allowed to see out her days in the comfort of a small palace close to the shabby home where she had raised Saddam.

A few hundred metres from his mother's palace Saddam built a 'family supermarket' into which juggernaut loads of Swedish furniture, Italian bathroom fittings, Japanese television sets and every other modern convenience were shipped to make their lives more comfortable.

Saddam realised that reward was as potent a weapon to enforce his will as punishment. He would use both at whim.

One night when he was working alone in his domed palace he called to the bodyguard on duty. The soldier edged open the door to see the carpet entirely covered by $100 bills. Saddam swung around in his chair.

'Come to me, walk towards me.' The president beckoned with his hand.

The man, who had been part of Saddam's guard for nearly a decade, was sweating under his heavy tunic as he stepped carefully on to the thick covering of notes. 'My son, you are loyal to me. You have done me great service and I am your father. Help yourself, as much as you want.'

The soldier gratefully did as he was told.

The image of Saddam as a paternalistic benefactor was reflected in the stories published about him in the Iraqi national press, which on his orders started to leak details of the 'beloved leader's' virtues as a family man.

The readers had heard of Sajidah, 'his loyal comrade in arms'. Now they were told of his five children – his sons Uday and Qusay and his daughters Raghad, Rana and Hala. There were reports and carefully crafted photographs of Saddam kissing his children as he worked with them in the family's vegetable garden. He told of his delight of spending afternoons fishing with his sons. And when sixteen-year-old Uday was asked what his ambitions were, he replied, 'I want to be a nuclear scientist.'

The president let it be known that he had set up a telephone hotline direct to his desk so that any citizen at any time of the day or night might call him to talk to the glorious leader about his or her problems – not that this helped the thousands who were killed, tortured and imprisoned in his first years of office.

The purges that had started within hours of his accession soon extended to the influential Shia community. Two Shia members of the Revolutionary Command Council were among those shot. Members of their clans were also rounded up, their houses taken from them and their possessions confiscated.

The predictable unrest among the Shiites of Baghdad led to the inevitable reprisals and random checks and arrests of any who were perceived as a threat to the new order.

Among those seized in the latter half of 1979 was a cousin of Hussein Shahristani. When he learned this, Shahristani immediately wrote to the president and asked why his relative had been imprisoned. The response was swift. The following afternoon the secret police arrived at his office in Tuwaitha.

6

A TALE OF TWO
SCIENTISTS

He didn't see the ambush coming.

On 4 December 1979, Hussein Shahristani was engrossed in his paperwork. His colleagues had been teasing him about how absentminded he was becoming. At times he was so deeply immersed in his research programme at Tuwaitha, he forgot to go home until very late at night. Once a dapper fellow, his hair was uncombed, his suits ruffled, and he was losing weight because of the number of meals he was missing.

He had promised his Canadian-born wife, Berniece, that they would have dinner that night with friends and was annoyed when two colleagues strayed into his room just as he was shuffling his papers into a near orderly jumble. The two men plonked themselves down on the brown settee, clearly intent on making themselves comfortable.

Shahristani told the men to help themselves to coffee, mumbling apologies that he couldn't hang around for long. He was also wary of offending this odd couple. Rumour had it that they were Saddam's eyes and ears at Tuwaitha. They must have been there for something, as Shahristani did not rate their scientific competence. He was on the point of throwing them out when they were joined by his best friend at the complex, Jaffar Dhia Jaffar. Shahristani wondered whether he should telephone Berniece and tell her another social engagement would have to be cancelled.

He was still wrestling with that unpleasant prospect when the office door slammed open and a security officer barged in. The chemist noticed that his guests didn't flinch.

'Doctor, I am sorry to trouble you,' the guard said before Shahristani could object to the intrusion. 'Might I have a word with you for just a moment?'

Shahristani looked to the odd couple to say something but they sat mute, as did Jaffar.

'Sure,' he said. 'Please go ahead. What do you want?'

The guard said he needed to talk to him in private and so Shahristani walked out of his office. The guard took his hand, almost as a parent would lead a child safely across a road. As soon as Shahristani was through the door, the guard grabbed his arm and twisted it behind his back, propelling him down the corridor and out of the building to a waiting car, with the frightened chemist demanding to know what this was all about.

There were two other men already in the car. They also refused to answer his questions. Shahristani was told, 'You will understand shortly.'

Shahristani had no idea where he was being taken. After a half-hour ride the car stopped. The chemist was dragged out. He recognised the grotesque outline of the headquarters of the Amin Al Aam, the internal security police. He was thrown into a room that was bare except for a desk and chair. The Amin officer sitting in the room refused Shahristani permission to say his prayers, but said nothing else.

After five hours the head of the security force strolled casually into the room and said to the chemist, 'How nice of you to visit us, doctor.'

For the next few minutes the security chief idly chatted to

Shahristani about a number of his colleagues, as though they were old friends reminiscing. As the officer lit a cigarette, Shahristani realised all those just mentioned had disappeared from Tuwaitha.

'Tell us, doctor, what it is you so have against our glorious regime?'

Before Shahristani could finish protesting that he could not care less about politics, the other Amin officer hit him across the back of his head.

'We know everything about you,' he shouted. 'Give him to me for a few minutes, sir. I'll bring him back to you talking like a parrot,' the self-appointed torturer said to his superior.

Shahristani couldn't see if the security chief nodded his assent because he was dragged by the hair, blindfolded and pushed down a flight of concrete steps. The fall into the basement torture chamber injured Shahristani's elbow, head and back. There, still blindfolded, he was stripped naked. His hands were tied behind his back and he was spat on. Two guards lifted him up and hung him by his wrists from the ceiling. They insisted that he would confess all his crimes within the hour. The pain was excruciating and he cried out for help, but as he did so his body was jolted by what felt like a thousand volts as the guards jabbed at him with electric cattle prods.

They were whipping him with electric cables and he could feel the skin on his back beginning to tear.

'Tell us how you helped our enemies destroy the facilities in France that were meant to be here in Tuwaitha,' one voice said. 'You wanted this project delayed, didn't you? You sabotaged it, doctor.'

Shahristani's protests of innocence were useless. He was about to faint from the pain in his shoulders when his two interrogators began chatting amongst themselves almost as if he wasn't there.

'He wouldn't have cooperated with the Jews. No, he is a religious man. It must have been his friend, Jaffar. Jaffar loves the Jews. Tell us, doctor, what Jaffar did and you can go home.'

Shahristani ached from every muscle and thought he would say anything if it meant ending this agony but he had no idea what his torturers were on about. He spat out what protests he could to defend his friend.

The guards noticed as the chemist began to lose conscious-ness and cut him down, letting him drop on to the concrete floor. One turned a hose of freezing cold water on him. The other jabbed him with the toe of his boot so Shahristani could not curl up into a ball to protect himself from the stabbing jets of water.

He told himself to concentrate on something, to think of Berniece, anything so long as he stayed conscious. By now he thought his bosses at Tuwaitha would realise what had hap-pened and be straightening out this ridiculous mistake.

But Berniece had not yet begun to worry. She was so used to his absences that she had not thought it unusual that their guests had feasted and gone and her husband still wasn't home. He did, however, usually telephone to offer some feeble excuse. She waited until midnight and called his office. There was no reply. She remembered then that her husband had always told her that if she was worried she should call Jaffar and so she dialled his number.

Berniece had first been introduced to Jaffar soon after the physicist had returned to Iraq in 1971 and was amused by his laconic humour. At their family get-togethers Jaffar proved himself an admirable mimic of some of their mutual friends and colleagues. When the two scientists found time to have a meal together, Jaffar enjoyed nothing more than talking about their time as students in England, which Jaffar called 'the happy days'. Jaffar would inevitably produce photographs of himself at Seaford College, where he had done his 'A' levels, as well as portraits of the shaggy-haired university student at Birmingham and University College, London.

Berniece would have liked their families to be closer, but

since arriving in Baghdad she had converted to Islam and took seriously the social and religious responsibilities of a Muslim wife and mother. Not so the gregarious Phyllis Jaffar, who had been brought up in west London and hated the creeping claustrophobia of small-town Baghdad with increasing intensity. From the few lunch parties she had attended with other 'Tuwaitha widows', she realised they felt as isolated as she did.

Phyllis answered Berniece's call. She sounded as though she had been asleep. Berniece blurted out her apologies for disturbing them so late and asked if either of them knew where her husband might be. Jaffar grabbed the phone.

'Don't worry,' he said. 'I'm coming straight over.'

Berniece thought it strange he should do that as she was only enquiring what corner of Tuwaitha her absent-minded husband had found to sleep in that night. Before she could figure out what was going on two policemen knocked on the door, asking if they could search the house.

Thoroughly confused, she stepped back from the door to allow the officers in. They explained that they were investigating some robberies in the area and were there for her protection. Quite how they intended to do this by going through the family's laundry basket and photo albums she wasn't sure. Before she could enquire, Jaffar arrived. Seeing the police, he slumped into Shahristani's favourite armchair. He said nothing while they remained and whispered to Berniece to do the same. The reassurance she had at his being there evaporated as she studied the worry creasing his face.

The moment she closed the door on the policemen Berniece begged Jaffar to tell her what was going on, though mindful that her three young children had been awoken by the commotion.

Jaffar said, 'I don't know, Berniece. Some men took him away. It must be a mistake. He will be with us by morning, I'm sure.'

In fact Shahristani was held incommunicado for another

thirty-two days. He was tortured and starved and then dragged in front of one of Saddam's kangaroo courts.

After the trial, Jaffar was one of the few in Baghdad who dared call on the Shahristani household. In the past, Jaffar had been able to reassure his own wife, confident of his own importance to Tuwaitha. He dismissed as stories the rumours that some husbands had been ordered to divorce foreign wives, or had simply disappeared. Jaffar would chide Phyllis for listening to such hysterical rubbish, explaining that these men had been moved to other parts of the project elsewhere in Iraq.

'And, besides, how could they possibly do without me?' he would tease her.

Jaffar had never been modest about his abilities and achievements and his house was liberally decorated with photographs of him receiving some degree or other, clutching some trophy he had won playing squash or shaking hands with some dignitary. He enjoyed the prestige that his professional status and family conferred.

He had set about impressing his elders in the nuclear fraternity as soon as he returned to Baghdad in the early 1970s. While Shahristani immersed himself in his work, Jaffar would delight in inviting guests back to his parents' rambling home in the affluent Keradeht Miriam enclave that was stuffed full of English antiques, grandfather clocks and brooding portraits of his ancestors recalling an older and more gracious age.

Those who visited the Jaffars remarked that the atmosphere and the generous hospitality were resonant of the days when kings still ruled Baghdad and his father, an American-educated engineer, served as a minister in the royal court. His mother had even more impressive royal connections; she was reputed to be a princess by some distant tribal link.

The whisper that swirled around the bazaars was that Jaffar's royal grandfather had unwittingly insulted King Faisal II by asking the king's entourage to divest themselves of their weapons before crossing the threshold into his home.

He had meant this kindly, hoping the king would regard this as evidence that in this house he would be safe. Instead, Faisal took offence and never visited them again.

Jaffar's retreat from domestic stress and Phyllis's unhappiness was the Alwiya English Club, and he became a daily habitué of the oak-panelled reading room. At the Alwiya, plaques still hung from the walls commemorating the achievements of the long-disbanded Baghdad Hunt, when the huntsmen in their traditional pinks used to chase jackals rather than foxes. An old picture of Iraqi President Bakr hung on the wall, replacing the portrait of Queen Elizabeth II.

The club was now frayed at the edges. The wing-backed leather armchairs were torn and the chintz prints were fading. Many of the heavy crystal glasses were chipped and were being replaced by cheaper tumblers imported from Egypt from which Jaffar refused to drink his whisky. The club's silver cricket trophies needed burnishing.

Jaffar once joked to Shahristani how he longed for the time when the club had tolerated only 5 per cent of its members being Iraqis. Shahristani frankly had little time for such diversions, not least because he did not wish to waste his $150 a month salary on the club's exorbitant prices and as a devout Muslim did not share his friend's fondness for claret.

In truth, the shabbiness irritated Jaffar. He seldom lost an opportunity to berate whichever barman had the misfortune to serve him the first drink of the evening. His moods were becoming more pronounced, excused by his coterie as the result of the pressure of work. The one indulgence guaranteed to mellow him was the roast beef and gravy lunches still served on Sundays in the dining room, which reminded him of his days as an English public schoolboy.

One afternoon, after just such a heavy lunch, Jaffar made a rare mistake. He could not stop brooding about Shahristani's continued imprisonment and the claret he regularly enjoyed began to fuel his courage.

'Why won't they let me even visit him?' he wondered out

loud to the barman, who preferred to ignore such conversations. Even in the Alwiya, Saddam had ears. 'We need him. I need him. He is like a brother to me. Surely, the president will listen to reason,' Jaffar muttered, not caring if anyone was listening to him.

At the mention of 'the president' the barman excused himself from the bar on the pretence of visiting the club's wine cellar.

Jaffar rubbed his hands through his lustrous black hair and almost knocked over his wine. The diminutive physicist convinced himself he had nothing to lose from an honest, heart-to-heart conversation with Saddam. He reasoned that the president, as head of the nuclear programme, would share his assessment of Shahristani as an indispensable member of his scientific elite.

That day he found Saddam in one of his more accommodating moods. The president insisted the two gossip a while before Jaffar made his request.

'Saidi, it is certainly not my place to question matters of security but may I draw your attention to Dr Shahristani's value to us? He is this country's most outstanding nuclear chemist. Since his arrest, valuable research has been interrupted. I cannot do his work because I am a physicist, so please, sir, can you help us in this matter?'

Saddam did not seem to register what the physicist was saying. That may only have been a tactic to see how far Jaffar would go, and Jaffar then made the mistake of letting his feelings show.

'I don't think it is reasonable to treat men of Dr Shahristani's calibre like dogs,' Jaffar shouted, and banged his fist on the desk for emphasis.

The bodyguard who routinely stood behind the president's chair moved towards the scientist but Saddam held up his hand and glowered at Jaffar.

In the instant his hand hit the desk Jaffar realised his mistake. He babbled apologies, waved his arms but dared not look into the president's face. All he noticed was an imperious flick from Saddam's wrist dismissing him from the room. The bodyguard almost physically lifted Jaffar out of the private office. Jaffar knew that any protests were pointless.

The physicist was terrified – and with good reason. He was shaking so badly he could barely turn the keys in the ignition. Within three hours, the secret police arrived at his parents' home and Jaffar joined his old friend in the interrogation rooms of the security service headquarters.

Jaffar was blindfolded and left to fret for six hours. It was after midnight when the guards came for him, his heels dragging along the corridor as he was taken to a torture chamber. Saddam had done his homework on the physicist, as he had with all the senior scientists employed at Tuwaitha; he knew how to break each and every one of them.

Jaffar was tied to a wooden chair and his blindfold removed. In front of him, kneeling on the floor, was a man of roughly the same age and build. The bearded figure, whose name he never knew, was pulled to his feet as a guard armed with a set of pliers began to remove each one of the victim's fingernails. Jaffar watched in terrified silence. The naked figure in front of him writhed with indescribable pain until the sufferer was put out of his misery by a hammer blow to the back of his head. The bleeding figure lay prone at his feet. Jaffar stared in mute disbelief.

One of his interrogators slapped his face. 'So, good doctor, this is what we do to Jew-loving traitors like your friend Shahristani.'

Jaffar vomited over his own feet. For the next two weeks the routine was the same. Jaffar was blindfolded and frogmarched down to the interrogation room, where he was forced to witness the torture and murder of other anonymous victims.

Then, without any explanation, Jaffar was moved one night in the summer of 1980 to the prison of the Mukhabarat secret police, who usually dealt with foreign enemies of the regime. Unbeknownst to Jaffar, his friend Shahristani was incarcerated inside the same building, a converted Baghdad synagogue.

Saddam's scheme was that Jaffar should witness the torturers' handiwork on his best friend. But he had no need. The physicist's spirit had been broken. For eight months he was shunted between the offices of the secret police and a mental asylum where doctors were told their latest patient had suffered a nervous breakdown.

Finally, when Saddam decided Jaffar had been punished enough, he ordered him to be brought to his office. Jaffar's jailers had to spend two hours cleaning him up. A fresh suit of clothes was brought from his home, along with his lemon-fragrance aftershave. Jaffar was sure this was some macabre charade, and he felt faint. He gulped great breaths of air as he was pushed into a police vehicle and driven to the presidential compound.

Saddam stared at him, then slowly extended his arms. 'My dear doctor, these fools sometimes overreach their authority. They were – how shall I put it? – somewhat overzealous.'

Saddam ordered a bodyguard to pour Jaffar a whisky. The scientist was shaking so much he could not hold the glass.

Saddam smiled at his obvious discomfort and continued, 'Now that I know you are loyal to me, you can have anything you wish to continue your excellent work.'

The physicist could scarcely control his tears and, still not having said a word, he reached out for Saddam's hand and kissed it. His silent assent had been given.

Jaffar knew better than to ask what had become of his friend. At the Amin prison Shahristani was dragged through the same cruel routine of watching others tortured. The first was a seven-year-old boy who had been hanged by his hands for so long that he told the chemist he couldn't feel them any more. Shahristani tried to comfort the boy, saying, 'Don't worry, you still have your arms, you will get better.'

As he tried to massage the circulation back into the child's arms, the boy described his crime. He had been at school and to amuse his classmates he had written on the blackboard, 'Saddam is a donkey.' A week after telling Shahristani this story, the child was executed.

When the guards realised they could not break Shahristani's will as easily as his colleague's, they trussed him up to a beam above the torture chamber and left him alone for two days. When they cut him down, he could not use his arms. The guards left his food on a plate on the floor and Shahristani had to lie next to it and eat like an animal.

Saddam, impatient with what he regarded as Shahristani's stubbornness, ordered Amin's most accomplished torturer to take charge. The chemist was thrown into the hands of a tat-tooed sadist known as Fadel, and was roughly confined in a different cell which he shared with ten others who had already been worked on by Fadel.

Three of Fadel's victims had had their backs broken by being repeatedly beaten across the spine. They lay helpless on the stone floor, completely paralysed and denied any medical help. Another of the prisoners was a doctor. He was forbidden to assist any of his cell mates and was bleeding profusely from the rectum. He told Shahristani that earlier that morning one of the guards had taken a glass bottle, broken off the top and then deliberately assaulted him with it. The doctor pointed to an old man crouched in the corner of the cell who held up both his hands. Holes had been drilled through some of his fingers. Others had burns on their backs and genitals. Some had had their hair torn out in clumps.

Shahristani was convinced he was about to suffer similar punishments. What may have saved him was Saddam's con-viction that he was crucial to his dream of full nuclear capability.

Two months after his arrest, Shahristani was allowed his first shower. He was not told why, but it was to make him suf-ficiently presentable for an appearance before a revolutionary court. The other five prisoners standing in front of the judge were not allowed to speak, and after barely ten minutes they were dragged back to their cells and handed a piece of paper informing them of their sentence. Shahristani could hear their wails as he tried to maintain his concentration and his dignity.

The oldest of the prisoners gazed at the sentence of twenty years scribbled on his piece of paper. He tried to grab hold of the guard's arm, saying, 'I was told, sir, that I would only get seven years. This must be the wrong paper.'

The guard kicked him and replied, 'There are no wrong papers, fool. They are all right papers.'

Shahristani was invited to plead his innocence. It was, of course, a pointless exercise. The judge did not listen, and appeared bored by the chemist's speech. He held up his hand and sentenced Shahristani to twenty years for the crime of 'being of Persian origin'. In Saddam's Iraq this was tantamount to treason.

The judge told him, 'Even if you prove your ancestors were living here for the past 1,400 years, you are still Persian. This in itself is a crime.'

Shahristani was too numb to protest. He was handcuffed and blindfolded and taken to a 'closed section' of the infamous Abu Ghraib prison. This new regime was harsher still. As he was dumped in his cell the guard leered at him and told him he was not allowed any visitors. For the next four months he was beaten daily and kept in a cell that was four metres square, where he slept in shifts because there were so many other prisoners.

Each man was given one cup of water a day that had to be used for his ablutions as well as to slake his thirst. The food was execrable and to amuse themselves the guards would order the cook to lace the daily rations with drugs so that the inmates suffered from diarrhoea. The only toilet was a hole in the floor in the corner of the cell.

Shahristani felt he was losing his grip on his sanity. In May 1980 he was almost grateful when the guards came for him, even though he feared this must be his day of execution.

Instead, the guards cleaned him up and drove him across

Baghdad and back to the Mukhabarat jail. It was another four months before Shahristani was given another chance of a reprieve. Numb from the beatings, he was awakened one morning to be told that his wife and youngest child had come to visit him. He suppressed his excitement, aware there must be some more sinister purpose to this invitation. He did not want Berniece to see him in this state but the guards refused to allow him to wash or change his filthy clothes.

His escorts marched him to an office in a part of the prison he had never visited and instructed him to look through a window. He cried as he glimpsed his wife, wrapped in her traditional black chador, holding the baby son he was seeing for the first time.

Shahristani was elated and tried to push his way through the door, but the guard gripped his arm. 'You know of course we could kill them now, kill them in front of you. Remember that.'

Shahristani noticed that another guard had slipped into the office where Berniece was waiting. This guard insisted on taking the child from her arms. He held the little boy during the ten-minute meeting allowed to husband and wife.

There was so much he wanted to tell her, so many questions he needed to ask about the rest of his family, but the haunted look in Berniece's eyes persuaded him to use the little time they had to reassure her that he was well and would soon be home. The ever-present guard laughed at that remark.

Back in his cell that night, Shahristani was still exhilarated from seeing Berniece and his son. He had to contend with another surprise when a senior officer opened the cell door.

'President Saddam is disturbed by your case and has said the Amin security should never have arrested you. We want to take you back and reinstate you at your post at the Atomic Energy Commission.'

Shahristani thought this another ruse and pleaded he wasn't mentally or physically ready for that.

The officer replied, 'That is for others to judge.'

The chemist was moved from prison to a comfortable villa where he was told he would be given time to recuperate, but he was still not sure why. One evening, without warning, Saddam's half-brother, Barzan, arrived along with Abdel Razak Al Hashemi, the deputy head of the Atomic Energy Commission. Hashemi stood guard by the door as Barzan walked across to the injured scientist, who lay half-paralysed on the carpet.

Barzan held out his hand. 'The president sends his greetings and is sorry about what happened to you. I hope you are recovering and that you are comfortable and that you will soon be able to return to work.'

Shahristani, who had still to recover the full use of his arms, complained he wasn't fit enough.

Barzan stared at the stricken scientist. With an edge to his voice, he said, 'You will go back to the Atomic Energy Commission and work with others to develop an atomic bomb. It is vital for our country, because it will give our leader a long arm to reshape the map of the Middle East.'

Whatever suspicions he had harboured, this was the first time Shahristani had been told of Saddam Hussein's secret programme to build a nuclear bomb. He was shocked.

'All my research has been in the peaceful uses of atomic energy,' he protested. 'I've had no expertise in weapons.'

Barzan interrupted the chemist. 'You will do this because it is an important service to your country. And let me tell you any man who is not willing to serve his country does not deserve to be alive.'

'I agree it is a man's duty to serve his country,' Shahristani said as he struggled to lift himself off the floor. 'But what you are asking me to do is not a service to my country.'

It was Barzan's turn to look shocked, but he controlled his temper and answered with a forced smile. 'Well, the important thing is we agree on the principle that we must serve our country. The rest are details we can discuss later. I can see you are tired now. Doctors will be sent to take care of you.'

The reason why he had been spared by the regime suddenly became clear to Shahristani.

Barzan left, remembering how the informers at Tuwaitha had reported the many irreverent conversations between Shahristani and his fellow scientists, about what they really thought of Saddam's regime. Every peal of laughter, every gibe had been recorded and passed on. When Shahristani dared to question the arrest of his relative, this was seen as proof of his treachery. Jaffar's intercession on his behalf was confirmation that the nuclear community was full of traitors. Shahristani's refusal to work on the bomb programme was the ultimate betrayal.

By the time Barzan reappeared at the villa at the end of September 1980, the Iraqi Air Force had launched a pre-emptive strike on Iran. Iraq was now at full-scale war with its neighbour, a pointless conflict that was as wasteful as the Somme. By the time it ended eight years later it had cost over a million-and-a-half lives.

Barzan seemed in a conciliatory mood for this second meeting, even though Shahristani made it clear in the first few seconds that he had not changed his mind.

'I've thought about what you have told me. In fact I've thought about little else, but I have no other answer. I know my scientific limitations and what you are asking me to do is beyond my scientific capability. That's it. I understand the threat and the consequences of saying no.'

Before Barzan could say anything Shahristani made his own stab at compromise, adding quickly, 'Nevertheless, please tell me what precisely you would like me to do.'

Hashemi, the Atomic Energy Commission deputy chief, interjected, 'Perhaps he can work on extracting uranium from the phosphate rocks at Okasha.'

Shahristani was happy to oblige, realising that there wasn't enough material in the desert wasteland near the Syrian border to make a firework, though mining the uranium would enhance Iraq's prestige as an emerging nuclear player.

Confident that his ordeal was now behind him, Shahristani asked if he might have laboratory facilities in which to work.

Barzan replied with obvious agitation, 'Yes, I understand your needs, doctor, but we're busy with the war. Perhaps we can make this arrangement later.'

Saddam's half-brother made several more visits to the villa, the last one in June 1981, shortly after Israeli jets bombed the French Osirak reactor at Tuwaitha. Shahristani was furious as he listened to details of the bombardment, protesting that his work there had nothing to do with any military plan. His guests smiled, wrongly believing Shahristani had been converted back to their cause.

As Barzan described the damage that had been done, he stressed how scientists at Osirak had assured him the reactor core had remained untouched. 'We can go in. Get the French fuel and make it into a bomb,' Barzan said, his eyes reflecting an obvious excitement.

Shahristani laughed nervously and shook his head. 'You simply can't do that. Don't you see that once you put fuel in the reactor and start the process, the uranium becomes so radioactive that no one could dare approach it? You can only work it through the lead shield of a hot cell and then you need a special facility to reprocess that fuel. All that is so complicated it's impossible to build in Iraq, and no one will sell it to us. It can't be done.'

Barzan interjected. 'We thought of all that. We don't care about the radioactivity. We can bring soldiers, as many as necessary, and we will send them in to where the uranium is kept.'

Shahristani could not quite believe what he was hearing. 'But they will die after only a few seconds of standing next to that fuel.'

Barzan smiled and said, 'We have many soldiers. We will send them in one at a time for one minute, then pull each one out. They can go to a rest house and die there.'

Shahristani shivered at the idea of this relay of death.

It was Hashemi who changed the subject rather obviously.

He asked Shahristani if there was anything to eat in the villa as he had missed dinner because of their meeting. Shahristani guessed another game was about to be played at his expense. As the three men shared a plate of kebabs, Hashemi introduced the name of Dr Jaffar into their conversation. Berniece had managed to let her husband know that Jaffar had visited her and that he had been briefly imprisoned himself after pleading for Shahristani's release.

At the mention of Jaffar's name Shahristani suppressed the natural instinct to sound excited. He chewed slowly on an olive, pursed his lips and let Hashemi continue.

'You know he was arrested also,' Hashemi said.

Shahristani willed himself to stay calm.

'He disappointed us, as have you, but that is behind us now – for him and, we pray, for you. He is back at work and he sends his greetings to you.'

Shahristani ached to be back in his laboratory with his old colleagues. He threw out his own bait. 'As the scientific programme was effectively supervised by the two of us, and if he is still there, then perhaps you can arrange for the two of us to meet and to cooperate again.'

'You know he is much wiser than you,' Hashemi replied brusquely.

Shahristani nodded, desperate to keep the conversation going to tease out what information he could about his friend.

Hashemi continued: 'When Jaffar saw that his future was really to serve his country and cooperate with us, he didn't hesitate. He came forward. Now he's once again a top adviser to the president and he's living in a palace.'

Shahristani was shattered by the realisation that his friend had sold out. He kept telling himself Jaffar would have done so only under terrible duress. He didn't even hear himself say, 'Well, that is his decision.'

Shahristani knew that what Jaffar had to offer was substantial. Jaffar's experience in the laboratories of Birmingham University and Imperial College and the even wider range of contacts and experience gained at the Centre for Theoretical Physics at Trieste and at the European nuclear research centre, CERN, in Geneva, gave him an insider's understanding of the type of infrastructure that Iraq needed to manufacture its bomb. He was also an expert in computer sciences. This combination of skills made him the natural scientific head of Department 3000.

It was true that Jaffar was back at work. It was also true that Jaffar had suffered. For nearly eight months he had been detained in a sanatorium. His repeated pledges of loyalty every time his guards entered the isolation ward to hand him his food were ignored. During these long, lonely months Jaffar persuaded himself that as an Iraqi scientist he should be proud to work on his country's most prestigious project.

The state had paid for his university education, provided him with the facilities to pursue his research and so had the right to develop its nuclear technology in any way it wanted, particularly if it was well known that its enemies were doing the same. He reasoned that Iraq was merely protecting itself and asserting its right to develop its native expertise.

Jaffar was also proud enough to believe that the nuclear project could never succeed without his particular gifts. His conviction that he was indispensable was reinforced when his research papers were delivered to his room. He was ordered to carry on with his work but forbidden to talk to any of his fellow scientists.

Rumours had swept Tuwaitha about his sudden disappearance, but Jaffar decided he could turn this to his own advantage. His seemingly principled stand against Saddam would impress the few dissidents at Tuwaitha, while in front of the regime he would play the game.

Jaffar had always been a consummate performer. When he suddenly reappeared at work one morning in his laboratory in Tuwaitha, he seemed to colleagues to have lost none of his poise. Only those closest to him noticed the subtle changes in his behaviour. He was no longer the one making jokes about

Saddam. He never complained about the shortage of facilities. After work he would drive straight home rather than stop off at the Alwiya. His genius was undiminished, but what was suddenly noticeable was a newfound patriotism.

He was still a man of strong feelings, but he had exchanged his loathing of Saddam for a hatred of the West. Now he would tell stories of being passed over for academic jobs in London because he was an Arab.

The transformation was all the more remarkable for a man who had been so trusted and admired by his friends in Britain. He was one of the few foreigners with easy access to the nuclear research centre at Harwell. His invitation had been approved by Britain's MI5 secret service, which was sure this anglophile would prove an invaluable asset when he returned home to Baghdad.

During his time at Harwell Jaffar immersed himself in the technology of electromagnetic isotope separation, known in shorthand as EMIS, which was the old-fashioned way of obtaining bomb-quality uranium. This idea had been pioneered some forty years earlier in Los Alamos, New Mexico, where scientists of the Manhattan Project, such as Nobel Prize-winning physicist Ernest Lawrence, grappled with the conundrum of separating uranium 238 from lighter, weapons-grade uranium 235.

Lawrence's solution was to build massive contraptions called calutrons. These looked like giant saucepan lids but were powerful magnets to separate the uranium atoms. They were built at Oak Ridge in Tennessee. The United States and the other nuclear powers would move on to more efficient technologies, such as high-spinning centrifuges and lasers. But in their efforts to end the Second World War the scientists relied on Lawrence's calutrons.

The civilian residents of Oak Ridge hadn't a clue about what was rising up behind the razor wire surrounding the compound. They were infuriated at the frequent power failures that blacked out their homes and defrosted their fridges as Lawrence's calutrons sucked up every available watt of power to produce a grain of uranium 235.

It was a cumbersome and time-consuming business and required about as much power as it took to light up Chicago. The process was happily abandoned and declassified after the first bombs were dropped on Hiroshima and Nagasaki.

The Oak Ridge scientists dumped their research into university libraries, and this is where Jaffar found it. He knew the technology was freely available and he made it his business to scoop up every fragment of research and reassemble it in his own laboratories outside Baghdad.

The ever boastful Jaffar claimed to have improved upon Lawrence's design and so called it the Baghdadtron. These giant magnets were sprawled across the new Tarmiya complex that comprised more than fifty buildings and cost over $2 billion to build in three-and-a-half square kilometres of desert.

It was crucial to Saddam's nuclear jigsaw, but the West would not see it. Satellites photographed every corner of Iraq to spot targets to bomb before the 1991 Gulf War, but they completely missed Tarmiya. Jaffar knew they would. The Iraqis had planned it that way.

The protective fences, video cameras and sensors were ringed far away from the main buildings. The American spy cameras never thought to widen their lenses to scan the entire desert perimeter. His enemies never imagined Saddam would rely on such an old-fashioned method of making a bomb, for he was known to have a passion for the latest technology and the Israelis, among others, were convinced he would be after weapons-grade plutonium.

Jaffar delighted in the deception. He told those who asked why Iraq was not concentrating on getting hold of the most recent technology: 'Why should we? This works and nobody will think that we had the wit to use it. It is like choosing to drive a Model T Ford rather than a Mercedes, my friends. The Model T is much, much slower, but it gets you there, even if it takes longer than the Mercedes.'

'The principle is simple,' Jaffar told them. 'Imagine you have a marble and a table tennis ball in a soup bowl. You spin the bowl as fast as you can and the harder, heavier marble will inevitably move to the outside of the dish. You do the same with uranium, for hour after hour, at tremendous speeds. The heavier 238 atoms end up at the edges of the calutrons, the cherished 235 drifts to the middle where it can be collected.'

The trouble with the process was the slowness of it. The Iraqis had to repeat the process thousands and thousands of times using a gaggle of these calutrons, and then got only enough uranium 235 to cover a fingernail.

Jaffar convinced his impatient masters that Iraq had the electrical power and the money to get it right. Besides, if they had tried to acquire the latest technology the West would have discovered what they were up to.

About this time, Saddam insisted that Department 3000 change its name to Petro Chemical 3. Obsessed as always with secrecy, Saddam thought anyone stumbling across the file would think it was just part of Iraq's oil industry. All the recruits to PC3 were extensively vetted.

Foreign scientists invited to Baghdad had absolutely no idea of the billions of dollars that were being poured into the nuclear programme. Nor could they guess at the rising stature of Jaffar, director of nuclear physics at Tuwaitha, vice-chairman of the Atomic Energy Commission and soon to be deputy minister of industry and military industrialisation.

These appointments were never publicised and Dr Jaffar was particularly careful in front of former colleagues from the West to suggest he had not changed. As always he was absorbed by the latest breakthroughs in science, but Jaffar was still amusing company. Over drinks he enjoyed exchanging gossip about old friends.

He regularly corresponded with Richard Wilson, a Harvard professor of physics whom he asked for advice about getting his son into the university's business school. Wilson was one of those invited to Baghdad and given a guided tour of the new facilities by Jaffar. It was a test to see how well they had disguised Tarmiya's real purpose. The Harvard professor never spotted the subtle changes at what he still thought was an old-fashioned nuclear research centre. Escorting such an eminent scientist through the complex gave Jaffar the chance to parade his intellectual snobbery.

With his Iraqi colleagues he was a different man. No one was more dedicated than the sober Dr Jaffar. He worked so late in his new laboratories that colleagues wondered how he ever found time to enjoy the enviably large villa that Saddam had given him. They were also curious of what his wife, Phyllis, made of his protracted absences. The truth was that Jaffar was grateful for the excuse to avoid his wife's increasingly erratic behaviour. Their disagreements were becoming more violent and Phyllis talked endlessly about leaving Baghdad.

Jaffar was so desperate to avoid going home that he eagerly volunteered to lead the Iraqi delegations sent abroad on secret buying missions. He applauded Saddam's new rule that wives would not be allowed on these trips in case the scientists took the opportunity to defect. Jaffar was never sure why the Iraqi secret service, who watched his every move, had not worked out that he was more likely to defect if it meant never having to go back to Phyllis. He knew his villa was bugged and wondered what the eavesdroppers made of the couple's fights.

Abroad, Jaffar proved himself a master tactician, able to reassure foreign suppliers of Iraq's peaceful intentions in developing nuclear power while knowing what hardware he needed to buy to pursue the military option. He was careful on these trips about how much he drank in front of others and curbed his natural instinct to gossip over dinner about the regime – certain that Saddam would have at least one spy sitting at the table.

Only when he was alone in his hotel room would he drink whisky to help himself sleep and think back to more innocent times when he and Shahristani used to go on these shopping expeditions for Saddam. One night when insomnia had gripped him, and he resisted calling room service for another whisky, he remembered a trip the two of them had made to Florida with their boss, Abdel Razak Al Hashemi.

He laughed out loud remembering how Hashemi had leaped at the invitation from his American hosts to visit a casino after spending a long afternoon haggling over various deals. Hashemi was chaperoned for the evening by a woman interpreter whose legs he had been staring at through most of the business meeting.

Shahristani and Jaffar didn't see their boss again for four days until they were packing to go home. At one stage they joked that Hashemi might have defected. When he reappeared at the hotel, he was grey with fatigue. He produced a bulging wallet to show how much he had won at the roulette tables. Suddenly nervous that these two might betray him, Hashemi spent the flight home on the specially chartered Iraqi Airways jet begging his 'dear understanding friends' not to mention his absences.

On their first day back at work Hashemi asked Jaffar into his office, saying he needed reminding what it was that they had bought in Florida for the nuclear programme. As Jaffar produced the contracts and explained how much they had spent out of the budget, Hashemi blushed. Jaffar joked that perhaps his boss might like to pay for some of it out of his roulette winnings. Hashemi put his fingers to his lips, imploring Jaffar to stop teasing him, fearful as always as to who might be listening in to their conversation.

While Jaffar's rehabilitation continued in the nuclear fraternity, Shahristani remained locked up with his secret service guards at a villa on the edge of Baghdad. Berniece was allowed occasional visits, but nobody else.

Barzan knew that he had failed in his job to persuade Shahristani to return to the fold. At what was to be their last meeting, Barzan had looked into Shahristani's eyes and realised that whatever he did to the chemist, he was not going to change his mind about working on the bomb.

For months Saddam was so preoccupied with his army's failures in the war with Iran that he had not bothered to ask Barzan for a progress report on his efforts to rehabilitate Shahristani. The scientists working on his nuclear programme had during this time experimented with ways to send a radioactive shower over the waves of Iranian troops pouring across the marshlands of Iraq's frontier. The plan was to use strips of zirconium metal, irradiated in a nuclear reactor and packed into a missile warhead which, when it detonated, would spread for miles across the enemy lines. The trouble was the radioactivity did not spray far enough.

Angered after reading a report of the failure of the zirconium plan, Saddam summoned his closest aides to check on the progress of PC3. Saddam was less than impressed by what they had to tell him.

The sweat trickled under Barzan's collar as one technocrat after another trotted out excuses for their delays. He closed his eyes when one of those present suddenly asked what had become of Shahristani, and why he was not lending his expertise to solving some of their problems. For a few seconds there was silence. Barzan stared at the floor. His brother erupted with a volley of insults about Shahristani.

Barely an hour after Saddam had been reminded of his obduracy, the secret police barged in to Shahristani's bedroom and gave him two minutes to dress. He could not call his family and was forbidden to take any clothes or other belongings as, blindfolded, he was taken back to Abu Ghraib.

The prison governor smirked as Shahristani was forced through the humiliating routine of being strip searched, deloused and dragged back to a cell. What Shahristani did not know was that he had been sentenced to indefinite solitary confinement. He was allowed no books, radio, or paper to write on. He sat on the freezing stone floor counting the bricks and then playing geometric games with them to retain his sanity.

He was not permitted to leave his cell. His food was passed

through a hatch so he would see no one and talk to no one. And he was never told how long this torment would continue. As he tried to sleep on the thin, lice-ridden army blanket, Shahristani wondered what had become of other colleagues he had met during his first month in prison.

7

BOMBING OSIRAK

Entombed in his cell, Shahristani cursed his decision to return to Baghdad to work for Saddam. Jaffar had felt the same during the months he too was held in an asylum. But it is possible that their imprisonment saved their lives. The Israelis were on a manhunt. They had orders to assassinate the men Saddam needed to create his nuclear empire, whatever the cost, and at the top of this list were Jaffar and Shahristani.

The operation to eliminate Iraq's scientific elite had begun four years before on a cool October morning in 1975 when the chain-smoking prime minister, Yitzhak Rabin, received a telephone call at first light from his old comrade and foreign minister, General Yigal Allon.

The two had been friends since teenage days at the Kedourie agricultural school and Rabin teased the general, who was older by four years, that old age meant he couldn't sleep properly. Both had fought in the Palmach brigade, where they learned the dark arts of sabotage and assassination.

'Itzik, I have to see you,' the general said sharply.

Allon had been his commander in the Palmach nearly thirty years earlier and Rabin knew better than to refuse such a request. Twenty minutes later, the burly general sat slumped in his chair as Rabin jabbed an unlit cigarette into the Foreign Ministry folder splayed out across his desk.

'Why has no one else realised this was happening?' Rabin asked in his distinctive growl.

The general simply shrugged. The cigarette was now almost bent in two as Rabin stabbed at the jumble of telexes from Israeli agents in Europe and beyond, warning how Iraqi scientists had embarked on an expensive shopping expedition to buy nuclear hardware. The priority was to purchase a 500-megawatt nuclear reactor from France. Although French Premier Jacques Chirac balked at that request, he was still willing to sell them a smaller research facility based on the Osirak reactor.

Rabin recognised the unmistakable signs of what Saddam really wished to acquire. Israel had done the same when it built the Dimona nuclear plant. He held up a press cutting from only a few weeks before that had photographs of a beaming Vice-President Saddam Hussein being fêted by French ministers during one of his rare excursions abroad to seal the deal.

'The French only care about themselves and their precious export deals,' Allon scoffed.

He was reminded of how his ambassador in Paris, Ben Eitan, in his first conversation with Jacques Chirac was led to believe that if any Arab country threatened Israel then France, with its nuclear muscle, would of course leap to its defence. In the same breath the French premier promised to invite the ambassador to his home that weekend for Sunday lunch so they could discuss this further. Months later, Eitan was still waiting for the call.

Rabin tossed aside the diplomatic responses from London and Washington which in effect told Israel not to be so excitable. 'I thought Kissinger would see the dangers,' Rabin said. 'If no one will help us we must do it alone. Let us kill this child before it is born, Yigal.'

The general permitted himself a wry smile. This was the response he wanted, but he dared not tell the notoriously short-tempered premier that he had no idea how to go about it.

Mossad prided itself on its invention but it had never managed to insinuate an agent in the heart of Baghdad's regime. A few prominent Iraqis had been on the payroll but never lasted long before being caught and hanged. Allon considered this not the time to dwell on Mossad's shortcomings. During the next two hours, he and Rabin mapped out a coded message to be sent to Israeli agents ordering them to monitor what Iraqi delegations were buying on their shopping trips. The general pointed out how there had been a recent rush of young Iraqi scientists sent to Rome, Paris and elsewhere to study. Now the Baghdad regime was suddenly hiring the brightest Arab technicians with ridiculously generous salaries.

'They must be watched, Itzik,' the general said. 'And then we must eliminate the best of them before they complete their work.'

Rabin closed his fist over the general's hand. 'We must be patient, Yigal, and not make any more mistakes.'

Rabin was referring to the disastrous operation two years earlier when Mossad was tasked to assassinate the Palestinian terrorists responsible for the murder of eleven Israeli athletes in the Olympic village at the 1972 Munich games. Millions had watched that tragedy unfold on their televisions. They learned that Israel does not wait long for its revenge.

The retaliation began in Lebanon. Commando units sailed into Beirut on inflatable dinghies and climbed into rented Mercedes cars that were waiting for them on the corniche. The teams split up and headed for the apartments of three PLO leaders. All three were shot dead within minutes of each other and the commandos slipped back out to sea.

Four months later an Israeli assassination team, known as 'a Kidon', turned up in the Norwegian resort of Lillehammer, certain they had tracked the man responsible for planning the

Munich outrage. He was also the commander of Force 17, which was responsible for protecting PLO leader Yasser Arafat.

The Israeli agents stalked the man for days and as he locked his car outside his apartment they opened fire. Only the next day did they realise they had killed a Moroccan waiter in front of his pregnant Norwegian wife. Mossad had left so many clues that it was fingered for this 'wet job' and embarrassed by the international condemnation. Israel suspended its overseas hit teams. As Rabin and Allon surveyed their mission to stop Saddam's bomb, they knew they dared not antagonise European allies the way they had upset the Norwegians.

Rabin knew the risks but he did not hesitate to sign the executive order to Yitzhak Hoffi, the Mossad chief.

Hoffi was not in his headquarters in the glass tower block close to the American embassy in Tel Aviv. He had driven down the coastal highway towards the affluent seaside enclave of Herzlia, where most Western diplomats prefer to live, and turned along the narrow road that leads past the hotel and health spa known as the Country Club. Buried behind scrubland on the gently rising slope is one of Israel's worst kept secrets, the site of Mossad's training school, the Midrasha. Hoffi had an office on the top floor which looked down on some of Tel Aviv's best beaches.

There, standing by the bullet-proof picture window, the Mossad chief studied Rabin's order. He did not need his prime minister to remind him that to thwart Iraq's nuclear ambition would stretch Mossad's resources as well as its ingenuity. Neither did he need telling that his agency was under scrutiny after the debacle in Norway.

This operation would mean recruiting new faces to make up 'Yarid' squads, the covert teams whose job it would be to keep an eye on suspect manufacturers and scientists. He thumbed through the intelligence files that included a handful of photographs of the scientists the Iraqis trusted enough to allow to travel abroad on buying missions. Hoffi sniffed as he read how much money the Iraqis were spending in the cocktail bar of the Meridien, their favourite hotel in Paris. He made a mental note to have more of his own people get jobs there.

The truth was that Israel's intelligence-gathering needed liberal doses of luck and the help of 'sayanim'. These were Jews who could be relied on for a favour, though most would spend their lives never getting the call to help. Their identities were jealously guarded even from curious prime ministers. Hoffi remembered the middle-aged secretary who identified one of the first French firms to offer its help to Saddam when she stumbled across a letter from the Iraqi clients insisting that the firm screen employers 'so no Jews or Israelis' could ever work there.

Stapled to the back of the file were the handwritten notes from the Nobel scientist Emilio Segra, an Italian Jew who moved to America in 1938 to escape the Nazis and who was later recruited by the Manhattan Project to build the world's first atomic bomb. Segra was one of the original sayanim. Twenty years earlier, he had helped Mossad to track down those of Hitler's rocket scientists hired by Egypt's ambitious president, Gamal Abdel Nasser.

Segra was again playing his part. He noticed the Iraqis had started making serious overtures to the Italian Atomic Energy Commission and passed on to an old friend, Professor Yuval Ne'eman, a nuclear physicist and scientific adviser to his country's intelligence community, his suspicions about companies like SNIA Techint in Rome which were lining up to supply Baghdad with sophisticated laboratories.

There was talk of the Italians' providing a 'technological hall' where the Iraqis could separate plutonium from spent fuel. Saddam was so excited by that prospect he called it the '20th of July Project', named after the date the Ba'ath Party had seized power. The Mossad chief made a note to add the SNIA offices to his list of possible targets.

In May 1977, while Hoffi and his spies busied themselves on this operation, Israelis made the surprising choice to dump their decorated war hero Yitzhak Rabin for the abrasive Likud leader, Menachem Begin, who promised to be even more resolute on their Arab enemies.

Thirty-six hours after moving into the prime minister's office, Begin called in the Mossad chief and was shown the files on what had been called 'Operation Mount Moriah'. As he read through an outline about Iraq's ambitions, the concern was evident on Begin's face. He pushed his glasses tight against the bridge of his nose and kept clenching his fist. Begin motioned for his secretarial staff to leave the office.

When they had closed the door he asked, 'What did Rabin do about this?'

'Not much,' replied Hoffi, making no time for diplomatic niceties. 'He just asked us to watch what the Iraqis were buying. He thought they were still in the planning stage.'

The obscene noise Begin made in response eloquently reflected his contempt. 'Well, we must do more to stop this madness than just send diplomatic requests. Hurt them, and hurt them hard,' he said.

That year Begin gave orders for a campaign of sabotage and assassination. Israeli forces launched their most ambitious and dangerous raid since the Entebbe rescue operation mounted against the Ugandan dictator Idi Amin. The consequences of getting 'Mount Moriah' wrong were incalculable. Begin kept the operation secret from all but a handful of trusted lieutenants, all of them certain to endorse his battle plan.

The operation began in France. For eighteen months, starting in 1977, Mossad made it its business to infiltrate the French manufacturer CNIM, which was building Iraq's reactor core at its plant on the Mediterranean coast near Toulon, the shabby relation that the billionaires next door on the Côte d'Azur prefer to ignore. A CNIM security guard on the Mossad payroll had warned that the two nuclear cores, dubbed Tammuz 1 and Tammuz 2 by the Iraqis, were about to be shipped to Baghdad.

French immigration officials were more concerned with preventing Arab immigrants from slipping into the port of Marseilles than they were about three European-looking tourists who arrived on Belgian passports on 4 April 1979. Two days later another four tourists appeared in Toulon. The seven agents met for an evening meal in a modest hotel in the town. Their waiter thought it odd that none of them were drinking.

Later that night, the team drove in two rented trucks to La Seyne-sur-Mer, a picturesque harbour choked with pleasure boats where the CNIM consortium had stored the cores in a hangar on the quayside.

Security was not up to much. The team leader signalled for his agents, who included a nuclear physicist, to cut through the wire fence on the far side of the hangar. Once inside they could hardly miss their intended target, as behind the double doors sat three wooden crates clearly stamped 'IRAK'.

It was just after three in the morning when the Mossad agents attached explosive charges to the cores. To cover their escape, others from the team stage managed a raucous diversion just outside the main gates when a young woman appeared to have been knocked down by a speeding car. As concerned security men rushed to her assistance, two powerful explosions lit up the Mediterranean sky, scattering flaming debris on to the corrugated roof of their guard post.

Few believed the claims made the following morning by an unheard-of French environmental group that it was responsible. French forensic teams certainly knew better. In the tangle of the wreckage, they found three explosive charges that had not gone off which they recognised as military ordnance used to blow up tanks. Mossad had utterly destroyed a $17 million contract and 300,000 hours of work.

Back in Baghdad the news that the cores had been blown up, delaying the nuclear programme by at least two years, sent Vice-President Saddam Hussein into one of his black rages. Saddam demanded to know who was responsible, though he suspected the Israelis from the start.

For the next two weeks the cable traffic between Baghdad and Paris was like a river in flood as the Iraqis first demanded compensation from the French and then, as wiser counsels prevailed among Saddam's advisers, a commitment from Paris that the cores would be replaced at France's expense.

Mossad knew Saddam would waste little time in rebuilding Osirak, which was why Begin made it clear that money was no object to blunt Iraq's efforts. Israeli agents returned to France for the next stab at Saddam. For more than a month they had been tailing the increasing numbers of Arab scientists being trained at Saclay and other French nuclear research centres.

Mossad tried to bribe other foreign scientists at Saclay to befriend the dour and obdurate Iraqis. They seldom joined colleagues after work for a glass of pastis, nor would they gossip about their frustrations at work or, more important, their problems at home. Each one had it drummed into him before leaving Baghdad that foreign conspirators would stop at nothing 'to endanger the mother country and her glorious achievements'.

Back in the country club outside Tel Aviv, the Mossad high command suggested a different approach. 'What assets do we have at Saclay?' Hoffi asked his planning group. 'We are paying some of them $1,000 a month and what are we getting for our money?'

While Hoffi and his colleagues were discussing the dubious merits of funding an Arabic restaurant near Saclay as a way of entrapping the Iraqis, the telephone rang. It was the Mossad operations chief in Paris. This was to be their first decent breakthrough in months.

'I think we have a connection,' the station chief told Hoffi.

Hoffi had to wait for the following day's diplomatic bag to arrive from Paris before he could study photographs of Mossad's Mata Hari. He permitted himself a smile. It was, after all, the oldest trick in the book.

'But if it works, who am I to criticise?' Hoffi said to his trusted lieutenants who argued against such a crass approach.

Marie Claude Magal, a Paris prostitute in her early thirties, had been on the payroll of Mossad for years. She was still an attractive figure, blonde, long-legged. Most important for Mossad, Marie Claude was also discreet. She had done a few insignificant favours in the past. Mossad employed her, at a generous rate, to linger around the arrivals hall of Orly airport. She was to study the faces of the Arab passengers who disembarked from the regular Iraqi Airways flights that flew to Paris, and to engage the visitors in casual conversation.

She was rebuffed every time. Mossad began to despair that this ploy would ever work when one of its paid informants inside the French Atomic Energy Commission offices at Saclay, a fifteen-minute drive from Orly, tipped them off about one possible target. A visiting scientist from Iraq in his early forties was moaning to his colleagues about his disastrous marriage. Recently his wife had embarrassed him when she appeared in the office to lecture her husband about spending too much time at work.

Mossad believed his sense of humiliation would make him easy prey for Marie Claude. What Mossad wanted was for the scientist to gossip about the comings and goings of more important figures in Saddam's nuclear team. The agency did not have to wait long. One man who was due to check into the Meridien Hotel, opposite the Palais de Congrès in Paris city centre, excited the Mossad team monitoring Marie's secret liaisons.

Just after 8 PM on 13 June 1980, Marie was stretched out on a settee in the open-plan lobby in a skirt that barely covered her underwear. She pretended to be listening to the jazz band and spurned the advances of at least three wealthy visiting businessmen. As the tall, well-dressed Egyptian emerged from the double doors, she eased herself up from the leather settee and teetered in high heels across the polished marble floor of the foyer.

She recognised Dr Yehiya El Meshed from the colour photograph her Mossad minder had given her that morning, along with an envelope containing 5,000 francs. Marie had no idea of

El Meshed's worth to Saddam Hussein. He had a PhD in electrical engineering from Moscow and had been one of the prize assets of Egypt's Atomic Energy Commission before Saddam hired him in 1975.

The blonde didn't care about El Meshed's qualifications. Her first job was to make sure she got into the same elevator as the Egyptian. She squeezed through the double doors just as they were closing and pressed the button for the ninth floor.

'Which floor would you like, sir?' she asked, pushing her hair back behind her ears.

Flustered and not a little aroused, El Meshed replied that they were going to the same floor. As she turned away, the scientist found himself staring at her taut figure visible through her black, form-fitting, shift dress. When the elevator doors opened, Marie turned left and deliberately stumbled into El Meshed, who savoured the exquisite perfume Mossad had provided her with that morning. Marie thought this one of her easier conquests, but she was mindful that her paymasters had impressed on her the need to be cautious and not upset their quarry.

'Are you following me?' she said in a teasing voice. Before the obviously embarrassed El Meshed could answer Marie Claude added, 'Because if you are, I don't mind such flattery from such a handsome man.'

By now the couple had reached Room 9041. As El Meshed fumbled in his jacket pocket for a key, Marie Claude reached into her handbag for a cigarette, clearly anticipating that her admirer would light it. He mumbled an apology and though she didn't hear what he said Marie let out a squeal of delight.

This was the signal for the Mossad assassin waiting inside Room 9041. She reached out for El Meshed's hand but he was trying to pull away from her. He was so absorbed in trying to stop her from following him into the room that he did not notice the stocky gunman slipping into the bathroom.

Sweating and breathing hard, El Meshed put the Do Not Disturb sign on the outside door handle.

'Get out! I have already told you I am not interested!' As he pushed Marie back from the door, he shouted, 'I shall call the manager if you do not go!'

Her curse, 'Bastard', was the last thing he heard.

At noon the following day, the chambermaids decided to disturb the occupant of Room 9041. They wanted to get home early that Saturday, and they did not care if the guest had company. After knocking several times, they let themselves in. The first woman through the door screamed.

El Meshed, still fully dressed in coat and tie, was sprawled between the two double beds. His skull had been crushed by a massive blow. The blood-soaked carpet silently testified that the scientist had been left to die of his wounds. Papers from his briefcase were strewn on the floor. His personal diary was missing, but his wallet, stuffed with 1,400 francs, lay untouched. Detectives found that one of the white towels in the bathroom had been smeared by a woman's lipstick. Police assumed that the Egyptian had been killed by a prostitute. That idea was supported by the statement of a couple four doors away, who remembered the young woman in the figure-hugging frock walking with the swarthy scientist along the corridor.

Detectives interviewed Marie Claude, but she played the role of the dumb blonde to perfection. She told how El Meshed had rebuffed her charms, and, annoyed by her chatter about 'how all rich Arabs are the same', the police sent her away, warning her that they might need to talk to her again.

They did not get the chance. Eleven days later Marie Claude Magal was knocked down and killed in a hit-and-run accident as she left a bar on the Left Bank. She had decided to try to tempt one more client that night. When a car drew up on the Boulevard St Germain, she walked around to the driver's window. As she bent down to begin her familiar routine, another car turned into the street. Just as it drew level, the driver of the first car pushed Marie backwards into the path of the oncoming vehicle. She was killed almost instantly. The two cars disappeared in different directions as she lay bleeding in the road.

The police never found her killer, nor El Meshed's. Marie's mistake may have been that she asked Mossad for more money after reading a newspaper report of Meshed's importance.

El Meshed's French colleagues in Saclay read the news of his murder with anxiety. None of them believed he had been the victim of a prostitute, or a thief. This was precisely the message the Israelis wanted to deliver – that no one working on Saddam's bomb was beyond their reach. There were several other deaths in the next twelve months. Some were the victims of accidents or illness. Others, like the Iraqi electrical engineer, Dr Salman Allami, were thought to have been murdered.

Two days after Allami arrived in Geneva to take part in a conference at the prestigious CERN laboratories he collapsed and was left completely paralysed. He died a month later at the Cantonal hospital where doctors diagnosed Lou Gehrig's disease, a degenerative motor neurone disease that wastes away the muscles. What they couldn't explain was why the engineer died so quickly from the illness.

Just before he slipped into unconsciousness Dr Allami whispered to one of his colleagues, 'Don't let them get me.'

Forensic tests proved nothing conclusive but the suspicion persists that he was poisoned. As usual Mossad neither admitted nor denied the accusation.

The agency also ducked insinuations that it had any part in the murder of Gerald Bull, the Canadian rocket scientist and designer of the so-called 'super-gun' that Saddam hoped would deliver a nuclear warhead above the skies of Tel Aviv. Ever since he was a schoolboy Bull had been fascinated by rockets, and in the garden of his home at North Bay, Ontario, he would design and build his own crude models.

He had a PhD by the time he was twenty-two, and was recognised by his peers at McGill University as a maverick thinker as he preached the virtues of using a gun to deliver satellites rather than strapping them to the top of a billion dollar Atlas rocket. It did not take long before American defence chiefs took an interest in his work and gave him one of their discarded sixteen-inch navy guns, some radar tracking equipment and a couple of obsolete trucks to play with. The Pentagon thought the scruffy eccentric worth that minimal investment, if only to track his progress.

Bull moved his operation, by now called HARP – the High Altitude Research Project – to Barbados, a location which appealed to his sybaritic lifestyle. The Americans didn't appear to mind as they could easily keep tabs on him. Few could keep pace with him at the rum punch parties, but Bull needed little sleep and never seemed to suffer from hangovers.

In 1964 he joyously proved his point when from his long-barrelled gun he launched a rocket-propelled Martlet shell a record distance of 185 kilometres above the earth's surface. Doused in brandy at that night's celebrations, Bull protested he still wasn't satisfied and boasted that using his technology he could launch a projectile weighing up to 272 kilograms and up to five metres in length over 1,700 kilometres into the sky.

NASA was sceptical but the American military and the CIA considered him worth persevering with, and in 1972 they arranged for him to acquire US citizenship. The Pentagon refused to subsidise all his whims and was quite prepared to let others fund his work as well. His minders encouraged Bull to lend his expertise to the South Africans, even though officially Washington was supposed to be respecting an arms embargo on the apartheid regime in Pretoria. Bull did not care whom he worked for as long as they shared his vision and, more particularly, they paid his bills.

Bull's technology was precisely what the South African defence forces needed to upgrade their artillery in their bush war with the Moscow-backed Angola rebels. The scientist easily dodged the United Nations arms blockade by deftly shunting weaponry around the world before it was delivered to Pretoria. Unfortunately the South Africans chose to advertise their new gun just as President Jimmy Carter was elected and Washington was gripped by his moral crusade. Bull was arrested.

He was sure the CIA would bail him out. Instead the agents persuaded Bull to say nothing about his past connections with the organisation, arguing they would underwrite the fine he was bound to get. Nobody from the Agency was in court to see Bull slump over the rails of the dock when in June 1980 a judge sentenced him to a year in jail and a $105,000 fine, ignoring his noisy pleas that his work had been sanctioned by the CIA.

While he was in Allenwood jail in Pennsylvania, his company, Space Research Corporation (SRC), went broke and the embittered scientist swore to get even with those who had abandoned him. After serving a little over four months he was released, moving to Belgium, where he started up SRC again in a one-bedroom flat, making it clear he was willing to work for anybody. Spain, Yugoslavia and China were among his customers, but another showing interest in hiring his services was Iraq.

Bull was working late in his office in the winter of 1987 when he received a surprise telephone call from the Iraqi embassy in Bonn inviting him to visit Baghdad. Iraq was still at the receiving end of Iran's human wave attacks and the tide of the Gulf War had not turned in Baghdad's favour.

Saddam told his technology adviser, Dr Amer Saadi, to secure Bull's services whatever the cost. The German-educated Saadi, who had a PhD from Munich and was a brilliant chemist in his own right, arranged to meet Bull in Bonn, the unlikely centre for Iraq's international procurement efforts.

Over a generous lunch Saadi, who was number two at the Ministry of Industry and Military Industrialisation, known as MIMI, persuaded Bull that he could finally achieve all his ambitions with Saddam's funding. The two men talked of how Iraq wanted to be the first Arab nation to put satellites into space. Bull was enticed and explained how by tying together five of Iraq's Scud missiles, he could easily conquer space.

When Saadi reported this conversation back to Saddam, the Iraqi leader insisted that Bull be brought to Baghdad so he could see if he was worth the $20 million he was being asked to spend on his projects. When the hand-delivered invitation arrived at the SRC's office the egocentric Bull left it on his desk for colleagues to see. His first day in Baghdad was spent being lavishly entertained by Saadi and another equally brilliant scientist, Amer Rashid.

Both men were enthralled with Bull's ideas for the rocket programme, known as 'Project Bird', and with his ambitions to build a super-gun, known as 'Project Babylon'. As the afternoon wore on in a private hotel dining room, Saadi excused himself from the conversation to call Saddam, excitedly telling him that Bull was even better value than he remembered.

Saddam wanted to see for himself. That night a bullet-proof Mercedes arrived to drive the scientist to the presidential palace. Bull squatted uncomfortably on a silk cushion in a reception room with windows that opened on to a garden irrigated by dozens of fountains.

For three hours, with just an interpreter and the ever-present bodyguard in the room, Bull and Saddam shared a bottle of Black Label whisky as the scientist sketched out his ideas on a notepad for the vice-president.

As Bull staggered home a little unsteadily, Saddam roused his son-in-law and minister of military industrialisation, Hussein Kamil, from his bed and ordered him to the palace to plan Project Babylon – Iraq's super-gun. The Iraqis suspected that Mossad was among Bull's other clients, but they were confident that the handsome budget they had given him would ensure his loyalty.

Late in the evening on 22 March 1988 the sixty-two-year-old Bull and his girlfriend left the SRC offices on rue de Stalle. The rain was falling as they drove back to his apartment in the Cheridien complex in one of Brussels' more fashionable quarters. Bull was finding it harder than he had expected to persuade firms in Britain and Germany to supply parts for his 156-metre-long gun barrels, and the strain of meeting delivery dates was beginning to show.

He bickered with his girlfriend. She wanted to go out for dinner. He wanted to stay in. That night Bull won the argument. The scientist walked briskly towards the plate glass doors of the apartment entrance, while his girlfriend went to park the car. He glanced over his shoulder and quickened his step. In recent weeks he had spotted the same two men sitting in a car directly across the road from the apartment.

A week earlier, he had noticed the crystal glasses in his cocktail cabinet had been very obviously rearranged, but the intruder had taken nothing from the flat. Bull determined that this manoeuvre was so heavy-handed that it must be a calling card from the Israelis suggesting that he drop his current employer. The previous weekend he had dined with two visiting Israeli businessmen who had delivered the same message over after-dinner liqueurs.

As he stopped to pick up his letters from the concierge, he noticed that his shadows had taken the night off. Since the break-in, he had taken to carrying his most valuable plans with him in a battered briefcase that grew bulkier by the day. Bull wheezed as he lumbered to the elevator.

The lights in the sixth floor corridor snapped on automatically as Bull came out of the elevator. He fumbled with his key, and the assassin stepped out from behind an alcove. He shot Bull five times in the back of the head and neck with a 7.65 mm Beretta from a distance of less than a metre. The assassin did not need to check that his victim was dead. When Bull's girlfriend arrived five minutes later, the corridor was empty. Seeing Bull's prone figure, she assumed he had suffered a heart attack.

Belgian police never found the killer, though they still suspect Mossad.

Israeli saboteurs had also been busy. In August 1980, a squad arrived in Rome and planted bombs at the offices of the SNIA Techint company and at the flat owned by the general manager. SNIA had ignored warnings against selling Iraq the 'hot cells' a laboratory required for reprocessing plutonium. The damage was deliberately superficial and there were no casualties, but the message had been delivered. Within days other companies in Europe thought it prudent to discontinue their relationship with Saddam. The French stubbornly refused to be cowed. They rebuilt the Osirak reactors and delivered them to Baghdad.

As the nuclear centre at Tuwaitha with its distinctive concrete dome rose up from the desert floor, Mossad sent an urgent relay of messages to Menachem Begin. Saddam's ambition to possess the bomb appeared unstoppable. The Israeli cabinet despaired of enlisting diplomatic support from among its apathetic allies to block the project, and in October 1980 Begin summoned his crisis team to consider a more drastic option.

'How can we destroy it?' Begin asked his army chief of staff, Raful Eitan, in his high-pitched scratchy voice.

The broad-shouldered Raful drew a deep breath and said, 'We have three options and there are desperate risks attached to all of them. But we dare not leave it any longer.'

In his hand he held the latest Mossad report, which predicted that the Osirak reactor at Tuwaitha would be operational by as early as September 1981. Once the reactor was functioning, Raful pointed out, they dared not attack because of the radioactive debris that would rain down on Baghdad and spread across the region. The Iranians tried bombing Tuwaitha nine days after the start of their war with Iraq, but their F4 Phantoms had managed only to damage a cooling plant. It was enough to make the foreign scientists panic, and most left.

Raful quickly outlined the three military options. The first was to drop a team of Israeli special forces deep inside Iraq.

They would be flown on camouflaged Hercules transports carrying helicopters to take the sabotage squad into the heart of the nuclear complex.

'The chances are radar would pick them up before the Hercules even had a chance to land,' Raful explained before questions could be asked.

Raful was equally dismissive of Begin's favoured plan to send a handpicked force 800 kilometres overland to blow up the reactor. Raful handed around aerial photographs of Tuwaitha. The pictures showed how Saddam had ringed the complex with electric fences, sensors and video cameras and installed concrete bunkers at fifty-metre intervals.

'Menachem, our boys would not stand a chance,' Raful told his prime minister. He added that the likely result would almost certainly be another Middle East war.

That left only one option – a long-range bombing raid by Israeli jets. For the next four hours, Begin's most trusted advisers thrashed out a battle plan that would get their planes across hostile Arab territory and in and out of Baghdad without being shot down.

Raful pointed out they couldn't use the most direct route, which would have taken them over Syria, which had just installed Russian-built surface-to-air SAM 6 missile batteries. Instead, the planes would drop south over Saudi Arabia on a two-and-a-half-hour flight to Tuwaitha. The extra distance that safety required would need more fuel, but Raful ruled out topping up the F16 bombers and their F15 fighter escorts in midair because that exercise would be picked up on Arab radar screens. They decided that the F16 Flying Falcons would have extra fuel tanks slung under the wings, but that meant they couldn't carry the full complement of bombs.

To have any hope the pilots would have to skim the desert, maintaining radio silence. They would fly tucked in such tight formation that they would look like a jumbo jet on the radar of any traffic controller. The F15s would fly just above the bombers, carrying jamming equipment to deceive Iraqi radar. Once they turned northeast to Baghdad on their final bombing run to Tuwaitha, the fighter escorts would climb to 18,000 feet to watch for any of Saddam's jets.

The planes would be over Baghdad for just two minutes. It meant the eight F16s would home in on the concrete dome of Tuwaitha at fifteen-second intervals, flying no higher than twenty metres above the reactor. Begin threw up his hands.

'Never mind the anti-aircraft fire, won't our planes be hit by the debris from the reactor?'

The chief of staff answered, 'Trust me.'

That night the plan was sent to a thirty-two-year-old air force officer, Colonel Zvi, who was regarded as the country's best military strategist. For the next thirty-six hours he pored over every possible permutation of what Begin had renamed 'Operation Babylon'.

Overnight two dozen of Israel's best pilots were moved to the Etzion base near the tourist resort of Eilat on the Red Sea. The pilots were not told why. Among them was a twenty-eight-year-old, known as Avi, who had as much combat experience as any in the Israeli Air Force. It was Avi who first noticed that what these pilots all had in common was their fluency in Arabic. Day after day they practised flying ever lower over the Negev desert. Avi was sure they must be planning to bomb the SAM missile battery sites in Syria.

Once, during a casual conversation, he asked the base commander if his hunch was right. He was told that he would be sent back to his original squadron if he continued such speculation.

'You will know the target only when you have to know,' the commander said. 'I don't want to hear anybody gossiping about what we are doing.'

Begin was so fearful of leaks that 'Operation Babylon' was discussed only with Foreign Minister Yitzhak Shamir and with Agriculture Minister Ariel Sharon; together they made up what was called the Committee of Three. But despite

Begin's best efforts, the original attack date of 10 May leaked out just as the pilots were being driven to their aircraft.

The prime minister pretended he had given up on the idea and sent a message to Raful asking him to prepare an alternative date a month later. On a sunny Sunday morning on 7 June, while tourists were staking out their territory on the beaches of Eilat, a message was flashed to the pilots that take-off would be at three o'clock that afternoon.

The rest of the base realised something was happening when the weekend's leave was cancelled and the phones were cut off. The last was a precaution insisted upon by Raful, who remembered how the Entebbe raid almost had to be scrapped because a lovesick crewman called his girlfriend to apologise that he wouldn't be home as he was on his way 'to deliver a surprise to Idi Amin'.

Ground crews were curious as they watched the pilots heading for the air-conditioned, underground operations room for their final briefing from Raful and the air force commander, Major General David Ivri, who had arrived by helicopter a half-hour before. Nobody outside that room knew the true purpose of the mission. As technicians loaded the Mark 84, 900-kilogram 'Iron Bombs' under the wings of the F16s, they speculated on the possible targets. None of them guessed the flight plan was to Baghdad.

The briefing room fell silent as Raful announced their target.

'I won't hide from you the dangers involved, but you all know that it can be done. It has to be done.'

The pilots ran through their route for a final time and were told about the rescue mission if any of their number had to eject. Just before three o'clock they were driven out to the tarmac and strapped inside their cockpits. From then on until they returned four hours later, after leaving Osirak a smouldering ruin, none of the pilots exchanged a single word.

8

THE AFTERMATH

Saddam could see the spirals of smoke rising from the ruins of Tuwaitha as his helicopter dipped to the desert floor. Army engineers had spent the previous forty-eight hours clearing as much of the debris as they could from what remained of the shattered dome of the Osirak reactor after the Israeli raid. The men were anxious to complete their task before the presidential visit; however, their work was hindered by the need to comb through the rubble searching for delayed-action bombs and booby traps.

Among the worried men in the reception committee lined up on the makeshift air strip that morning was Jaffar. He had only recently returned to work at Tuwaitha. Through the sandstorm kicked up by the helicopter's rotors, Jaffar could see the gaping holes punched into the reactor's concrete wall. He wondered what Shahristani would make of the damage. He and his missing friend had nurtured Osirak from the start. A sense of outrage ran through Jaffar.

As Saddam stepped down from the helicopter, Jaffar joined the others chanting his name and punching the air with his fists.

As the helicopter's engines were stilled Jaffar turned to one of his colleagues who was fidgeting in line. 'We spent a billion dollars on this,' he said, nodding in the direction of the smoking ruin. 'And now we are left with nothing. I hate the Israelis for what they have done.'

Jaffar had to lengthen his stride to keep pace with Saddam's entourage as they walked briskly to within fifty metres of the shattered reactor. He could feel the heat on his face from the fires still burning beneath the mounds of rubble. Others in the group jostled to stand as close to Saddam as they could, but it was Jaffar that Saddam turned to.

'In the name of God the most merciful, we will build this again and make it a thousand times more powerful and ensure that our enemies can never again strike at us!'

Saddam's acolytes crowded closer still, their sycophantic chorus so loud that Jaffar had trouble hearing what Saddam was saying to him. His response was to nod feverishly and to try not to get elbowed out of the way.

On the twenty-minute flight from Baghdad, Saddam had thumbed through the scientists' preliminary report detailing how the air raid had smashed the core and destroyed the main control room. As he picked his way over jagged lumps of concrete and metal, he realised that if Israel was willing to risk a war to knock out a reactor that hadn't even been fully built then they must fear his pursuit of the atomic bomb beyond all else.

He resolved to spend more than ever to restore Iraq's nuclear capacity. He had the money, with $30 billion in his reserves and promises of even more from his Arab allies to continue his war against the mullahs in Iran. The international powers had condemned Israel's actions, as they had to, but the French went even further and agreed to rebuild Osirak. It was not a promise they kept, but that morning as he wandered around the site Saddam made up his mind that Iraq would ultimately rely on no one but itself.

In all, he spent less than an hour stamping around what

was left of the reactor. He was assured as he flew home that the phoenix would surely rise.

Two weeks after the Israeli raid, Saddam summoned a meeting of his council of ministers. Before the cabinet could settle into their seats, Saddam got to his feet. Without the use of notes, he delivered a spontaneous forty-minute speech about how the Israelis wanted to keep the Arab nation in the dark ages so that they alone could retain a nuclear monopoly.

'We have said for some time that the Zionists would try to attack vital installations in Iraq with the goal of paralysing development and scientific and economic progress. They would have the Arabs do away with high-school and university education in such subjects as chemistry, physics, mathematics and astronomy because these branches of science could be used for military ends.'

Looking in turn at each man around the table, he delivered his next sentence with deliberate care.

'Every nation that is truly seeking peace and security and that honestly respects freedom and the independence of peoples should help the Arabs in one way or another to acquire the atomic bomb so that they can confront the real atomic bombs the Zionist entity possesses.'

This was a rare public admission by Saddam that he was going to build the bomb. That was glossed over later that day when, in an unexpected move, he gave an interview to the ABC television network. Unbeknownst to almost all of those in the room, Saddam had agreed to be interviewed by celebrity anchorwoman Barbara Walters to make his pitch for American support.

Saddam spent hours debating what to wear for his television interview. His hair was tinted at the edges with black dye and he had his own staff carefully apply the television make-up to mask the lines at the corners of his eyes. He decided what he was going to say before the first question was asked. Saddam is not a man used to being interrupted. He ignored Walters and launched a verbal barrage against the Israelis.

At the same time, he was careful not to lose his temper. His voice did not have its usual shrill edge, but even so his message was plain. Speaking just fast enough for the network's translator to keep up, he told the million-dollar-a-year interviewer: 'The American people should ask themselves whether it is possible to maintain good relations between the USA and the Arabs, especially when the American administration is openly allying itself with the Zionists by giving them political, military, economic, scientific and financial support.'

If the White House and others had been paying attention they would have heard Saddam give fair warning that he was going to buy his way into the nuclear club, no matter what.

At his cabinet meeting a few hours earlier, he had set up the new Military Industrialisation Organisation (MIO). This body was a cumbersome mouthful, but it would eventually run around sixty secret weapons establishments. As ever, the communist influence from the days of Moscow's grip on Baghdad was hard to shake. Although Saddam would inevitably make all the critical decisions, he insisted on six-month plans and tedious inventories and demanded that this committee meet every week at his palace to review progress.

Jaffar was among those seconded to this committee. His job was to authorise the purchase of all the hardware and expertise that would be needed for the chemical and biological as well as the nuclear facilities that Saddam was planning.

The physicist found it awkward when Saddam would occasionally defer to him about some scientific matter that needed explaining. There was no question that Saddam wanted to continue at Tuwaitha, though it was obvious they would have to disguise their true intentions in the future with better security. They spread blueprints across the table showing how the power lines, ventilation shafts, water supplies and approach roads could all be disguised.

Their ingenuity was boundless, particularly when it came to plans for duplicating every key establishment at various remote sites around the country. Scientists working in one would never be told what their counterparts were doing hundreds of kilometres away. All this was the lesson of the Osirak raid. The Israeli strike was to make it harder for the world to detect the weapons of mass destruction that Saddam was amassing.

Every meeting would end with Saddam's wearily asking his nuclear experts why they couldn't match the success of his chemical weapons laboratory at Muthena that had been operating in secrecy since 1976. There, west of Baghdad and on the banks of the Euphrates, his chemists had been brewing the toxins that would soon wash over the waves of teenage Iranian conscripts forced to march across minefields and marshlands carrying plastic keys around their necks that the ayatollahs promised would open the gates of paradise. The keys were no protection against the choking, yellow mustard gas that rolled towards them, blistering their eyes and lungs. They couldn't even see the sarin and tabun nerve agents that within seconds paralysed the respiratory muscles.

Saddam would endlessly watch videos of what these poisons could do, replaying the grotesque contortions of death filmed on the battlefield. He would force those on the MIO committee to do likewise, urging them to devise ever more potent weapons.

He was so enthralled by the work at Muthena that he favoured building an underground nuclear reactor near the ten-square-kilometre chemical factory. Jaffar, on the other hand, was shrewd enough to realise that no country, no matter how much money it was offered, would risk building another facility that the Israelis would target.

In the first weeks of the committee's discussions Jaffar's energies were concentrated on preventing Iraq from walking out of the Nuclear Non-Proliferation Treaty. At every meeting he would argue with the men in military fatigues who sought a confrontation with the other signatories of this nuclear cabal that had failed to protect Osirak.

Saddam listened in silence as Jaffar spelt out the logic of

staying inside the club. 'If we walk out now, our enemies will say this is proof of our real intentions. I say we keep them guessing. Better we stay inside and learn how to deceive them.'

Such duplicity appealed to Saddam, who agreed Iraq would continue to pay lip-service to its international obligations while secretly pursuing its own nuclear agenda.

Jaffar's days were now spent commuting between the nuclear laboratories at Tuwaitha and Tarmiya and his office in the presidential complex. While bulldozers were shunting away the debris from the bombed reactor as foundation for the thirty-five-metre-high embankments that would soon surround the complex, he was busy designing six new laboratories. They were so cleverly disguised that even when you walked through a door you wouldn't realise there were any number of secret entrances hidden behind library shelves, blackboards and the pine-panelled offices.

He was so desperate to prove his loyalty that Jaffar even agreed to Saddam's orders that scientists should divorce foreign wives. He finally left his English-born partner, Phyllis. With her gone, Jaffar could devote all his energies to devising how to deliver Saddam the bomb.

The idea he came up with was thirty-six years old. It was so simple he chastised himself for not thinking of it sooner.

For months now he had been pirating the blueprints from the Manhattan Project. He brought some of these diagrams and drawings with him the night he explained to Saddam and the others on the committee what he needed to start building the bomb. They were the calutrons.

The starting point was raw uranium. Iraq had phosphate mines near the borders with Syria from which uranium was extracted as a by-product. Extra supplies of raw uranium were obtained from abroad. Jaffar described how this was easily converted into what is called 'yellow cake'. This in turn could be processed into a powder and fired from a gun towards the magnets.

Like a physics teacher, Jaffar also explained how greedy this process was for electrical power. He told them how the scientists at the Oak Ridge plant in Tennessee, where the first calutrons were built, had used up more electricity than the whole of Canada needed to keep going for a year.

His audience looked at him in disbelief as he recounted how the Manhattan team had to plunder America's entire silver reserves to use as cladding around the magnets because every available ounce of copper had been requisitioned by the arms industry in the Second World War. Iraq could easily buy the copper it needed and did so from Finland without attracting any suspicion. Any big imports they explained as being for their own war effort against Ayatollah Khomeini's regime in Tehran, and the West was happy to oblige.

Jaffar knew that pirating the calutron technology was far from perfect. He admitted to colleagues that even the slightest variation in power or temperature would throw this finely balanced process off course. It was so messy that the precious material would splatter all over the insides of the vacuum chamber, so the whole process had to be stopped every few hours for everything to be scraped clean.

The committee listened as Jaffar described other ways to build the bomb using lasers, gas diffusion and centrifuges, but he stressed these would be harder to get hold of. The advantage with employing old-fashioned calutrons was that he could build almost all the components at factories in Iraq.

Jaffar perfected his own designs and took them to a variety of factories which were told to stop building window frames and car parts and to begin manufacturing the components for his calutrons – or 'Baghdadtrons'. For the most critical items he built four secret plants at Al Radwan, Al Amir, Djilla and Sehee, which together formed a crescent to the west of Baghdad.

There was no shortage of scientists now willing to serve the nuclear programme, particularly after Jaffar promised they would be excused from military service if they agreed to go abroad to study.

To satisfy Tuwaitha's thirst for electricity, Saddam agreed
to build a huge power plant nearby. The cables were buried
beneath the sand to hide them from spy planes. The electrical
lines strung along the pylons that could be seen perched on top
of the barricades were a ruse. The pylons were strung together
with high-tension wire that would slice the wings and tail fins
off any enemy aircraft that tried to repeat the Israeli raid.

The crucial test of whether they could get away with this
deception was the twice-yearly visits of the nuclear inspectors
from Vienna. These inspectors remained convinced of Iraq's
honourable intentions. They walked along pathways in
Tuwaitha that passed right beside secret laboratories, blithely
unaware of what was going on. The IAEA inspectors were
never allowed to see inside Tuwaitha. They didn't even know
it existed.

Saddam was pleased with how well Jaffar had covered his
tracks, and this swift rehabilitation excited jealousy amongst
the other scientists at Tuwaitha. He was given a new apartment in the presidential compound and would boast about
the red telephone installed on his desk that was a hotline to
Saddam. Colleagues envied the limousines he drove and the
posse of armed guards who accompanied him everywhere.

Jaffar was confident he could dictate the pace at Tuwaitha
but had not reckoned on the sudden ascendency of Hussein
Kamil. Others in the family had tried to muscle in on this
project when they realised how much the nuclear programme
meant to Saddam. The man that Saddam chose to be his minister of industry and military industrialisation was yet another
who had served his time as a presidential bodyguard in the
handpicked Amn al Khass. Saddam chose Hussein Kamil.

The muscularly built lieutenant bore more than a passing
resemblance to Saddam. It was while he was working as a
motorcycle outrider for the president that he began to style his
hair to accentuate the likeness. Kamil's own sadistic streak
became evident whenever he was required to shadow Saddam
on his occasional tours of Baghdad's prisons. He would join in

torturing suspects with obvious relish and his practised cruelty ensured swift promotion.

When asked to accompany the president's wife and his favourite daughter, Raghad, on a shopping trip to London, he followed the pair on their exhaustive excursion around every expensive store in Bond Street without complaint. At dinner, he would amuse mother and daughter with gossip gleaned from his fellow bodyguards about the sexual excesses of the Baghdad hierarchy. By the time the party returned home the affection between Raghad and her minder was apparent.

Barely a year after his marriage, Kamil was seen at Saddam's shoulder on every trip he made to the war front. From being a lowly lieutenant he was promoted to colonel and then brigadier in less than two years, though like so many in the president's entourage there was no evidence of any military skills. He was, however, slavishly loyal, which was all that mattered. Raghad was ambitious for her husband and pestered her father to put him in charge of the national security council. Saddam indulged her, but Raghad was not satisfied until her husband was appointed to run the nuclear programme.

It was obvious to everyone at Tuwaitha on Kamil's first visit that his scientific knowledge would disgrace a schoolboy. Strutting about the complex, he nodded sagely as Jaffar pointed out the various elaborate processes going on in the laboratories and design centres. Kamil would fiddle with the expensive lathes and presses the Iraqis had imported, pretending he was familiar with how these machines would fashion the vital components the scientists needed to pursue their work.

When his armoured motorcade was safely out of sight the scientists would delight in recounting how, when visiting a particular factory, Kamil asked why production was so slow. The weary foreman explained he needed more steam.

'So what's the problem?' Kamil responded. 'Go out and buy as much as you need.'

Rivals of Jaffar realised that the boorish Kamil, whatever

the depths of his ignorance, held the purse strings for the projects they sought to pursue. The scientists courted the new minister, none more so than Dr Mahdi Al Ubeidi. He wanted to create an empire to rival Jaffar's and accordingly played up to Saddam's son-in-law.

Two months after he was appointed a minister, Kamil presided over a meeting with his nuclear experts and asked Jaffar why it was taking so long for his calutrons to produce the promised HEU. Jaffar stammered his excuses, explaining the complexity of the technology and the constant fine-tuning required to produce micrograms of the nuclear material. Al Ubeidi interrupted.

'Perhaps it is time, minister, that we concentrate on a more *modern* approach,' he said, accentuating 'modern' for deliberate effect.

Before Jaffar could respond, Ubeidi pushed a sheet of calculations towards Kamil. These illustrated how the Iraqis could easily double the amount of weapons-grade uranium they were after simply by using the more technically efficient centrifuges.

Jaffar attempted to splutter a reply, but Kamil held up his hand and silenced him.

'And where do I get these centrifuges?' Kamil asked.

It was Al Ubeidi's moment.

'We can buy them from West Germany, and I know the men who can help us do it.'

9

SHOPPING TRIPS ON THE RHINE

The raucous chorus of a Bavarian folk anthem poured from the bar of the Alwiya club. In recent months Jaffar's favourite watering hole had been taken over by the burgeoning number of German scientists and engineers in Baghdad. Many of them were shipped into the city to work at Saddam's chemical weapons factory at Muthena.

When the belly dancers wafted off the stage in a fog of cheap perfume the Germans would commandeer the piano – much to the annoyance of Jaffar. He now spent as little time as possible at the Alwiya. His rival took advantage of his absence.

Al Ubeidi was shamelessly cultivating the Germans, who had already earned considerable kudos for the success they were having in developing ever more unspeakable toxins at the Muthena plant. Nobody gathered around the piano that night bothered with the pretence that the Germans were there manufacturing pesticides, as the Iraqis liked to claim. The lethal brews they were helping produce would later be used on men, women and children from Kurdish villages in northern Iraq who thwarted Saddam.

Dr Mahdi Al Ubeidi looked a bit like Jaffar. He had the

same slight build and the jaundiced complexion that comes from spending too many hours slaving in laboratories under fluorescent light. The gifted mechanical engineer was, also like Jaffar, trained in Britain, an experience that was shared by most of this elite corps on the PC3 nuclear weapons programme. One name this old boys' network never mentioned on such nights was that of Hussein Shahristani, who had been sent back to prison for refusing to rejoin their ranks.

Over platefuls of kebabs and imported sweet Bavarian wines, the German scientists regaled their Iraqi hosts with graphic descriptions of what their latest invention had done to the dozens of beagles chained up in their research centre. Al Ubeidi swallowed his revulsion, knowing these men could be of value to him.

Saddam never wanted foreigners in the ranks of his nuclear programme, but his son-in-law and many of his senior scientists told him that progress was impossible without them. The day after Kamil presided over his first meeting as minister of industry and military industrialisation, he sent for Al Ubeidi and Dr Amer Saadi, the Munich-trained chemist, to ask about the German connection. Kamil realised his father-in-law was annoyed by the slow progress of the nuclear programme and he knew his job was to sort that out.

'Tell me more about these Germans,' Kamil ordered as he paced about his new office, occasionally distracted by some decorative improvement he wanted to make.

Al Ubeidi sensed that the short-tempered Kamil was easily bored.

'Some of them worked for Hitler,' Al Ubeidi blurted out.

Kamil had been fingering the silk curtain material and was holding it up to the light of a crystal chandelier. He stopped and turned to Al Ubeidi.

The mechanical engineer explained, 'The Americans tried to get hold of scientists like Walter Busse and many others after the war. But they hated the Americans and the British for what they had done to the Fatherland. Some, like Busse, managed to escape Berlin. He went to work for Nasser in Egypt, building rockets and jet engines to take on the Zionists.'

Al Ubeidi's sales pitch worked. Kamil picked up the hotline telephone on his desk to his father-in-law. Saddam needed little persuading. A few days later, Iraqi agents were told to approach Busse, who had made his reputation during the Second World War as an engineer in Hitler's army. After a stint working in Cairo, Busse had slipped back to Germany in the early 1960s. He was careful to disguise his Nazi past and managed to find himself a job in a top-secret consortium that was trying to enrich uranium-using centrifuges.

This was not the first time that the Iraqis had heard Busse's name. He had already been talent-spotted in Rio de Janeiro, where his German employers, MAN, had sent him to help the Brazilians overcome teething problems with their peaceful nuclear programme. In 1986 Brazilian industrialists had identified Iraq as a promising market for their engineering and arms exports and there began a steady stream of government officials and businessmen travelling between Rio and Baghdad.

During a visit by Iraqi officials to Rio, the head of the Brazilian arms giant Aviebras took one of his guests aside at dinner and told him, 'We are so lucky to have secured the services of Dr Walter Busse – he is a genius.'

Intrigued by the high praise that was being heaped on a nondescript German, the Iraqi asked for more details – which were sent directly to Kamil that same night. Rummaging around on his desk Kamil reached for the file marked with Busse's name in red ink.

The German was now in his late seventies and was suffering from diabetes. He had retired to his apartment at Bernau in the Bavarian foothills. Six months after his retirement, Busse was bored and hunting around for a final challenge.

Kamil listened as the two scientists persuaded him why Baghdad needed to diversify its production of enriched

uranium. Al Ubeidi told him it could do that only by invest-
ing in the latest technology and that meant using centrifuges.
He said that Dr Jaffar's method of trying to get enough
HEU by just improving upon the old-fashioned calutron
process was taking longer than anyone had anticipated.
Kamil nodded.

If Jaffar was affronted when he subsequently learned of Al
Ubeidi's proposition, he was diplomatic enough to conceal his
true feelings. His main worry was that Kamil would starve
him of the millions of dollars he still needed to keep his cumbersome calutrons working. What was also galling was that his
competitors, under Al Ubeidi, were holed up in better
equipped laboratories on the other side of the Tuwaitha
complex.

As deputy head of the Iraqi Atomic Energy Commission,
Jaffar was allowed through the secret network of corridors to
see what Al Ubeidi and his team were up to. He hated making
such visits, as his competitors would taunt him over his snail-
like progress.

Unlike Jaffar's calutrons, which rely on magnets to separate
the lighter uranium 235 atoms from uranium 238, the centrifuge uses what scientists sometimes describe as an 'egg
beater'. The raw uranium is first converted into a gas – uranium hexafluoride (UF_6) – and then fed into the centrifuge,
which looks like a giant milk churn with a profusion of stainless steel pipes poking out of the lid. These pipes eventually
link together thousands of these milk churns in what engineers call a cascade.

Inside the centrifuge the 'egg beater' rotates at 60,000 rev-
olutions per minute, forcing the lighter U235 atoms to the
middle of the cylinder, where they are siphoned off. This
process has to be repeated literally thousands of times to get
the right mix. The problem is that each time the centrifuge
spins at colossal speeds, a fractional amount of U238 pollutes
the mix. So what is drawn off each time has to be put through
the whole process again and again to achieve sufficient purity.

The rotors used to spin the centrifuges take such a hammering they have to be replaced at regular intervals, which is time-consuming and costly because of the special steel used to make them.

Al Ubeidi had drawn a diagram for his boss, Kamil, so he in turn could explain to Saddam why this process took so long. He pointed to an equation showing that to produce electricity from nuclear power stations, the U235 obtained from centrifuges need only be 3 per cent pure. For a bomb, it should be 93 per cent pure. Kamil stared at the numbers in silence.

The scientist felt Kamil's obvious disappointment.

'It sounds slow, but I promise, Excellency, that once we have all our cascades up and running at full capacity we can deliver between ten and fifteen kilograms of 93 per cent highly enriched uranium.' He paused for a moment and then, confident he had Kamil's full attention, he went on, 'This is enough for one bomb a year. And it is just the start.'

Kamil knew the pioneers of this technology, the two superpowers, had conspired to make sure nobody else got hold of the secrets of how to turn lumps of uranium ore into a speck of bomb-grade fuel. Fortunately for Iraq, a three-nation European consortium, Urenco, combining the expertise of British, German and Dutch scientists, was fast getting in on the act.

This is where Kamil would find his mercenaries. One of the German subcontractors was MAN Technologie, which had once employed both Walter Busse and a chemist named Bruno Stemmler, whose skill was designing these centrifuges.

Stemmler, then in his late fifties, was a malcontent. He believed his employers had never sufficiently rewarded him for his designs and so was receptive when Dr Busse invited him to join him working for Saddam. When Stemmler first turned up in Baghdad in the autumn of 1987, he was met at the steps of the plane by an enthusiastic group of Iraqi officials who fussed over his luggage and documents, steered him to a waiting limousine and then accompanied him to a suite at the Al Rashid Hotel. A cautious man, Stemmler declined the copious amounts of champagne and cognac he was offered at dinner.

This was just as well, as shortly after dawn he was awoken abruptly by one of his Iraqi minders. As Stemmler struggled to dress, the official said, 'You are very honoured. Our president says we can show you something nobody from your country has seen.' Curiosity got the better of his irritation.

After two hours crammed in the back of a Mercedes with a team of Iraqi scientists, Stemmler wished he was back in bed. The car suddenly swung off the road into a large industrial complex which had armed guards at the entrance.

One of his hosts said, 'Welcome to Factory Ten.'

Once inside, Stemmler was shown sets of blueprints covering the entire length of a two-and-a-half-metre-long trestle table. They were labelled in English and Arabic. As he ran his hand across them, Stemmler saw they were almost identical to those he'd been using at MAN's laboratories on his own prototype of a centrifuge. The documents had clearly been stolen, and though Stemmler had his suspicions that his old colleague Busse was responsible, he did not ask.

Impressed by his discretion, the Iraqis escorted the scientist across the complex to a two-storey building with a heavy black metal door. Sunk into the ground was a fully working centrifuge. Stemmler noticed the engravings on the equipment, which bore the names of many prestigious manufacturers from the US, Britain and Germany.

Most of the building was still under construction. There was no air conditioning, some of the lights didn't work and the centrifuge Stemmler was shown was in an otherwise empty room about half the size of a football field. His escorts excitedly told him of plans for more buildings nearby.

They jostled him to the edge of the pit and helped him down a ladder. He had to jump the final few steps as the bottom rung was missing. The Iraqis turned on the centrifuge. He immediately noticed there were no feed-extraction tubes.

The Iraqis were not yet enriching uranium at Factory Ten. As the machine vibrated still faster, Stemmler examined every part of the milk churn, warning his Iraqi audience that if the centrifuge failed, it would explode like a grenade.

Over the hum of the rotor, the Iraqi scientists shouted down to him that they were having problems with their vacuum system. Stemmler was unsure if their enquiry was genuine or some kind of test, as this had been the same problem he had struggled with at MAN.

Stemmler clambered awkwardly up the ladder and spent the next two hours showing them his tricks of the trade. He knew such scientific shortcuts would significantly cut the time it would take them to create a successful cascade of centrifuges at the Design Engineering Centre they would soon be building at Rashdiya, north of Baghdad.

One of his shadows, known to him only as Mohammed, told him, 'We can be very generous, my friend, if you help us learn more about what you call cascades. Couldn't you get inside Urenco headquarters back in Europe to find more out about these cascades?'

'I don't have the security clearance to get inside such facilities,' Stemmler replied, and clumsily changed the subject.

He was aware that Mohammed did not believe him. His colleagues back in Germany didn't believe him either when he told them that his many visits to Baghdad were to discuss irrigation and energy development schemes. He certainly didn't tell them he had been paid 120,000 Deutschmarks in two equal installments. Nor did he let on he was recruiting others to work for Saddam. Among them was Karl Otto Brauer, a retired rocket engineer who had worked on Hitler's V2 programme and was later recruited by the Americans to assist Werner von Braun at NASA on the Apollo Space Program.

Saddam had indicated that he would seize help from any quarter. Iraq's nuclear colonisation had begun when he was still vice-president and the Russians had given them their first reactor, the IRT 2000. The French were next with their two reactors – Osirak and the smaller Isis – that were built side by side at Tuwaitha. The British had trained most of the elite corps of scientists who were working on PC3. Now it was the turn of the Germans, who would make millions by selling the Iraqis what they needed.

One of the German habitués at the Alwiya club was a trader named Anton Eyerle. One night he thrilled his Iraqi hosts by proclaiming loudly, 'Saddam Hussein is a strong man for whom it is worth fighting.'

Eyerle adored his time in Iraq, which puzzled his German colleagues.

'This is just as it was in my youth,' explained Eyerle, who was said to keep an old radio console popular during the Third Reich days at his office at Kaufbeuren in Bavaria. On it he would play some of Hitler's speeches.

If the Alwiya was a sanctuary for the Germans, no shopping expedition to Germany by Saddam's nuclear agents was complete without an evening or two at Club 56 in Bonn, and there were any number of Iraqis volunteering to go on sales missions to Germany.

Club 56 is not one of Bonn's more fashionable addresses, requiring a taxi drive to the outer suburbs, but it is where the Iraqi engineers and their minders preferred to seal the day's haggling over contracts. In the opaque pink light, Aly Muttalib Aly, the senior Iraqi diplomat at the crowded table, ordered three bottles of Johnny Walker export. He was officially designated the commercial counsellor at Iraq's Bonn embassy but the professional diplomats knew he had a direct line to Saddam.

In the far corner of the club, scarcely visible through the cigarette smoke, were four men who were noticeably more abstemious than Aly's guests. These were undercover agents for Germany's BVD intelligence service who, like their British counterparts in MI6, were always curious to know what the Iraqi delegates had bought.

Ever since Saddam set up his covert procurement programme for his nuclear bomb project, PC3, the core of his
international operation was to be his drab two-storey embassy
in Bonn. German companies, in particular Siemens AG and
H&H Metalform, were crucial to the hardware and machine
tools that Saddam needed. His agents had warned the Iraqi
president that he should put together his bomb almost like a
child's Meccano kit, buying pieces from as many different
outlets as possible to make it harder for his enemies to monitor PC3's progress.

Western governments, in particular the French and the
Germans, argued they were giving Saddam a jigsaw to assem-
ble, but they would keep a few pieces back so that no matter
how hard he tried he could never complete the puzzle. What
they didn't realise was that the Iraqis were wise to this game
and had worked out which pieces were missing and where
they could find them.

Aly was beguiled by playing his own games with the businessmen sitting opposite him. He always dragged them to
Club 56 so that he could revel in their embarrassment as they
flinched from the over-amorous attentions of the hostesses.
He grinned at the antics of the visiting Iraqi scientists who
came to satisfy their often bizarre sexual tastes rather than
enjoy the gourmet menu.

Aly was one of Saddam's most trusted operatives in military
intelligence and knew they were being watched. He scanned
the other tables in Club 56 until he caught sight of the
German agents sitting rather stiffly with their half-empty bottles of beer. Aly called over his favourite waitress with the
bobbed black hair.

As she bent over to listen to what he had to say, affording
him a pleasing glimpse of her cleavage, Aly stroked the back
of her thigh under her short red mini-skirt and whispered
an instruction in her ear. Minutes later she reappeared with
a bottle of chilled champagne which she placed in front of
the four embarrassed agents, who promptly finished their

beers and scampered out of the club, to Aly's obvious amusement.

With them gone, his mood became more serious. 'Right, gentlemen, before we forget why we are here, let us agree that the dozen lathes we require can be shipped on time and cause no problem with your customs. I will sign the cheque here and now if you can assure me you can meet our deadline,' Aly said, reaching into the pocket of his double-breasted jacket to pull out a leatherbound wallet. He was the man who decided where to allot the $500 million Saddam was going to spend in Germany over the next eight years.

While Aly chatted to a German salesman about the steel rotor tubes needed for the centrifuges, two of the visiting Iraqi engineers sloped off to some of the adjoining rooms that the club provided for more intimate relaxation with its hostesses.

Saddam may have been spending a substantial chunk of his oil revenues on German engineering, but he expected these big companies to pay the entertainment bills, which at Club 56 seldom came to less than 3,000 Deutschmarks a night. At two in the morning a fleet of limousines would take the Iraqis on to the Bristol Hotel, where they would invariably lose a small fortune at the blackjack tables.

Whether the Iraqi president approved of this relaxed way of conducting business, he never said. His only concern was that freighters leaving Hamburg docks were regularly loaded down with crates of oxidation furnaces from Degussa AG, centrifuge balancing machines from Reutlinger und Sohne KG and electron beam welders from Leybold Heraeus.

He put out tenders to equip every government building with an underground nuclear bunker. He studied designs for shelters that could hide 48,000 soldiers. The German specialists, Boswau and Knauer, built Saddam his own nuclear sanctuary 100 metres below the Tigris that could withstand any blast.

The one rule Saddam did insist on was that his engineers should never stay at the same hotel as the European salesmen.

He dared not risk any of his emissaries becoming so familiar with the businessmen that they might let slip the true reason for these shopping expeditions and reveal the secrets of PC3. If any of the businessmen guessed what the Iraqis were really trying to build they were sensible enough never to ask questions.

Their work was done on the ground floor of the Iraqi embassy, where Aly would preside over a long, rectangular table scattered with order forms, contracts and design drawings. Gathered around him were businessmen from half-a-dozen European countries making their pitch. One of the more frequent callers at the chancery was Mark Gutteridge, marketing director of Matrix-Churchill, the British machine-tool factory the Iraqis later bought lock, stock and barrel.

The Iraqis acquired the Coventry firm because their traditional German suppliers became too busy trying to meet orders from Saddam's sworn enemies, the ayatollahs in Iran. The Iraqis had bought 50 per cent of H&H Metalform, but that still wasn't enough to absorb their demands for machine tools.

One morning in June 1982 as the businessmen exchanged pleasantries, folded away their copies of the *Financial Times* and waited for Aly to join them, Mark Gutteridge remarked, 'I noticed our friend from German security had a new Audi this morning. Our importance has clearly increased.'

They could afford to mock the clumsy attempts by the BVD to shadow them because all those present knew they were immune from official interference. Gutteridge hinted he was in regular contact with British intelligence but boasted he enjoyed a 'hands-off tag', meaning he was free to do as he chose in Germany.

After his early commuter flight to Cologne that day, Gutteridge had taken a taxi to the front entrance of the embassy, a solid white metal gate without decoration or inscription. As usual, he announced his arrival over the intercom, gazing up at the single surveillance camera positioned beneath the red, white and green Iraqi flag. His name was instantly recognised by the receptionist and the heavy gate swung open, leaving him a short walk to the main door.

Gutteridge delighted in saying 'Good morning' to the Iraqi guard with a pistol strapped to his trouser belt. In the two years Gutteridge had been coming and going, the guard had yet to utter a word of reply. As he went through the door Gutteridge glanced at the time on his wristwatch, knowing this was likely to be a marathon session, as there was a $29 million contract on the table.

Once inside, Gutteridge and the other businessmen knew their limited route. Twenty metres along the corridor decorated with tourist posters of Babylon and the Tigris they were steered into the same office on the right-hand side. The salesmen joked about how strange it was they were never allowed to stray any further, except when they were escorted to the toilet.

'I suspect there will be no outing to Club 56 on dirty strasse,' he whispered to a German colleague seated next to him, with some relief for that small mercy.

The slim-built Coventry businessman strained as he heaved the outsize Delsey suitcase crammed full of documents on to the oak table. His instincts were right. For the next thirteen hours nobody left the room, except when they were escorted to the lavatory. The Iraqis were led by a tough and persistent negotiator, Dr Safa Al Haboby, who bickered over delivery dates and design faults. Haboby's impatience clearly reflected Saddam's agitation to accelerate PC3.

It irritated Gutteridge that the Iraqis seemed more solicitous to his German colleagues, but then he recognised they were spending more money than anybody else so he could hardly complain. What he didn't think fair was that he was expected to pay half the bills at Club 56, which they were visiting with increasing regularity.

Like most of the salesmen there Dietrich Hinze, the technical director of H&H Metalform, was anxious to conclude their business as swiftly as possible, joking to Gutteridge and others that his liver could not take the strain of another drinking session at Club 56.

The sales strategy was brilliant in its simplicity. These companies used the likes of Busse and Stemmler, whom the Iraqis trusted, to explain how Baghdad needed more German technology. In this way firms like H&H would continue to profit. Or at least they did until July 1988, when Iraq ended its war with Iran and the true character of Saddam's regime was unmasked.

There was revulsion when it was realised that Saddam had fired shells of mustard gas and turned his front line into a modern Somme and Passchendale. Untold numbers of young Iranians felt their skin blister and burn as the gas that smells like a mixture of garlic and damp hay wafted over their trenches, choking them to death.

Three months earlier Saddam had used the same poison to slaughter thousands of villagers at Halabja to stamp his authority on the Kurds whom he accused of helping his Iranian enemies. The public was appalled when it discovered that Western firms had helped build his chemical weapons plants, and European governments looked for scapegoats.

Dietrich Hinze and the others – including H&H's managing director, Peter Huten – were prosecuted for selling sensitive material. Hinze and Huten were among those sent to jail, where they would tell anyone who would listen in the prison yard that the country's intelligence agencies gave them the nod to what they were selling.

The Bonn government was forced to investigate their claims, and their inquiry turned up an enormous number of German companies that had perhaps unwittingly helped Saddam acquire his deadly armoury.

Culprits like the Thyssen Rheinstal company and a consortium led by Ferrostaal helped build foundries at the Taji weapons complex. It was German firms who constructed the chemical weapons plants at Muthena and the military base at Al Faluja, forty-eight kilometres west of Baghdad. This was where scientists produced nerve agents like sarin and tabun which shut down all the body's organs so its victims are left twitching on the floor, drowning in the fluid from their own lungs.

One of the most prominent German contractors in Iraq, Karl Kolb GmbH, was represented in Baghdad by one of its major shareholders, Klaus Franzl, an old friend of the Munich-trained chemist Dr Amer Saadi. The pair were regularly amongst the last to leave the Alwiya club and the Bonn inquiry discovered an oil painting of Herr Franzl wearing a Third Reich medal.

Saddam told his agents in Bonn to spend what they needed and in 1984 German companies sold him $860 million worth of technology. Within another year 150 German firms opened offices in Baghdad, where street traders now preferred the Deutschmark to the dollar.

When Saddam decided to improve the range of his Scud missiles it was German companies which led the charge to cannibalise the old Soviet rockets in what was known as Project 1728. Havert Consult from Frankfurt built plants for rocket fuel, Leifield and Co (Leico) perfected missile engines and Mercedes Benz sold him tractor trailers that were later converted into missile launchers that would be used to fire Scuds at the coalition forces and against Israel, Saudi and Kuwait in the Gulf War.

The well-known German arms dealer, Friedrich-Simon Heiner, even hired former members of GSG-9, the equivalent of the SAS, to set up a special 'anti-terrorist unit' for Saddam. The order for that job came from IPC, whose only address was a post office box in Baghdad and which was owned by Hussein Kamil and used as a front for his nuclear procurement programme.

Saddam had lectured his son-in-law about spreading his patronage so that Iraq never had to rely on any one partner, and Kamil obediently shared out the order forms around the world. He bought hot cells that could handle the radioactive

bomb-grade uranium from Italy. Control panels were pur-
chased from Brazil, valves from France and copper cooling
coils from Finland. He ordered uranium ore from Niger and
Portugal and he hired construction firms from Yugoslavia.
Two Swiss firms sent components for centrifuges, including
parts made from 'maraging steel' that was strong enough to
withstand the crushing vibration.

Every company claimed it thought it was making spare parts
for cars, baby food factories and air conditioners. The eventual
repugnance felt in the West at this arms bazaar forced all those
countries to ask who had given what to Saddam. The public
inquiry ordered by Prime Minister Margaret Thatcher into
how British firms helped arm Baghdad, with the help of MI6,
was to give her some of her most uncomfortable moments in
Downing Street.

British companies were accused of making parts of the
barrel for the super-gun and customs agents seized centrifuge
components and plans from Matrix-Churchill, although the
government was aware of its work. The firm complained that
long before this raid in 1987 it was known that its chairman
was Dr Safa Al Haboby, who was the senior Iraqi official
doing most of the buying for the nuclear programme.

The British connection extended to scores of Iraqis study-
ing at universities who were later recruited to the PC3 bomb
project. Others were regularly invited to tour factories and
sensitive installations, like the four in 1989 from the Al Qa Qaa
bomb factory who were given training in Hertfordshire about
the X-ray photography used to capture and analyse the instant
a nuclear device explodes.

The flow of deliveries to Baghdad abruptly stopped by the
end of the decade, leaving Saddam and his officials to invent
ever more underhanded ways to obtain the parts. The Western
firms still prepared to do business with Saddam would become
victims of their own greed. When Iraq failed to pay its debts,
many of these companies were bankrupted.

By the time the West woke up to the menace of Saddam

Hussein, almost all of those who had enjoyed drinking bitter Arabic coffee at the table at the Iraqi embassy in Bonn were bankrupt, imprisoned or dead.

Another to suffer was Club 56, which was left to mourn the end of Aly's celebratory evenings.

10

THE CHARM WAR

The folded piece of paper fell from the diplomat's trouser pocket as he moved around the table filling his guests' glasses with a vintage Montrachet. Saddam Hussein's man in Washington, Nizar Hamdoun, appeared not to notice what he had dropped.

He stepped on the crumpled note as he fussed over a congressman who was known to be a close friend of President Reagan. Hamdoun affectionately patted the politician's shoulder, enthusing about the main course they were about to be served, which was a personal favourite of his chef. Few refused an invitation to his townhouse on Carlton Street, where the quality of the food was surpassed only by the gossip.

As Hamdoun shifted his attention with seamless charm to the bejewelled wife of a wealthy Jewish industrialist, the congressman reached down and picked up the discarded scrap of paper.

'Nizar, you have dropped this,' the congressman called after him. 'Better take it back before we look; it may be a state secret.' Hamdoun laughed the loudest as he feigned indifference to the paper, which he flicked open in his left hand, still pouring the wine into his guest's glass.

His expression changed. He furrowed his brow and affected to shove the note into his jacket pocket. Prompted by his guests to explain his apparent change of mood, Hamdoun paused for a minute, pulled out the paper, stared at it for a few more seconds and then began to smooth it flat on the damask tablecloth with the palm of his hand.

'This came in the diplomatic bag from Baghdad this morning. Our war with Iran is going badly, as you know, and I didn't believe this.' He repeated, flourishing the paper, 'I didn't want to believe it.'

Without looking up from the mysterious document he knew his audience was in his grip. He gently slid the paper to the congressman, who was next to him.

'This was taken from an Iranian officer who was leading an invasion force across Iraq's Fao Peninsula.' Hamdoun quickly retrieved the document and held it against the candlelight.

'It's their battle plan,' he said, tracing the line of red arrows that showed the Iranian army racing through Iraq, pushing down into Saudi Arabia and taking the oil wells, then moving across into Jordan.

Hamdoun knew he was appealing to the powerful Jewish lobby sitting at his table when he stabbed his finger on the final destination – Jerusalem.

'These madmen have to be stopped, whatever the cost,' he murmured, almost as if he was talking to himself. Hamdoun knew he was preaching to the converted.

Iraq was officially still in a state of war with Israel. That didn't matter to Saddam's envoy, the head of the Iraqi interests section in Washington. Hamdoun understood the power of the Jewish lobby in Washington. He made it his job to win them over.

He had played the trick with the map before. In fact, he had performed this party piece when he was meeting foreign journalists at a breakfast gathering that morning, dropping the same dog-eared map as he pretended to be shuffling his notes. The same piece of paper fell out of his handkerchief when he dabbed perspiration from his forehead as he was addressing car workers in Detroit. He let this supposed secret slip from his wallet as he handed his business card to a White House aide, and the much-travelled document had also floated down to the foot of his lectern when he was lecturing a group of Ivy League students.

The dried bloodstain that was smeared across Baghdad on this map was typical of the man's theatricality.

Nobody at the table noticed the map was written in Arabic and not Farsi, as it should have been if this battle plan had truly come from the uniform of a captured Iranian soldier.

It didn't matter that their host was a master of deception and disguised his own violent past as a member of Saddam's Mukhabarat secret police. That night's handpicked guests were, like the rest of America, traumatised by what the mullahs were doing in Tehran.

Everyone in that elegant Washington salon had flinched at the television pictures of American diplomats being beaten on the steps of their own embassy by Iranian students who had taken over the building in 1979. The student revolutionaries held their fifty-two American hostages for 444 days.

They felt impotent rage night after night as they watched blindfolded hostages plead for their lives and confess to being CIA spies while the mob behind them set fire to the Stars and Stripes, chanting 'Margh Bar Omrika' (Death to America). They all felt revulsion when they watched Iranian conscripts dragging the incinerated corpses of American troops around the desert after their airborne rescue mission, Operation Eagle Claw, crashed in April 1980.

When an Iranian-backed suicide bomber, cloaked in a white shroud and reciting the Koran, drove his truck laden with explosives into the US Marines barracks in Beirut, killing more than 200 people, America was united in its loathing of the mullahs in Tehran.

America was waging an undeclared war against Ayatollah Khomeini's regime in Iran. Saddam Hussein's cunning was to convince the Americans that he was doing the fighting for them and the least Washington could do was show its gratitude.

Saddam's key purchases abroad and the frantic building of his nuclear infrastructure at home should have set off alarm bells in Washington and other Western capitals. But it was Saddam's good fortune that the expansion of nuclear weapons research was overshadowed by the fall of the shah of Iran, the rise of Ayatollah Khomeini and the eight-year-long Iran–Iraq War.

While the scientists back in Baghdad debated how best to build the bomb, the more immediate threat to world stability was coming from the Iranian mullahs who swore to export their Islamic revolution to the rest of the world.

When the shah sat on his Peacock Throne, Iran protected America's interests in the Gulf. Once the shah was forced into exile by Khomeini's Islamic revolution, Washington had to find a new ally. Saddam saw his opportunity and played the Iranian card for all he was worth.

His envoy in Washington played his part. The avuncular Hamdoun with his trademark hand-stitched white suits and black silk shirts scorned what the mullahs were doing in Iran.

'In my country no woman needs to cover her head,' he would tell his dinner guests. 'These people in Tehran are from the dark ages. We will never allow religion to drag us back to their sort of barbaric behaviour.'

This was the kind of reassuring language the Americans wanted to hear. Comforted by the likes of Hamdoun, the State Department did not enquire too deeply about what was going on inside Iraq.

Hamdoun was the first Arab diplomat to so shamelessly charm Washington. America still didn't enjoy full diplomatic relations with Baghdad, but Iraq's chargé d'affaires was a man with whom they could do business. The Iraqis recipro-cated. When Ronald Reagan won the 1980 presidential race with his running mate George Bush, the Foreign Ministry in Baghdad was among the first to send flowers and effusive congratulations.

Like everyone else in the West, the Reagan administration was petrified that Iran, with the help of the firepower America had sold it in the shah's days, would overrun Iraq and then move on to the oil fields in Saudi Arabia. Suddenly Hamdoun was getting invitations from Washington high society.

He was paying former ambassadors $5,000 a month to act as lobbyists and sponsored a business forum in Iraq embracing companies that employed some of Reagan's cabinet. As a treat during their time in Baghdad, the businessmen were entertained for two hours by Saddam Hussein, who was at his most engaging for their visit and went around to each one of them thanking them for their efforts on Iraq's behalf.

Saddam signalled his new affection for America by sending his wife, Sajidah, to New York. It was the early hours of the morning when a switchboard operator had to awaken the Iraqi ambassador to the United Nations.

'Your Excellency,' the operator said to the drowsy envoy, 'it's the president on the line.'

The two men had known each other since childhood and had been part of the Ba'ath Party coup in 1968. In those days they called each other 'comrade'. That morning Saddam didn't bother exchanging pleasantries. 'Salah, my wife needs to have a minor operation. I want it done in America, not in Moscow or in London. I want you to look after her.'

Two hours later a coded telex relayed details of the nineteen bodyguards in Sajidah's entourage, led by Hussein Kamil, who the ambassador knew was fast gaining influence with Saddam. He knew better than to enquire why Kamil, who shadowed the president's wife everywhere, would be using an assumed name for this trip.

While he pondered how to accommodate all this company in his four-floored townhouse on 72nd Street, the FBI arrived to ask if they could have a room so that seven of their agents could set up a surveillance operation to protect the First Lady of Iraq.

Ambassador Salah Omar Ali met his FBI visitors at the front door, shaking hands with each of them and offering them orange juice as he asked how he could help. He was amused to see that three of the agents wore clumsy earpieces with wire which curled up from under their Brooks Brothers shirts. These men said nothing, leaving it to a grey-haired agent in a shiny blue suit to explain that they needed a room to install their command centre to shadow Sajidah's every move.

'This is for her own protection, sir, and indeed yours,' the agent said in a slow Texan drawl. 'I understand Mrs Hussein will be accompanied by her own staff, but as you know, Mr Ambassador, these men are not permitted to carry weapons while they are here.'

Saddam had anticipated such a move and had lectured his old friend about the need to keep the FBI at arm's length without arousing its anger or curiosity. He was fearful the agents might use their time inside the residence to bug the building and he could not afford to have Washington eavesdrop on what he was really buying in America.

Ambassador Ali nodded politely while the FBI agent went through his list of requests, but at the mention of installing their surveillance equipment on the same floor as Mrs Hussein's bedroom the ambassador held up his hand.

'I'm sorry, gentlemen, but that won't be possible. You see we are in the process of renovating our embassy and we simply don't have the space, but I'm sure we can accommodate you quite comfortably.'

As he was speaking he led them through the main dining room, out of the French windows into the garden and across a lawn to a conservatory about twenty metres from the main house. The FBI team traipsed morosely behind the ambassador, knowing they could not complain about being billeted so far away. The envoy graciously pointed out the toilet facilities and the telephone line he had installed for them to call his kitchen whenever they felt hungry.

Saddam laughed when Ali reported that evening how he had forced the FBI to set up camp in his garden.

The ambassador had known Sajidah from their hometown of Tikrit and between her medical appointments he took her to see the Statue of Liberty and to climb the Empire State Building. What she enjoyed most, though, were the several days she spent touring Bloomingdale's department store, accompanied by the ambassador's wife, nineteen bodyguards and the seven FBI agents who proved useful to carry around her many purchases.

This was not her first trip abroad. Sajidah was used to shopping in Paris and London. On one visit to Britain she dropped into a West End jeweller and demanded a jewel-encrusted gold sword with a matching scabbard. Embassy staff let it be known to the incredulous staff that the cost was irrelevant as Saddam wanted this sword as a personal gift for King Faisal of Saudi Arabia.

While she was in New York, Saddam would telephone her at six o'clock every evening to ask how she was, whom she had met and whether she was being shown the respect due to the wife of America's new best friend. After only a few minutes of this stilted conversation she would pass the receiver to Hussein Kamil and leave the room, as would everyone else, while he would recite his list of military purchases that day. Iraq had been taken off the State Department list of countries supporting international terrorism and, although there was still an arms embargo, Kamil had managed to buy $12 million worth of security equipment.

He was also promised a lot more.

'Saidi, the Americans promise they will help us, but they say they have to be cautious.'

Saddam grunted.

'We will have no problem in purchasing what we need from Europe, South Africa and South America,' Kamil said, as he explained how the CIA would help Iraqi officials travel through New York on their many clandestine arms-buying missions.

By the time Sajidah was well enough to return home, the US Defence Department had helped customise Saddam's private jumbo jet so it could dodge a missile attack. America wasn't to know then that it was doing all it could to protect a man whom less than a decade later the CIA would be spending millions trying to kill.

When Kamil left New York he took with him a secret communications system for his father-in-law. Customs agents at John F. Kennedy airport were told to wave him through, even though his souvenirs from this trip included a cache of pistols and automatic weapons.

The next step in this diplomatic dance was entrusted to Nizar Hamdoun. His English was colloquial and in the first twelve months as head of his country's interests section he worked hard at losing the abrasive edge to his voice.

Other envoys marvelled at his stamina. The lights burned late most nights on Carlton Street and there were lavish parties at the Grand Hotel where Hamdoun would regularly enthral 500 guests at a time. He toured over thirty-five states, visiting schools, factories and obscure civic organisations. He sat through hundreds of lunches and lectured at scores of universities in his charm campaign.

At his soirées he let it be known that Iraq had expelled wanted Palestinian terrorists like Abu Abbas, who had led the hijacking of the *Achille Lauro* cruise ship. In fact, Baghdad was actually funding terrorist operations, but making sure that Iran got the blame.

Late one night in June 1982, the Israeli ambassador in London was shot on the steps of the InterContinental Hotel. In revenge Israel invaded Lebanon, blaming Palestinian groups for the assassination attempt. It was really Saddam who had paid the gunmen.

When in 1987 an Iraqi Mirage F1 fired on an American warship, the USS *Stark*, which was cruising off the shores of

Iran, the pilot claimed he had mistaken the frigate for an Iranian battleship. In the darkness he slammed two Exocets into the *Stark,* killing thirty-seven American sailors.

Saddam offered immediate apologies and compensation for the bereaved families, but wouldn't let American investigators speak to the pilot or listen to the garbled radio transmissions that the Iraqis blamed for the fatal error. Nevertheless, President Reagan went on television three days later to call the attack a genuine mistake.

The president was so convinced of Iraq's innocence that he ordered the CIA to hand Baghdad spy satellite photographs pinpointing the front-line positions of the Iranian forces. The agency then looked the other way when Saddam poured tons of poisonous chemicals over locations like the Majnoon Islands to beat back his enemy.

The White House helped broker more than a billion dollars' worth of credits for Iraq to buy American grain and farm machinery, which meant Saddam could use his own money to buy military hardware rather than food. The Reagan administration helped Saddam pay for his secret arms purchases using the Atlanta branch of an obscure Italian bank. Saddam badly wanted cash because the war with Iran was eating away his reserves and he needed money to buy the components for his nuclear programme.

The CIA was so absorbed watching Ayatollah Khomeini, in what they called Operation Staunch, that the Agency never bothered investigating the Russian Antonov planes that slipped in and out of Iraq. The giant transporters would touch down at night at Habaniya air base, 100 kilometres west of Baghdad, and disgorge their cargo of enriched uranium fuel. Encased in lead, the uranium was loaded on to tank transporters that would take it on roads closed to all other traffic to the Tuwaitha complex.

No one ever knew the amount Moscow was sending for what Iraq still insisted was for its nuclear research.

It was Dr Jaffar's job to ensure that on their six-month

visits the inspectors from the IAEA would never discover how much weapons-grade uranium Saddam was amassing. On the eve of every visit Jaffar would discuss in laborious detail with Saddam how best to divert the visiting IAEA team. The inspectors, who were usually Russian or Hungarian at Iraq's request, were delighted by the ever more extravagant reception waiting for them at Baghdad airport. The tedious business of customs and immigration was ignored as the party was led from the aircraft to waiting limousines that whisked them to the Al Rashid Hotel.

In the foyer the manager would be waiting, flanked by attractive secretarial staff carrying flowers and bowls of fruit for the 'honoured guests'. The finest suites were reserved for them and there was ample time for relaxation before an evening's entertainment provided by their ever-attentive hosts.

Air-conditioned Mercedes ferried them to Iraq's nuclear headquarters at Tuwaitha, where the only entrance was through a long tunnel made of earth and concrete. As the inspectors emerged into the sunshine, a guide was waiting for them. He greeted them in English and led them down the red gravel pathway, fringed on both sides by bougainvillaea and neatly clipped hedges that separated the offices and laboratories.

Explaining the layout of the complex, the guide walked around the administration building and turned left, passing a group of workers who were planting young date palms.

'As you can see, we employ more gardeners and horticulturists than scientists at Tuwaitha,' the guide joked.

His guests politely joined in the laughter, unaware that at that moment they were passing a laboratory where the Iraqis were illegally experimenting with plutonium. They strolled on past an auditorium where young researchers had listened that morning to Jaffar explaining the complexities of constructing a calutron. The inspectors did not know that beneath their feet, under the freshly mown lawn, was another secret laboratory set up to extract weapons-grade uranium by gas diffusion.

At the end of their three-hour tour, the visitors were led into the director's office, where a tray of sweet Arabic coffee, ice water and sandwiches was waiting for them. Each man was handed a folder bound in green leather that was stamped with Iraq's symbol, the triple-headed eagle.

As they enjoyed the refreshments, the inspectors flicked through the achievements Tuwaitha had recorded in the past six months. They also examined the known stockpile of nuclear materials that Baghdad was permitted to hold. Etiquette dictated that inspectors were not to ask or to check whether Iraq was telling the truth. This was the only facility the IAEA team was ever allowed to see.

The formalities the inspectors observed prevented them from learning that Iraq was illicitly importing toughened 'maraging' steel, vacuum furnaces, copper wire, magnets and hundreds of other vitally needed components to make a bomb.

In eight years Saddam would spend billions of dollars building his nuclear weapons facilities and, incredibly, nobody noticed.

11

THE NUCLEAR EMPIRE

The fruit of Hamdoun's diplomacy and Kamil's clandestine purchases was visible in a fast-emerging nuclear empire made up of twenty-four nuclear installations, as well as research centres, small factories and countless support facilities spanning the length and breadth of Iraq like an uncharted galaxy.

Starting from Baghdad, the cluster was thickest in and around Al Atheer south of the capital. It thinned out further west along the border with Syria, leaving a wide open space all the way north to Al Jesira, inside Kurdistan, where raw uranium was being converted into hexafluoride gas or granules of tetrachloride powder. By 1990 this secret empire was employing 20,000 skilled personnel and consuming hundreds of millions of dollars every year.

The enormous cost of setting up PC3 and the massive sums required to keep this programme going preyed on Kamil's mind as he walked around Al Atheer on a bright spring morning in May 1990.

He had flown by helicopter from Baghdad to open the first phase of the weapons-design plant – officially designated the National Materials Centre for Industry and Technology –

which the smiling director, Khalid Al Sa'id, assured him was every bit as modern as anything the Americans had.

Sa'id mentioned to his obviously bewildered visitor the names of the two American scientists most commonly associated with the early successes of the US atomic bomb programme. 'One day the world will remark on our Edward Tellers and our Robert Oppenheimers trained at these laboratories,' he told Kamil.

At Kamil's insistence, Sa'id escorted him on a tour of the most important and expensive facilities. All the time the director gave him a running commentary on how the scientists used induction furnaces, plasma coating machines, computer-controlled drills and cold isostatic presses to shape explosive charges. He could not tell from Kamil's impassive expression how much of it the minister was taking in.

The director had tried to separate the 300 scientists working at Al Atheer to discourage gossip. He had divided them into working groups and segregated them in different laboratories around the complex. Each team was assigned its own responsibility – neutron generators, bomb design and assembly, explosive lenses and the delivery system. This last group was made up of rocket technicians who had been instructed by Saddam to see how the bomb could be fitted to the nosecones of the Scud missiles bought from Moscow.

They paused for cold drinks, then continued on to the metallurgy, welding and electrical workshops, ending up outside the underground bunkers where army engineers had stored 250 tonnes of HMX high explosive for the nuclear detonators designed and produced by Iraqi scientists.

Kamil had a checklist in his hand. Each time they stopped in front of a new purchase he would scribble down the cost of each piece of equipment. By the time the two men and their armed escorts walked back to the director's office, the sum of $567,000 was written down on Kamil's inventory.

The sums perturbed him. As the minister in charge of PC3 he had to justify all this expenditure to Saddam. He worried that the results so far were hardly giving value for money.

The invasion of Kuwait was still four months away and the crash nuclear programme had not yet been sanctioned, but Kamil was aware of a new, more aggressive mood in Baghdad and the sense of urgency swirling around Saddam's private office.

His wife, Raghad, had overheard her father hectoring another of his ministers about the delay in the nuclear programme and passed on this gossip to Kamil that morning. She recounted how Saddam had told the minister that he had ordered the execution of British newspaper journalist Farzad Bazoft a few weeks earlier because he was sure that the man was a spy and that the West was monitoring his nuclear activities.

Sa'id was confident the first bomb would roll off the Al Atheer assembly line in 1992 as planned and his private prediction to colleagues was that Iraq would have a stockpile of at least a dozen nuclear bombs by 1998, earning it the status of the world's eighth nuclear state after the five great powers, India and Israel.

'Mr Minister, sir, everything is running on time,' Sa'id assured Kamil. 'In six months the second phase will be completed and our team will be ready to handle as much weapons-grade uranium as Dr Jaffar sends us.'

The two men were alone, facing each other across a low table in Sa'id's shaded office.

'Our real achievement,' Sa'id added, 'is with the design of the bomb.' Lowering his voice to a barely audible whisper, Sa'id leaned towards the minister. 'We have five blueprints we can draw upon when we are ready. The team is sure of it; all of them have been simulated on our computers and they work perfectly. Our theoretical calculations are aimed at coming up with designs for the implosion mechanism,' he added, briefly lapsing into the jargon he used with his scientific colleagues.

Kamil listened in silence for the next two hours as Sa'id

took him step by step through the different stages of bomb production. Other scientists had briefed him along similar lines at least a half-dozen times before, but Sa'id was one of his favourites. There was always a chance that his exposition would highlight some tiny but important detail that the others had missed out.

'As you know,' Al Sa'id began, 'the heart of a bomb is explosive atomic material. It comes in two forms. The starting process in both cases is raw uranium that ends up as either plutonium or the highly enriched, weapons-grade uranium we call HEU. The production methods for each are completely different.

'The plutonium route needs a reactor to "cook" uranium fuel until it is converted into plutonium. Plutonium remains within the cooked fuel until it is taken to a chemical reprocessing plant where it is dissolved and extracted. When we started in Department 3000 our assumption was that plutonium would be easier to obtain than HEU. But after the Zionists attacked Tuwaitha and destroyed our reactor, we had to think again.'

Kamil nodded, taking in the details of plutonium and uranium production as best he could.

'Yes, yes, I know all that,' he gestured to Sa'id, signalling him to continue. The memory of Israel's aggression still rankled.

'Since then my respected colleague, Dr Jaffar, has been experimenting with the production of HEU from calutrons. Dr Al Ubeidi, you know better than any of us, Minister, has been trying to achieve the same result with centrifuges. We need ten kilograms of HEU for the bomb. A lump about the size of a grapefruit, and twice as heavy as lead, will be packed around the outside with powerful plastic explosives to compress the material to the size of an orange.

'We are now experimenting with the neutron initiator that starts the nuclear chain reaction at that critical microsecond when the grapefruit's just been squeezed.' Sa'id paused. Like the rest of his colleagues, he knew of Kamil's academic limitations and did not want to blind him with science, but he was also keen to take the credit for what his team had achieved.

'Sir, here at Al Atheer we have been working round the clock to master the squeezing process,' he said, using his hands shaped in a circle to illustrate his point. 'You have seen the underground bunkers where we test our explosive lenses. True, we still lack sufficient HEU, but we have been working with substitutes to make our calculations accurate to one billionth of a second. Believe me, you have every reason to be proud of our progress.'

Sa'id did not go into the details of the natural uranium layer his team had designed to boost the power of the bomb. Nor did he mention the steel 'tamper' or casing they had calculated they would need to surround the inner core of HEU to prevent it from blowing apart prematurely. These finer points of bomb-making were guaranteed to make Kamil's eyes glaze over.

The scientist need not have worried. Kamil was sufficiently impressed by what he had seen and, most important, by what he had heard. The report Kamil was formulating in his mind was sure to win him at least a grunt of approval from Saddam.

Kamil was pleased his protégé did not patronise him. He liked visiting Al Atheer, where he thought the staff showed him proper respect, not like Dr Jaffar's arrogant upstarts at Tuwaitha. That was his next appointment, and as the helicopter hovered above the thirty-five-metre berms surrounding the national nuclear research centre on his way back to Baghdad, Kamil felt depressed. He was wearing the uniform of a lieutenant-general, but even this artificial prop could not boost his sagging morale.

It was the only place in the whole of Iraq where he felt uncomfortable. He had been three years in office as the minister in charge of Tuwaitha and still could not find his way around the scores of neatly labelled laboratories, buildings and annexes.

If Al Atheer was a satellite of the nuclear empire, Tuwaitha was its sun. But whereas Al Atheer owed its existence to Saddam and the Ba'ath Party, the academic traditions at Tuwaitha had begun in 1956 when Iraq was ruled by a monarchy that didn't feel threatened by freethinkers and intellectuals. The many thousands of scientists working at Tuwaitha on full-time contracts, with their impressive academic pedigrees from abroad, refused to be bullied by Kamil. Men like Jaffar would just look away when he shouted at them.

When Saddam first appointed him minister of industry and military industrialisation in 1987, Kamil tried stamping his authority on Tuwaitha by cutting back some of what he considered to be dead-end projects. At his insistence, an unpromising line of research into producing HEU by gaseous diffusion was dropped. Laser separation was another area from which money was diverted to support the centrifuge and calutron laboratories. Scientists from these departments who were told their projects were being postponed or even cancelled did not hide their resentment.

A few complained to Jaffar, but the physicist refused to interfere in what he described as political decisions. His advice to any protesting scientists was that they should approach Kamil directly. After his own time in prison Jaffar was never going to put himself at risk again. He made it clear to the dissenters that he wanted no part of their protest, however principled or well-meant it might be.

Kamil had heard of Jaffar long before he met the physicist. The boorish peasant from Tikrit instantly loathed the urbane aristocrat of Baghdad. He is not subservient enough, Kamil thought to himself as he watched Jaffar approach the helicopter. He did not just dislike Jaffar, he distrusted him as well.

'Who knows what he really thinks of us after all those months in prison?' Kamil once asked his father-in-law.

'Fear keeps him honest,' Saddam replied. 'If he wants revenge he will have to bide his time in a very long line.'

Kamil telephoned Jaffar every day and the two met several times a week as members of the minister's committee charged with overseeing the production of all weapons of mass destruction. At the Tuwaitha helipad that afternoon Kamil steeled himself to repeat the same question he had asked Jaffar at least a dozen times in six months: 'How much longer before your machines start producing the HEU we need?'

Jaffar's monosyllabic answer, 'Soon,' infuriated him. As he had watched Jaffar at their committee meeting earlier that week, Kamil had caught himself thinking how this one scientist alone was responsible for spending at least $3 billion or possibly $4 billion of the country's money. The cash had not stopped flowing since the day Jaffar convinced Saddam that old-fashioned calutrons were the only reliable way to produce weapons-grade uranium undetected.

Tuwaitha alone had swallowed up more than $1 billion in research and development for magnetic cores, vacuum chamber parts, electrical control panels and other esoteric components which Kamil had not heard of, but which Jaffar argued were vital for the electromagnetic isotope separation process used in his calutrons.

When Jaffar ran out of space inside Tuwaitha's perimeter, he persuaded Saddam to let him build additional facilities in the nearby villages. Whatever else was in short supply in war-weary Iraq, Saddam's orders were that Dr Jaffar's requests were to be met in full. When Jaffar announced in 1985 that he was ready to produce HEU in kilogram quantities, the prototype calutrons were moved out of Tuwaitha because there wasn't enough space. They were shifted to a vast empty area of the desert at Tarmiya, around seventy kilometres north of the capital.

He borrowed ideas of how to disguise it from the Americans, who had designed dummy road and rail links to hide their Oak Ridge facility cut into the Appalachian hills on the banks of the Clinch River. Jaffar added other touches of his own. Power lines were buried miles under the sand, and from the air all the roads leading to the complex looked like dirt tracks. Its water supply was hidden and millions were spent on masking the security installations.

After what happened at Osirak it was Kamil's conviction that Iraq should never be so vulnerable again. He pinpointed the most important of the new facilities and insisted they be replicated many kilometres away so that if one were attacked, its twin would survive. The idea came to him one morning as he was shaving that these duplicate installations should be built back to front so that any saboteur knowing the layout of one plant would be confused that nothing was in the same place in the replica. All this would cost a fortune, but secrecy and security were the only concern.

Tarmiya's twin was built 300 kilometres further north at Ash Sharqat, which alone added $500 million to Iraq's nuclear bill. The same, expensive sleight of hand was used at Al Faluja, the plant for manufacturing centrifuges, which had its duplicate 100 kilometres south at Al Furat, while the explosive lenses factory at Al Qa Qaa had sister facilities at nearby Hatteen. The trouble was that Tuwaitha was just too big to clone.

That afternoon at Tuwaitha the conversation once again turned to money. While Kamil silently fumed, Jaffar explained he needed another $120 million to produce the feedstock for his calutrons. 'The raw uranium we have bought from Niger and Portugal has to be converted into uranium tetrachloride and building the plant is turning out to be more expensive than we anticipated.'

Kamil did not understand.

'Surely we are producing our own uranium now as a by-product of the phosphate mines?'

Jaffar sighed, barely disguising his irritation at the minister's ignorance.

'Uranium itself is not the issue. We have our own stocks and we have imported enough from Brazil, Portugal and Niger. Now it has to be processed and turned into a powder before it can be fed through to the calutrons. We have done this at laboratory levels, but now we need industrial-scale facilities.'

Kamil quietly conceived of ways to blunt Jaffar's influence. The minister had tried encouraging his scientific rivals, but Jaffar's participation was indispensable to the nuclear project, and the physicist knew it.

Jaffar remained the scientific head of PC3, but at committee meetings on the fifth floor of the ministry it was Engineer Al Ubeidi, as Kamil liked to refer to him, who was encouraged to make his own pitch for more resources.

Kamil enjoyed stirring the rivalry between the two scientists. It suited his crude philosophy of divide and rule, but it did not save him any money. Al Ubeidi had suggested a short-cut to get the uranium. But his centrifuge method, which was supposed to be cheaper and more efficient, was now devouring as much money as Jaffar's antiquated calutrons.

At his grandly named Engineering Design Centre, Al Ubeidi was grouping together hundreds upon hundreds of centrifuges in what he called 'cascades' to spill out the weapons-grade uranium they needed.

Rival teams of engineers using computer-controlled machine tools were working at Al Furat near Babylon to manufacture home-grown centrifuges. The scientists all had to approach Kamil with their requests.

Just a week after approving Jaffar's request for an additional $120 million, Kamil was approached by Al Ubeidi. The minister stared at him in disbelief as the engineer explained his urgent need for $100 million to build a factory to produce the feedstock for his centrifuges. Kamil dreaded the thought of having to ask his father-in-law for more money.

'We simply must have it, Minister, sir,' Al Ubeidi pleaded. 'The uranium we have must be converted into uranium hexa-fluoride gas. We have managed with laboratory facilities so far, but now we are ready for large-scale production. I'm sorry it's an expensive process, but we have no choice.'

12

FAMILY AT WAR

Saddam was in an exuberant mood as he watched a video of two of his senior generals being tortured for their part in a rather clumsy assassination plot. Kamil sat quietly as Saddam shouted obscenities at the screen and thumped his fist on the desk while the traitors confessed how they planned to fire a rocket at his car as he was leaving the home of his latest mistress. The president whispered to an aide that his mistress should be moved to a new, more discreet address that afternoon and not told why.

He snorted with pleasure as the hour-long video ended with the two officers being shot in the mouth as they whimpered for mercy. Kamil knew this was the moment to interrupt.

'Saidi, I visited the nuclear centres at Al Atheer and Tuwaitha today and your scientists are working harder than ever for the sake of the country.' Kamil paused for a moment and then said, 'I have approved another $220 million for their work.'

He watched Saddam's response as he pushed the file across the desk towards his father-in-law. Saddam adjusted his reading glasses on the end of his nose and for several minutes studied the latest estimates. The president glanced up at him and then scratched his signature on the bottom sheet. Kamil knew as he picked up the paper that his illicit share from these orders was assured and would find its way into one of the many Geneva bank accounts owned by his family.

Saddam knew all about these kickbacks. He trusted nobody but realised that he had to rely on some to carry out his orders. He preferred members of his own family to benefit from his patronage. Indeed, he encouraged such corruption when it suited him.

Kamil, on his father-in-law's instructions, had recently bought $120 million worth of state-owned factories as part of a publicity drive to privatise Iraq's industry. When he told Saddam he couldn't pay, his magnanimous father-in-law summoned the Revolutionary Command Council and ordered them to gift the factories to Kamil 'in appreciation for his services to the country'.

What made this gesture all the more galling for the rest of the Council was that they knew Kamil was salting away a fortune in bribes.

The exorbitant commission Kamil was charging on every nuclear deal allowed him to keep $30 million in cash and $10 million in gold hidden in his house. It was this money that Kamil packed into thirty Samsonite suitcases five years later when he fled Baghdad – fearful that Saddam's eldest son, Uday, was going to kill him because he was jealous of the money Kamil had siphoned off from the nuclear programme.

While Saddam used Kamil's network of phoney companies to buy his nuclear hardware from abroad, he entrusted his half-brother, Barzan Tikriti, to launder the family's money. It was easy for Barzan, because he had been appointed Iraq's ambassador to the United Nations in Geneva and was able to misuse his diplomatic position to set up any number of secret accounts.

By far the most grasping of all the family was Uday. He needed to finance his sybaritic lifestyle and he behaved as if

Iraq belonged to him. He kept over eighty cars in the bomb-proof garages built within the presidential compound and paid for an armed retinue whose job, apart from protecting him, was to procure women for him.

When one army officer objected to Uday's crude attempts to seduce his wife at a party the heir apparent pulled a gun from inside his jacket, shot the man dead and then dragged the woman from the room. He pestered one university student so much that the young woman set fire to herself after he threatened to murder her entire family if she did not succumb.

Often he wouldn't even bother going through the motions of courtship and raped any woman who took his fancy. His bodyguards ambushed young women off the streets and took them to parties that Uday held in cronies' villas around the capital. After being gang-raped and abused, many of these women were never seen again.

He took to strutting around Baghdad in a military uniform, though he never bothered to spend time in the army, not even during the eight years his country was at war with Iran. Saddam said it was because his son could not be spared from his other national duties, though no Iraqi knew quite what they were. When he was fifteen Uday had complained to his father that two very senior officers had failed to salute him when he spoke to them. Saddam had the soldiers court-martialled and ordered his troops to show his teenage son more respect in future.

When he developed an interest in soccer, Uday simply took over Iraq's leading club, Al Rashid, ensuring they won every competition from then on. He regularly burst into the dressing room to harangue the Iraqi national team for its ineptitude and once pistol-whipped one of the trainers who dared to try to stop him from slapping a player he blamed for missing a goal. When the team lost a World Cup qualifying match to Kazakhstan the insult was too much for Uday to bear, so he had the entire squad rounded up and beaten on the soles of their feet.

He appointed himself head of Iraq's National Olympic Committee and turned its eight-storey yellow building in Baghdad into his fortress headquarters. Behind the bullet-proof glass of his top-floor office he ran a burgeoning black market in smuggled whisky, cigarettes and medicines. He was briefly put in charge of the country's oil industry, but looted so much money his father had to take it away from him. Saddam signalled his disapproval by torching his son's cherished collection of cars.

Uday had embarked on his business career when he was twenty-four, buying the newly privatised National Meat Company. He ordered the National Bank to transfer 10 million Iraqi dinars into one of his offshore accounts at the official exchange rate of $3 to the dinar. He then brought the American currency back into the country and sold it on the black market, giving him enough to buy the company and pocket $20 million in cash.

More than once, when Saddam wanted to punish his son for his excesses, Uday was spared only by the intervention of his mother, Sajidah, who was fiercely protective of him. Mother and son knew better than anyone how to pander to Saddam's ego.

The birthday cake was so enormous it required five of Saddam's personal guards to manhandle it into the ballroom. A gaggle of women soldiers, wearing tee-shirts with Saddam's face over their combat trousers, led the procession of 300 well-wishers who came in clapping and chanting his name. Saddam, who was sitting alone reading the Koran in this vast amphitheatre, feigned surprise at the intrusion while his hand-picked guests fanned out around him in a semi-circle.

There were so many candles on the cake that the decorative icing in the colours of the Iraqi flag began to melt around the edges, dripping on to the uniforms of the honour guard. Saddam held out both his hands and bowed his head in a masterful show of humility as the chanting became more frenzied.

The chorus stopped only when from out of the perspiring crowd stepped Sajidah.

Walking slowly towards her husband, she began to recite a birthday eulogy. The fawning message had been prepared by one of the president's favourite speechwriters and approved by Saddam before it was delivered to his wife for her command performance.

The chanting erupted again as Sajidah handed him a golden scimitar and invited him to slice through the multilayered cake, causing more of the icing to spray over the guests.

Saddam discarded the scimitar as a guard handed him a freshly laundered napkin to wipe the icing off his hands. Rubbing his hands, Saddam accompanied his wife into the white marble corridor where a line of Iraq's most celebrated artists stood anxiously beside their portraits of the president. This was an annual ritual they were obliged to attend.

Stopping at the first canvas, he nodded appreciatively at a flattering depiction of himself in flowing white Bedouin robes that made him look considerably slimmer and younger. Sajidah pointed to how the artist had found room to include his favourite grey Arabian stallion in the corner of the painting. Saddam smiled, tapping the heavy gilt frame, and motioned to the aide at his shoulder who produced a cheque from his leather folder that was handed to the artist, who had the good sense to look suitably abashed.

'No, Saidi. Please, I could not possibly accept this,' he gushed. 'What I did was out of love for you. No painting can do you justice and it is an honour for me to present this humble offering to the father of the nation. The reward for me is to serve you.'

The other artists applauded and Saddam nodded, moving on to the next painting. The same ritual was repeated all along the line. Saddam inspected portraits of himself in military uniform, wearing fashionable suits and cloaked in tribal robes. He was seen on horseback, in schools, in factories, at prayer and taking the salute of his Republican Guard. There were paintings of him in a bewildering array of headgear from Homburgs to keffiyehs.

The smile never slipped from Sajidah's face and she amused herself by wondering where in the palace they would find space for these offerings when every room was already crowded with Saddam's portraits.

He stopped in front of a painting of himself with his youngest daughter, Hala, who was sitting at her father's feet, looking up at him as he read to her, her arm resting on his knee. The artist fidgeted beside the easel, fearing he had offended the president, who inclined his head one way and then another while whispering to Sajidah.

Suddenly, Saddam reached out and embraced the artist, insisting the portrait be moved instantly to his main office. Ignoring Sajidah, he led the way as two soldiers carried the portrait behind him.

Brushing past the two dozen other artists who had yet to present their work, Sajidah turned to her paid companion and sighed. 'I appear to have played my part for another year,' she said, as she watched her husband vanish into the distance.

She saw little of him these days. He excused his absences, and his refusal to tell her about where he was staying each night, by the need to safeguard her and the rest of the family from assassination. Sajidah knew better. She had her own courtiers in Baghdad who at obvious risk to themselves had for years been spying on Saddam's infidelities. Most of these affairs Sajidah ignored, but in recent months Saddam had become besotted with Samira Shabander, the wife of the chairman of Iraqi Airways, who seemed to be at every official function nowadays.

Samira had long been a coveted guest for Baghdad socialites. Her beauty was immediately obvious, with her fashionably cut blonde hair and unerring choice of French couture that accentuated her tall, slender figure.

By comparison, Sajidah was a dowdy creature. She had put on weight in the past few years and her outmoded dress sense, which looked as if it had been copied from magazines of the 1960s, did little to enhance her style. She had taken to dyeing her hair blonde. Baghdad's sophisticates mocked her bushy eyebrows and dark skin plastered with make-up, saying that she looked like a prostitute. No one would dare say this to her face.

It wasn't Samira's looks that worried Sajidah, or her obvious poise and confidence, or the fact she was clearly better educated and more worldly than the peasant girl from Tikrit. Sajidah's concern was the increasing influence Samira seemed to be having over Saddam. Samira was able to persuade him to attend more social functions that the First Lady loathed. Sajidah hated Samira for causing the rift between Saddam and her favourite son, Uday.

Samira had been invited to a party in honour of Suzanne Mubarak, wife of the Egyptian president, in November 1988, which Saddam was hosting in a candle-lit marquee on Jezirat Um Al Khanazeer, an island in the middle of the Tigris River, which overlooks the presidential palace. This used to be a favourite picnic spot for Baghdadis. In his early days as vice-president, Saddam would show up in his motor boat and descend on surprised families. Introducing himself, he would hand over bottles of wine and whisky and then would sit and share their food – without an invitation – almost as if he was a political candidate on the campaign trail. All this changed when he became president, not least because one of his first executive orders was to ban the public from 'Pigs Island', which became his private playground.

Swathed in a long, red silk evening gown that clung to her figure, Samira was at his side when Saddam arrived late at the party. Pushing their way through Saddam's usual sycophantic throng, the couple made their way towards Mrs Mubarak, who was not used to being kept waiting.

Taking her hand, Saddam mumbled a few apologies. He turned looking for Samira and, reaching out, pulled her closer to him, saying to Mrs Mubarak, 'May I introduce you to the First Lady of Iraq?'

For a moment Mrs Mubarak was puzzled. She had been briefed before arriving at the party to expect Sajidah. The photographs she had been shown were of a woman with an oval face and broad shoulders, one who was considerably older than the svelte figure standing in front of her. Samira affected an embarrassed smile.

The previous week Saddam had summoned Samira's long-suffering husband, ostensibly to discuss the future of the state-run airline. Saddam insisted the two meet alone. Once his office door was closed, Saddam asked with growling menace when the man intended to divorce Samira. The husband did so the following week.

Unlike his other mistresses, Samira would stay with the president at his palace in Baghdad, and she was flown on military helicopters to his many homes across Iraq. She would be summoned at short notice and never told where she was going or how long she would be expected to amuse the president before she was allowed home to her children. Saddam was never one to woo his women, but those closest to him noticed that he showed Samira an affection they had never witnessed with any of his other mistresses.

Word of Samira's introduction to Mrs Mubarak reached Uday within minutes from an acolyte who was only too ready to pass on this gossip in full expectation of a reward. The emissary was disappointed this time as Uday slapped him across the face and pulled his pistol from the leather shoulder holster.

'Tell me what she was doing there, you dog, or so help me I will kill you and every one of your family.'

The messenger was so frightened he could barely speak. He stammered his way through a garbled report of Samira's introduction as 'First Lady'. Mention of this provoked Uday to kick the man, who cowered on the ground.

Uday had been forbidden to attend the official party and had sulked off with some of his cronies, drinking at a government-owned villa on the banks of the Tigris. As usual, there were women in various states of undress in the room. Realising their evening was over they scurried to pick up their clothes when Uday screamed at the emissary, demanding to know more about this insult to his mother.

He tore out of the room and jumped in his white Mercedes sports car, his bodyguards struggling to keep up with him in a posse of identical vehicles as Uday recklessly weaved through the evening traffic towards the island. As he drove, Uday weighed up his options for revenge. He could not get close enough to his father since Saddam had some months before prudently ordered his guards to disarm his son before he was allowed in to see him. It would give him the greatest pleasure to kill Samira but she would be in bed with his father by now so was out of his reach for the moment. He would have to settle for Saddam's favourite manservant and food-taster, an Iraqi Christian called Kamel Hana Jajjo, who had introduced the couple and who for months had been carrying messages between the two.

'I warned this snivelling wretch what would happen to him!' Uday screamed at the bodyguard in the front passenger seat who tried not to flinch as the Mercedes narrowly squeezed past a bus that was turning across their path. 'I swear to God this reptile will know what it means to defy me and to insult the name of my dear mother.'

Uday shoved aside the guards at the entrance to the party and barged his way into the room just as Suzanne Mubarak was ready to leave what had been a longer and more eventful evening than she had anticipated. She couldn't see where Uday was going but like everyone else in the room she was aware of the commotion being caused by the unshaven figure in a brown leather jacket who was carrying what appeared to be a baseball bat.

Uday found his target smoking a cigarette with a group of Saddam's other servants and screamed at Jajjo to stand up. The old man looked terrified, unsure what it was he was supposed to have done wrong.

'You brought that whore into my house, you betrayed my mother and you insult me!' Uday yelled, lashing out with his baseball bat at the man's knees while his minders ensured that no one was rash enough to come to Jajjo's aid.

Uday continued to rain blows on Jajjo, who tried to cover his face with his left arm. His right was already broken. Spittle ran down Uday's chin and blood from a gash on the servant's scalp splattered on to his fawn slacks as he repeatedly jumped up and down on Jajjo's spine, screaming obscenities about Samira.

Jajjo was dead but Uday would not stop until one of his bodyguards eased him away and out of the marquee, where the majority of guests were oblivious to what he had done. It fell to Saddam's private secretary to wake the president two hours later with the news of Jajjo's death. While Saddam was getting dressed the secretary nervously recounted Uday's insults about Samira, who sat up in bed with the sheets pulled tight to her neck.

'Where is he?' Saddam shouted. 'Find him and bring him to me. Do it immediately or you will be punished!' he ranted while pulling a black sleeveless sweater over his pyjama top. He said nothing to his mistress as he stomped out of the room. It would be a week before Samira would see or hear from Saddam again.

Uday's arrogance had evaporated by the time he was dragged in front of his father, whose face was contorted with rage. Uday's hangover was beginning to bite and foolishly he affected astonishment to receive such a brutal summons from the presidential bodyguard. He didn't get to finish the sentence.

Saddam slapped him hard across the mouth. He would have fallen but a guard held him under his armpits as Uday shook his head to clear the ringing sound in his ears. Instinctively Uday raised his fist and then thought better of it as the body-guard supporting him drew his pistol.

'You have disgraced the honour of your family. What gives

you the right to behave like this?' Saddam screamed with such
ferocity that purple veins pulsated at his temples. 'You are not
above the law and this time you will feel its full force like the
coward and common murderer you are. Let God judge you
because I never want to see you again.'

Before Uday could make his protest Saddam turned his
back on his son and walked out of the room shouting, 'Get
that vermin out of my sight forever.'

Uday was frogmarched to a waiting car and driven to Abu
Ghraib prison. On the way, Uday first tried to bribe his captors to let him go and when that failed he spat out various
threats, warning them that when he was freed, as he surely
would be in a matter of minutes, he would relish taking
hideous revenge on them all.

The guards said nothing, though privately they enjoyed
seeing Uday so afraid. Before the convoy had reached the
prison gates news of his arrest had been passed to his mother.

Normally she would not dare try to see her husband without first making an appointment. But tonight Sajidah, still
wearing her nightdress under a fur coat, brushed past startled
palace staff until her progress was impeded by the two sentries
who stood outside the bomb-proof entrance to her husband's
private complex.

Most of it, including Saddam's private cinema and swimming pool in the eleven-room bunker, was underground.
Sajidah guessed that her rival would also still be inside there.
She stood shrieking at the two guards who looked across at
each other wondering what to do. The president's private secretary was awakened for the second time that night and,
bleary-eyed, he tried to pacify Sajidah by offering her coffee
while he promised to track down her husband and arrange a
time when they could meet.

Sajidah shouted that she was not going to wait and told the
guards they would have to shoot her if they wanted to prevent
her from entering Saddam's private quarters. The secretary
put his hands up in a show of surrender and, pleading for just

ten minutes, he scuttled off to alert Sadam that his wife was on the warpath.

Saddam had been expecting her and was by now properly dressed and determined not to give in on his decision to execute his son for murder. He deliberately kept Sajidah waiting another hour while he had his nails manicured and his hair trimmed by his personal hairdresser, so that by the time she was shown into the room her rage was such she could barely speak.

'How could you do this to our son? What he was doing was to defend me and so if you kill him then you should kill me too,' Sajidah said in her high-pitched voice.

Saddam was unmoved by her arguments and looked away. He lost his temper only when Sajidah insulted her rival, Samira, whom she blamed for this entire affair. At the mention of his mistress's name the expression on Saddam's face changed and he simply stood up and left the room, warning Sajidah, 'Hold your tongue, woman, and be mindful who you are talking to.' Realising her mistake, Sajidah attempted a more conciliatory tone but her husband simply carried on walking.

Meanwhile, once inside the prison Uday demanded to see the governor, who was an old acquaintance and a man he knew could be bribed. His worry was that many of those chained up in Abu Ghraib were there on his orders and would dearly love their chance of revenge. Uday needed assurances he would be protected. The governor was unsure whether Saddam would maintain his threat to put his son on trial and arranged for Uday to be housed in his own quarters, where he would at least be safe for the president to free or execute him.

Sajidah spent the next two days enlisting support to free Uday. She asked her younger son, Qusay, and her three daughters, Raghad, Rana and her father's favourite, Hala, to intercede on Uday's behalf. She was careful this time not to drag the fate of Samira into the argument, which was just as well as weeks later Saddam married his mistress in a private ceremony attended by none of his children. Together they had a son, Ali, who from the day he was born was given round-the-clock protection by Saddam's own guards for fear that his older children would harm this new rival for their father's patronage.

Sajidah's efforts on Uday's behalf were unceasing. She even persuaded Jordan's King Hussein, then a close confidant of Saddam, to pilot his own plane to Baghdad to plead for clemency for Uday. Saddam met the king and was polite, but remained noncommittal. Finally, Sajidah managed to get her brother-in-law, Barzan Tikriti, to offer to take the errant Uday to Switzerland as a nominal first secretary at the Iraqi embassy, arguing that exile from his self-indulgent life in Baghdad would be as great a punishment as any.

Saddam relented and sent his son to Europe – though Uday was clearly unabashed. Days after arriving in Geneva, he arranged to have several of his companions flown out and celebrated their arrival with an evening's drinking in one of the city's more exclusive nightclubs.

He presumed he could behave as he did in Baghdad, and when a languid blonde in a silver dress took his fancy he simply marched on to the floor of the discotheque and began pulling her away. When her boyfriend tried to stop him, Uday produced a gun and began waving it above his head as the dance floor emptied. Before he could do any mortal damage, two policemen appeared in the club. When Uday pointed the pistol at them he was bundled to the floor and arrested again.

His uncle Barzan had to use up a good many of his diplomatic favours to persuade the Swiss authorities that his nephew had immunity before they would let him personally put Uday on an Iraqi Airways jet that had been sent specially from Baghdad to collect him.

Barzan assured them that several extremely lucrative orders would be placed with Swiss firms in the next few weeks, believing that the Swiss, like most other European powers, were more interested in profiting from the money Saddam was spending abroad than in punishing Uday.

Such is the perversity of the Hussein family that, having banished his son, Saddam now welcomed him back as a returning hero. He appointed him leader of the Youth Federation and encouraged the compliant Iraqi press to rejoice in Uday's homecoming.

None was more pleased at the prodigal's return than Sajidah. She had always indulged him. As headmistress at the Al Karkh primary school in the fashionable neighbourhood of Keradeht Miriam, Sajidah would conduct a weekly ritual where she would gather the children beneath the flagpole, raise the Iraqi colours and order a volley of rifle-fire in honour of the nation. Clapping her hands, Sajidah would call out to the children and the other teachers to name the best student of the week in every class. In level six Uday's was unfailingly the name that was chosen. It didn't seem to matter that he seldom bothered to attend classes and when he did he spent his time rebuking the staff. One morning when a teacher was trying to comfort a weeping eight-year-old English girl, the daughter of a diplomat, Uday marched up, punched the child and screamed, 'Why are you bothering with her? She should be killed. All English people should.'

The choice for the best pupil in the next class down was invariably Qusay. Unlike the other children, Qusay chose not to wear school uniform. Instead he and those he picked for his gang would appear in jeans and tee-shirts. As an added flourish, the president's younger son would wear a crown of laurel leaves on his head like Caesar. 'He is only a boy,' his doting mother would tell the other teachers. It was the stock response she also offered to excuse his bullying of younger children.

It was no surprise that in her year Raghad was nominated. If it were at all possible, she was more spoilt than both of her brothers. One morning when she and her coterie of friends were reprimanded for being late, Raghad turned on her teacher, saying, 'Shut up, you bitch, or I'll rip out your heart.' The teacher was later dismissed for upsetting the child.

Rana was selected in her class, though by comparison with

her siblings she was the most diligent and the least offensive. This didn't mean she was incapable of tantrums. Dissatisfied with the result of one exam, on which she received the highest grade in the class, Rana ordered the teacher to take back the paper and mark it again. When it was returned an hour later there was an apology from the teacher and a perfect score.

The youngest sister, Hala, was the most precocious of them all. By the time she was sixteen Hala was renowned for borrowing her brothers' sports cars, which she drove recklessly around Baghdad. In the playground at Lake Habaniya, reserved for the children of VIPs, Hala liked to race Uday's Mercedes, imitating his style by driving with one foot placed on the dashboard. Her big brother would take the opportunity to go fishing, although he did not bother with rods and line. His satchel was stuffed with hand grenades which he nonchalantly lobbed into the pale green waters.

Saddam liked to boast that, unlike other rulers' wives, Sajidah preferred to 'remain close to her people by working with them in their communities rather than spending her time on shopping trips abroad'. He claimed her promotion to headmistress was evidence of how emancipated women were under his rule and that Sajidah got her job solely on her abilities. He insisted his wife's only income was her teacher's salary.

'Like everyone else she is called upon to give an account of her actions,' Saddam would say, though this did not explain how she was able to regularly replenish her wardrobe from fashion houses in Paris and London. Her style may have been gauche, but it was expensive. On many occasions, passengers at Baghdad airport suddenly found their flights cancelled because a plane was needed to ferry around the First Lady.

Like the rest of her family, Sajidah enjoyed various affairs – though she went to extraordinary lengths to keep them secret. She once had a servant's tongue cut out when she discovered the woman, who had been on her staff for years, was spreading rumours about one of her liaisons. She was particularly

angry because she did not want her husband to know that her
then lover was his most trusted bodyguard, Arshad Yassin.

Yassin was at Saddam's shoulder when he was sworn in as
president and had seldom left his side. He was immediately
noticeable, with his thick shock of fair hair and for the style
with which he wore his army fatigues – with the sleeves turned
up so he could show off his bulging biceps. Apart from his
obvious physical attractions, Yassin paid the neglected Sajidah
the attention she craved. He was also close enough to Saddam
to have overheard snippets of gossip that he could pass on to
Sajidah about which politicians were in favour. And he could
keep her informed about who was sharing her husband's bed.

When Sajidah finally tired of him she arranged for Yassin to
marry her youngest daughter, Hala, knowing her husband
would approve the choice. Her other two daughters had also
wed bodyguards, the brothers Hussein and Saddam Kamil,
who were also cousins of their brides.

Marriage was the swiftest avenue to promotion in Baghdad.
Soon after his wedding, Yassin graduated from his bodyguard
duties to becoming the custodian of Iraq's art treasures. He
immediately used this position to sell off many artefacts
abroad, using a chain of agents in Jordan to export antiquities
to private collectors in the West.

Blood ties were the only loyalty Saddam knew. Most of the
key jobs in the army and government went to relatives from
Tikrit, an obscure backwater that now had as many palaces as
Baghdad to accommodate the First Family. Sajidah's father,
Khairallah, who had raised Saddam like his own son, became
one of the most corrupt figures in Iraqi history. Businessmen
were forever complaining to the president about Khairallah's
excesses as the mayor of Baghdad, but he was the one man in
Saddam's eyes who was beyond reproach.

It was apparent that Sajidah had inherited her father's
knack for making money. In the early years of her marriage
she showed no inclination to profit from her power and, being
naturally shy, never involved herself in court intrigue, except

to protect her children's interests. Businessmen and others, seeking to impress Saddam, had always lavished gifts on her, but it was Uday who explained how she could turn this influence to real financial advantage. He encouraged his mother to acquire vast tracts of land close to his own farm at Salman Pak, where, unbeknownst to them both, Saddam had sited one of his chemical weapons plants. Under Uday's guidance it took barely two years for his mother to monopolise the country's dairy industry.

Now when businessmen approached Sajidah for help they would be invited to present her with ever more elaborately bound editions of the holy Koran as they sipped fruit tea in her salon. The ones most likely to win her favour were those who enclosed the most generous cheque inside the sacred book. They could tell her appreciation by whether she kept the Koran on her lap, signifying her approval, or whether she handed it without comment to one of her retainers.

Saddam was perfectly aware of all these schemes, but as long as they didn't threaten his authority or cause him problems he was prepared to ignore them. Occasionally he would insist on a family summit to chastise them for their greed and would, for appearance's sake, strip the worst offenders of some possession or other, but his family continues to loot Iraq with impunity.

Saddam's personal wealth is greater than all of theirs, though his real sleight of hand had been to cream off 5 per cent of his country's oil revenue to secretly finance his nuclear weapons programme.

The only two witnesses to this scheme are both dead, murdered by Saddam. One was his son-in-law, Hussein Kamil, and the other his wife's brother, Adnan, who had known Saddam since childhood but made the mistake of criticising the president's second marriage. Sajidah realised the danger and excused her brother's outburst by saying he was 'mad'. Saddam pretended to forgive the insult but two weeks later Adnan died in a mysterious helicopter crash. Nobody in

Baghdad enquired too deeply about the cause of the midair explosion.

Saddam went to extraordinary lengths to prevent anyone from knowing how he was financing his nuclear programme. He disguised where he was getting the money, then buried his purchases in a labyrinth of bank accounts and dummy corporations that the West still can't unravel.

Secrecy smothers his every move, particularly when it comes to his own movements. There is only one way into the thousand-acre presidential complex, across a heavily guarded bridge over the Tigris River. Once visitors pass the final checkpoint they are directed to one of the entrances appropriate to their status. There are watchtowers every fifteen metres and the guards are changed every hour.

Each of the men from the Amn Al Khass brigade lives in a luxury villa inside Saddam's fortress. They have their own hospital, restaurant, sports club and schools for their children. Every six months they are given a new car and they earn twice the salary of a cabinet minister.

They screen every visitor who comes to see Saddam – including members of his immediate family. Everyone is rigorously searched, and all are required to wash their hands at least three times. Saddam is not only fastidious about cleanliness, but he is also superstitious. His favourite soothsayer, an old woman from Tikrit, warned him years ago that an enemy would try to poison him by shaking hands. And members of his cabinet are required to keep a suit of clothes at the president's office. These are microscopically checked in advance of every visit.

Saddam built his own private office well away from the domed palace where all his family have apartments. Next door is his own interrogation centre and his Amn Al Khass bodyguards maintain a 250-metre exclusion zone around this area.

With certain foreign visitors, Saddam took every opportunity to impress with the control he exerted over his countrymen. None more so than King Hussein of Jordan. Saddam suspected his royal neighbour still harboured an ambition to follow his Hashemite forefathers by one day extending his rule to Iraq.

Once he went to Baghdad airport to meet King Hussein and on the drive back to the palace he suddenly turned to his guest and said, 'Would you like to see how well my people are living?'

The king was startled, but with his customary good manners he simply nodded, curious to know where he was going to be taken. Saddam grinned and spun the wheel of the Mercedes, stopping outside a breezeblock high rise. On his way to the airport, following some circuitous route for security reasons, he had spotted a lawyer's sign banging in the wind. The occupant was named Hassan al Hakim, noticeable to Saddam only because he had always regarded that family as sworn enemies.

While Saddam waited on the tarmac to greet his royal visitor, his bodyguards burst into Hakim's flat. The lawyer sat shaking as the armed guards searched every crevice, asking questions about whether he was expecting any visitors in the next twenty-four hours. Hakim tried to concentrate on his answers while frantically trying to think what it was he had done to merit a visit from the secret service.

After an hour one of his intruders told him that he was going to have a guest, then disconnected the telephone and sat in an armchair facing Hakim, refusing to say any more. Hakim jumped as the front door was flung open and in walked Saddam, followed by the diminutive figure of King Hussein, who was by now completely bemused at the course his visit was taking.

Saddam began firing questions at the lawyer as he strolled around the flat, turning the pages of a magazine on a coffee table and fingering the titles on the bookshelves. He threw in some insults about the Hakim clan, though personally the lawyer knew none of the people Saddam was talking about and protested as much.

Saddam smiled when he noticed there was a somewhat faded photograph of himself on one wall. Hakim, like any self-respecting professional in Baghdad, kept the portrait as insurance against some Ba'ath Party spy reporting him for not having a picture of the beloved leader, as all loyal Iraqis should.

The king sat mute through it all.

Hakim recovered his composure enough to remember his manners as host, and offered the speechless King Hussein and the president refreshments. The king simply smiled, unsure what was going to happen next. Saddam took up the cue.

'I can see you are loyal and I would like to reward you,' he told Hakim, pulling the lawyer towards him so the king could not hear the next exchanges. Hakim was told to leave his flat and go to the Rashid Hotel, where Saddam had arranged for him to have the use of a suite for the night, though he was not told why. On the drive to the hotel, a guard explained that the lawyer could order what he fancied but could tell no one he was there and could not make any telephone calls.

After Hakim had been ushered out of his flat, along with the king, who was wondering where this tour might take them now, Saddam had his staff move into the building, strip the flat and install a range of handcrafted Italian furniture, new curtains and a king-size bed.

That night a convoy of unmarked cars arrived at the same building and Saddam, in heavy disguise, was smuggled into this anonymous address to spend the night with one of his mistresses while Mukhabarat officers sealed off the entire area.

When Hakim was allowed to return to his flat he had no notion Saddam had stayed there but was told he could keep the refurbishments, including the expensive new satellite television and video.

Saddam's scope for such self-indulgent gestures diminished as the demands of a nuclear programme and a war-weary army began to take their toll. Over 375,000 Iraqis had been killed in the war with Iran. When it ended in April 1988 both sides ended where they had started. There was hardly an Iraqi family that hadn't lost someone in the war. Now both soldiers and civilians wanted their peace dividend.

Saddam thought some of his wealthy Gulf neighbours should pay. When they demurred, as in the case of Kuwait, he decided to take what he wanted.

13

LUCKY STRIKES

The American ambassador, April Glaspie, was fast asleep when the telephone rang. She had enjoyed an early supper with her elderly mother and the two had discussed plans for their holiday trip to Rome later that week. She groped around in the dark for the telephone receiver, troubled as to who might be calling this late.

The duty operator told her: 'Ma'am, it's the Iraqi Foreign Ministry on the line. They say they need to talk to you urgently and ask if you can go there right away.' The Iraqi official was left waiting on the line while the ambassador collected her thoughts. All she could think was that in recent days she had exchanged memos with the ministry about America's plans to hold military exercises in the Gulf.

The official, courteous as ever, apologised for the lateness of the call. He asked, 'Might you be so kind as to come to the ministry? We would very much welcome your views on some information we have just received.' He said no more, enquiring whether a half-hour would be long enough for her to make the appointment.

If there was one thing about this posting that irritated her it was the Iraqis' penchant for scheduling meetings long after most people have gone to bed. This time, the ambassador didn't think it worth waking her interpreter, for it seemed a routine matter. She would need her driver but knew he seldom went to bed much before now anyway.

The air was still warm that night of 25 July and she could savour the smells of the city rising up into the cloudless, blue velvet sky. The drive took her a matter of minutes through streets with just a trickle of traffic, mostly police patrol cars, delivery vans and battered orange taxis still plying for late-night fares. Inside the ministry there were the usual courtesies and offers of refreshment. After a half-hour, she was suddenly told she was to be conducted to the presidential palace to meet Saddam Hussein.

Glaspie had no time to collect any of her staff as her driver, flanked by motorcycle outriders, was directed towards the presidential palace. The ambassador was guided past the usual stringent security requirements into Saddam's office, where he was hunched over a table sifting through a pile of documents as assistants buzzed like demented wasps around the desk trying to anticipate the next request.

He looked up and, seeing Miss Glaspie, dismissed most of those in the room with a flick of his hand. She barely had a chance to settle herself into her chair before the Iraqi president began haranguing her about what the United States thought it was doing charging around in warships in the Gulf at such a sensitive time, and if it wanted to interfere in Iraq's affairs it should say so. Saddam never seemed to glance at a note as he continued his rant for over an hour, giving her no chance to interrupt.

The ambassador noticed a portable tape recorder on the desk and wished she had wakened her private secretary to witness this encounter.

Saddam has a ponderous style of speaking, slowly measuring each sentence as if talking to a child. His delivery noticeably quickened when he began talking about his neighbour, Kuwait.

'Don't they recognise what I did for them?' Saddam asked. Before the ambassador could open her mouth to defuse this rant, he ploughed into a litany of how the eight-year war with Iran had left him with an $80 million debt and how he was losing money due to falling oil prices because Kuwait and the Emirates were flooding the market. The 'final insult' was that the Kuwaitis were stealing $2 million a day from him by sucking oil from the Rumailah field, most of which – he claimed – was in his territory.

He stopped only because the telephone rang, and a nervous aide explained that Egypt's President Mubarak needed to speak to him. The ambassador recognised Mubarak's distinctive growl but couldn't hear what was being said. She noticed that Saddam had unclenched his fist and something approximating a smile formed at the corner of his mouth.

The president told her that Mubarak was confident a conference they planned in Jeddah would settle this dispute. As he finished his call, the ambassador finally got her chance to speak. Glaspie carefully recited the approved State Department line that the military exercises were just routine and that America hoped Saddam could sort out his differences with Kuwait peacefully.

She went on to say, 'We have no opinion on Arab–Arab conflicts, like your border disagreement with Kuwait.'

Saddam sat up in his chair, almost as if he wasn't sure he had heard correctly.

Glaspie retrieved her belongings and made her extravagant farewells to Saddam. Whatever the ambassador thought her message had conveyed, he was convinced the Americans had signalled their lack of interest in how he resolved his fight with his neighbour.

In the next few minutes, a half-dozen of his ministers would be awakened and ordered to his office. Saddam pulled out of his desk drawer a file he had thumbed through every night since the idea it contained was first mooted three months earlier.

He had spent most of that spring day in April with his son-in-law Hussein Kamil and a clutch of scientists, including Jaffar Dhia Jaffar, all of whom told him that without more money they couldn't deliver the bomb. Saddam flayed every man in the room.

'For twenty years I have spent more money on this project than anything else. This was the ultimate prize for our great nation, for the Arab people and the liberation of Palestine. And you sit here like dogs whining that you cannot do as you promised. I should have you shot!'

Jaffar flinched. A number of his colleagues had been executed as the price for failing to meet Saddam's expectations, and over 300 scientists in the bomb project had gone missing. Their families were never told what had happened to them. Some were in jail. Others, he knew, had been hanged. Jaffar still didn't know if his best friend, Hussein Shahristani, was among them.

Saddam raged on. If his PC3 nuclear programme needed more money, he would find it. While the scientists and his son-in-law sat locked in one room, Saddam had his finance ministers estimate how much money he could muster without depriving his army, decreasing food subsidies, or cutting back social programmes and provoking dissent at home – and curiosity in the West.

One of Saddam's vice-presidents, Taha Yassin Ramadan, came up with a violent solution. 'Saidi, the cause of all this suffering for our great people is the cowardly and treacherous behaviour of those who lick at the feet of the emir and his family. They have never paid for our sacrifices in our glorious war against Iran. Let them pay now. Kuwait belongs to Iraq. It is our 19th province. Let us free the Kuwaiti people from their corrupt rulers.'

Everyone else in the room held their breath, waiting for Saddam's response. Grabbing Kuwait meant he could steal $20 million a day from its oil fields.

His spies across the border assured him the emir had

enough gold and foreign currencies in his banks to easily fund some of what Jaffar needed. Saddam knew when he had the bomb nobody could thwart him again. He felt like a poker player who had invested so much in what he was convinced was a winning hand that he could not give in now.

Saddam's eyes narrowed. He eased himself around his chair, and pointed to the defence minister, Abdel Jabber Shenshall, saying, in an almost casual aside, 'Draw me a plan for lancing the poisonous boil, Kuwait.' Three months on, this was the file he held in his hands.

That summer Saddam began moving his tanks around the border Iraq shared with Kuwait, shunting divisions of troops from one side of the desert front line to the other while assuring other nervous Arab leaders that this was shadowboxing to concentrate the emir's mind. Spy satellites had picked up the Iraqi infantry's sand dancing along the border.

In August, the US State Department called a crisis meeting. The consensus was that Saddam was bluffing. But one veteran Pentagon intelligence expert, who had kept his counsel for most of the discussion, waited until the coffee and doughnuts were being served to make his pitch. While some at the table idly exchanged departmental gossip, the man said to no one in particular, 'I think he is going to do it. I think Saddam will invade Kuwait and will do it soon.' He was flicking through the latest satellite images and comparing them with a sheaf from the previous forty-eight hours. Without looking up, he knew he had their attention. He ambled awkwardly to the slide projector, making a mental note that he must start losing a little weight around the waist as these anonymous conference rooms in Washington seemed to be getting smaller by the week. As one of that morning's photographs appeared on the two-metre-square screen he traced with his red laser pointer how Republican Guard divisions had begun moving out of their barracks in Basra towards the desert border with Kuwait.

'He doesn't make those boys march up and down in the

desert for fun. They are the elite and he wouldn't move those people unless he was serious. Look at where his mechanised units are today compared with yesterday. Look at the fuel lines he is bringing forward, and listen to what Saddam is saying about Kuwait. He is pissed with them, and he is going to make them suffer.'

His boss looked perturbed. He pointed to Ambassador Glaspie's report of her meeting with Saddam. 'She is sure that Saddam wants to settle it peacefully. Mubarak says so. King Hussein says so. Let's not start moving the carriers there just yet. As Glaspie said, that would just spook him.'

Nobody in the room mentioned a war game the Pentagon had played in July called 'Internal Look'. It showed that the Saudi oil fields, just beyond the southern borders of Kuwait, could be protected from an Iraqi invasion, but only at an appalling cost. There were none in Washington that summer prepared to think the unthinkable about Saddam.

As the State Department meeting ended, 12,500 kilometres away the sinister figure of Vice-President Ramadan rifled through the final draft of the battle plan he was taking to Saddam. Less than twenty-four hours later, with the desert still wrapped in impenetrable darkness, a thousand Iraqi tanks turned over their engines and moved across the international border, rumbling unmolested down the main highway towards Kuwait City.

At precisely 1 AM, three Republican Guard divisions crossed the frontier, rolling south. Thirty minutes later Saddam's Special Forces landed by helicopter in the capital and picked off key government buildings without much of a fight.

The emir's panic-stricken staff bundled him into his armour-plated Mercedes and ordered the motorcade to head for the Saudi border – two hours' drive away. The emir's younger brother, Fahd, argued they should stay and fight. Two hours later, Fahd was shot dead on the steps of the Dasman Palace by an Iraqi Special Forces unit whose members ransacked the building for what they could carry. By early evening the capital was in Saddam's hands and he declared that Kuwait no longer existed except as 'the 19th Province, an eternal part of Iraq'.

Predictably, the United Nations Security Council went into emergency huddle and condemned the invasion in time for the evening news bulletins in Washington. Saddam did not expect them to do much more.

What he was waiting for was word from the task force he had assigned to head straight for the Central Bank of Kuwait. Saddam was enraged when he learned that the amount of money and gold in the vaults was barely enough to keep his nuclear programme going for a month.

Worse news was to follow when King Fahd, fearing Iraqi tanks might roll across into his kingdom next, invited the Americans to use Saudi Arabia as the base for Operation Desert Shield. With thousands of troops and fighter planes scheduled to descend on the region over the next fortnight, Saddam summoned his war cabinet to thrash out his options.

The euphoria of the previous forty-eight hours had gone. He had thought he would have more time to plunder Kuwait before his enemies decided to evict him. Saddam sat, shoulders hunched, chewing one of his Havana cigars, listening to his army chief of staff outline the alternatives.

'Saidi, we have eleven divisions in Kuwait. The Saudis have no defence.'

Saddam frowned and grunted his disapproval, refusing to be enticed into a further invasion. Only two men in that room knew the real reason why. Earlier that morning the White House had sent him a warning that if his forces stepped one foot inside Saudi territory, the Americans would launch a nuclear strike from its submarines cruising deep beneath Gulf waters.

He resolved to hold what he had.

Within weeks, he would tell Jaffar to relocate staff to secret centres to start work on the crash design for his 'mechanism'. If he couldn't have Kuwait, then nobody would. Detonating a nuclear device on one of the ring roads around Kuwait City would make his enemies think again about attacking him.

While the Allied coalition under the abrasive command of General Norman Schwarzkopf was funnelling manpower and machines into Saudi Arabia, Saddam was moving crucial nuclear materials to safer locations. Some of the enriched uranium, given to him by the French and the Russians, was sealed in lead-lined drums and buried at a farm a few kilometres beyond the barbed wire perimeter of the Tuwaitha nuclear complex. Tonnes of concrete were poured over the hiding place so that the relocated uranium could not be picked up by spy satellites. Only Jaffar and a handful of others knew precisely where it had been stashed.

Construction crews were ordered to partially dismantle some of the nuclear sites to make them look as if they were rusting, obsolete factories waiting for the bulldozers to move in. Some were enmeshed in scaffolding to resemble building sites and so delude the CIA. Others had part of the plant converted for the manufacture of useful goods, such as baby food, to protect them from being bombed. In spite of this expert camouflage, Saddam knew installations like Tuwaitha and Al Atheer were still vulnerable. What he couldn't know was that he had overestimated what the CIA, Mossad and the rest knew about his nuclear installations.

As a precaution, crates of key components for his nuclear warheads and designs for explosive lenses were shipped to Algeria, Sudan and Mauritania – the few friends he had left in the region. They were all paid for their trouble and the Mauritanian government showed its gratitude by offering sanctuary to Saddam and any of his family, should they ever need it.

In his briefing room in the National Military Command Center in Washington, DC, Defence Secretary Dick Cheney kept asking the CIA why Saddam was apparently content to just sit and watch Desert Shield growing to awesome proportions.

'What has he got that we are missing?' Cheney asked, turning to the reassuring presence of Colin Powell.

The four-star general had been a surprise choice as chairman of the joint chiefs of staff. Powell was a career soldier who had grown up in the Bronx. He had swiftly impressed President Bush with his easy confidence and his gift for explaining complicated battlefield tactics. Powell turned to the military aide sitting behind him who jabbed at his laptop.

'We know he has stockpiles of nerve agents, and the CIA believes Saddam has a thousand tons of other chemicals. He is working on some biological weapons, like botulinum, but the Agency doesn't believe he has the missiles to launch any of this at our lines. I'm not so sure.'

The spectre of yellow clouds of mustard gas or sarin blistering and asphyxiating Allied troops, and the possibility of a poisonous rain of anthrax spores choking the life out of America's young soldiers, terrified the generation of Vietnam veterans, like Powell, who were in charge of planning this war. Thousands of protective chemical and biological warfare 'Noddy' suits, gas masks and vaccines were shipped to the Gulf along with body bags and coffins. Allied commanders were secretly told to lease refrigerated trucks to store bodies and Powell tasked his staff to work out whether the contaminated corpses of American servicemen should be cremated on the battlefields rather than risk bringing them back for burial.

Powell reached over his shoulder for another sheet of paper. 'At least Saddam hasn't got nuclear. The CIA says he is still three years away.'

An audible sigh of relief ebbed around the room.

In a dreary basement beneath the river entrance of the Pentagon, Colonel John Warden finished reading the thick file. From the first days of the invasion of Kuwait, Warden, who had flown more than 300 combat missions over Vietnam, had been conjuring with Operation Checkmate – the most ambitious aerial assault ever contemplated. In front of him lay his timetable for the first day's bombing of Iraq.

The Checkmate plan was sent to the 'Black Hole', Schwarzkopf's underground headquarters in Riyadh, where it would be changed dozens of times in the next five months, as politicians and generals argued over the priorities of what to bomb. It was agreed that Iraq's air defences, its radars, missile batteries and communications centres would go first to protect the Allied pilots.

In Baghdad, the command and control headquarters that kept Saddam in twenty-four-hour contact with his generals would be obliterated on the first night, along with the Ba'ath Party's premises, key ministries and military barracks. A dozen Tomahawk missiles would be reserved for Saddam's palace in the vain hope they might catch him there and kill him. Among the 400 sorties to be flown on the first night, there would be bombing raids on Saddam's favourite retreat at Taji on the Euphrates River, his summer homes in Tikrit and Mosul and other choice hiding places.

Bush and other world leaders never publicly admitted that Saddam was a target, but waves of strike aircraft repeatedly pummelled buildings where he was thought to be. Two weeks after the war started, one of the few informers who managed to survive in Baghdad tipped off British intelligence that Saddam was heading for what was left of Basra on the southern tip of Iraq.

Just after dawn, Royal Air Force (RAF) Tornadoes spotted a convoy of eight identical motor homes flanked by land cruisers and jeeps racing south. Furious arguments crackled across the air waves as the Americans insisted that Saddam was their kill and that the RAF should wait until US Navy jets could reach them. By the time the Americans had scrambled off their carrier, the Iraqi convoy realised it was being stalked and split into small groups, tearing off across the desert with the frustrated RAF crews unable to tell which was carrying Saddam.

The second missed opportunity came when the Americans

mislaid crucial information that Saddam would be recording a broadcast in what was left of Baghdad's television station. Four missiles slammed into the studios, vaporising the entire floor where Saddam was. The president had left twenty-five minutes earlier.

This was all still to come as, two kilometres north of Schwarzkopf's bunker on the King Abdul Aziz Boulevard, in the basement of the three-storey headquarters of the Royal Saudi Air Force, Lieutenant-General Chuck Horner, the barrel-chested commander of the United States 9th Air Force, perused the map of Iraq. It covered an entire wall and was dotted with brightly coloured pins representing the final list of targets.

It was 15 January 1991 and, although no one in that room knew it, this war would begin in less than forty-eight hours. Schwarzkopf found time for a visit to the planning team – who felt as though they had not seen daylight for weeks. Horner was totally focused on the map and barely noticed Schwarzkopf's arrival.

There was a scrape of chairs as everyone else in the room stood up and saluted. The general was in no mood for pleas-antries and, striding up to the map, ordered Horner to explain the sequence of attacks. Around twenty officers hovered in the background. They noticed that Schwarzkopf was becoming increasingly irate.

'Why are we not bombing the Republican Guard with B52s from the first second this operation begins?'

Before Horner had a chance to explain, the commander-in-chief yelled, 'You lied to me! I told you to bomb those sons of bitches, and bomb them again and again from day one. If you don't do what I tell you, I'll find somebody who will!'

With that Schwarzkopf stormed out of the room, leaving Horner and his exhausted staff to change the target list yet again.

What was apparent was that each time they inserted a new priority, the few nuclear installations that they knew about slipped even further down the list. A mountain of intelligence assessments about the nuclear programme had just been dumped on Horner's desk, but nobody told him what to look for.

Analysts knew of the importance of Tuwaitha from what international inspectors and others had told them. The CIA checked with every company who had ever done business with Saddam to find out what they had sold him. Satellites had picked up convoys of trucks travelling in and out of places like Tarmiya and Ash Sharqat, but even these facilities were progressively downgraded to accommodate often hysterical demands for more obvious targets by politicians of a dozen countries.

The UN deadline, giving Saddam one last chance to pull out of Kuwait by 15 January, was fast approaching.

The previous morning President George Bush had met for breakfast with both Secretary Cheney and General Powell.

'Colin, whatever happens now, we cannot let Saddam escape with his army intact. We also have to destroy his weapons of mass destruction, no matter what.'

Powell did not reply immediately. He shared Bush's worry about the contamination that could occur if the Americans hit any one of the dozens of chemical and biological factories on the list of targets. Nobody at that breakfast table knew about the efforts in Baghdad to build Saddam's 'mechanism', or the immense progress Iraq had made towards becoming a self-sufficient nuclear weapons power.

What was also concerning the White House was a telephone call from the Soviet leader, Mikhail Gorbachev, claiming Saddam had agreed to a face-saving compromise, so there was no need for war. Bush could scarcely disguise his disappointment and was relieved when five hours later Saddam responded to the Kremlin's offer with a pompous ultimatum of his own. He was playing for time, calculating that his scientists would benefit with every day gained to perfect what would become known as the 'beach ball'.

Bush decided to inform only a handful of his coalition

partners that the air war would begin in the early hours of 17 January. He was livid when the CIA monitored the Kremlin trying to telephone Saddam with this news.

'What is the point of targeting his palaces and his hideouts if he knows precisely when we are going to bomb?' Bush fumed.

He considered altering D-Day, but by then a million hours had gone into perfecting the timetable for Operation Desert Storm.

The Black Hole, from where Schwarzkopf would command the war, was the size of a tennis court and four floors beneath the concrete fortress of the Saudi Ministry of Defence. The sign that the general was about to appear was unmistakable. An aide arrived with a glass of ice water, black coffee, orange juice and a bottle of cold mocha chocolate. Each was placed with geometric precision next to the commander's spectacles and a blank notepad.

Minutes later the door burst open and an aide announced, 'Gentlemen, the commander-in-chief!'

Schwarzkopf strode to his seat and nodded to the chaplain to say a prayer. As it finished, the general read a brief message to his troops and then jabbed at a portable tape recorder on his desk. The sounds of 'God Bless America' echoed around the room. As it finished, Schwarzkopf said, 'Okay, gentlemen, let's go to work.'

He was ordering into war more than 1,000 planes, 4,000 tanks, more than 150 ships and 650,000 troops. Banks of computers kept him in touch with ships like the *Wisconsin*, which fired the first Tomahawks, and with the air bases spread across the Gulf. For the first indication of how Baghdad was reacting Schwarzkopf, like everyone else, had to rely on CNN. His aides had rigged up a link to Iraqi television. They knew the second it went off the air at a little after 2 AM that the first targets in Baghdad had been hit.

President Bush was still wet from the shower when he was called to the White House Situation Room and briefed on the success of the first night. He dared to think that this war could be over more quickly than his military planners had predicted.

The illusion did not last for long. That same morning Saddam launched the first of his Scuds on Israel – six on Tel Aviv and two on Haifa. Ambulances screamed through the streets of both cities amid scares from civil defence teams that nerve gas had been detected in one of the incoming missiles. In fact, they did little damage.

The White House was nervous about how the Israelis would react. The Israeli prime minister waited a day before speaking to Bush. When he did, Yitzhak Shamir brusquely informed him that Israeli forces were about to launch raids into western Iraq.

Those in the Oval Office listening in on the conference line knew that if the Israelis made good on their threat of retaliation, it would shatter the coalition. At first Shamir appeared to dismiss Bush's reassurances, but his attitude changed when the American leader offered him millions in aid, and banks of Patriot missiles that Bush promised would intercept the Scuds. Above all the Israelis could dictate a large percentage of the daily targets they wanted bombed in Iraq.

Horner was speechless when this new complication was communicated to him. Once again he had to ask his staff to revise the target list. The few Iraqi nuclear installations on the inventory were downgraded even further. Some slipped off the list completely.

Saddam had taken to spending his nights in private villas in the most built-up parts of Baghdad so the bombers couldn't reach him. A trembling Dr Jaffar was driven through the blacked-out and deserted streets as the sirens wailed. He was to report to Saddam on the progress of 'the mechanism'.

The scientist explained that weapons-grade uranium had been chopped up in preparation for dissolving in the LAMA hot lab of Tuwaitha. 'Saidi, the process has started, the teams are working twenty-four hours a day with no thought to their own safety, but only to serve you.'

Saddam said nothing. In his mind's eye he was calculating how long it would take to move the finished bomb to Kuwait for testing. Jaffar was dismissed. But it would not be long before he had to return.

The following day the scientist had the unenviable task of telling Saddam that an overnight attack on Tuwaitha had destroyed the secret LAMA laboratory crucial for recasting the uranium fuel into a nuclear explosive. Jaffar was petrified as he explained to a scowling Saddam why there was now no possibility of building 'the mechanism'. The president sat with his head buried in his hands.

Saddam dismissed everyone in the room. He sat in darkness for an hour, wondering how much of his cherished nuclear programme could be salvaged. His only tactic now was that he must survive this war, no matter how long it lasted. He prayed that his concealed laboratories and research centres would survive with him.

The F117 pilot responsible for sparing Kuwait from centuries of radiation had no idea what he had achieved. He was limping his plane back to the Saudi air base of Khamis Msheit, and he was running desperately short of fuel. The weather had closed in around the air crews that day. Planes were stacked one above the other waiting anxiously for their chance to strike.

To help the pilot conserve his fuel, flight controllers told the pilot to check through his target list and find somewhere to drop his last bomb. Over Tuwaitha the computers in his cockpit coughed up the grid reference for the main administration building. Distracted by the streams of anti-aircraft fire and surface-to-air missiles, he paused for just a fraction of a second before releasing his laser-guided missile. That minuscule delay destroyed the most significant single building in Saddam's crash programme. It would be another ten months before the Allies would begin to understand just what the F117 had hit.

The weapons-design centre at Al Atheer was hit in the last sortie the Stealth bombers would fly in the war, and only

because it was another of those unfinished factories that the
analysts couldn't quite decipher. Just to be on the safe side it
was put on the list of targets because it was sandwiched
between the army's high-explosive testing centres at Al Qa
Qaa and Al Hatteen. The Allies wouldn't know the full extent
of what had been going on inside Al Atheer until Saddam's
son-in-law Hussein Kamil defected in August 1995. But
another fortuitous strike by an American pilot would reveal
more of Saddam's nuclear jigsaw.

Banking through thick cloud the F14 Tomcat homed in on
the Tarmiya complex, just north of Baghdad. It had been
designated a Grade B target, which meant no one knew precisely what it was but from the air it was big enough to justify
attention. Intelligence agents presumed it was a munitions
factory and warned the air crews that night 'to expect fire-
works'.

The pilot picked out Building Thirty-Three, the largest in
the complex, and looked over his shoulder as the groundbuster
bomb peeled back the factory roof like the lid of a sardine can,
revealing what looked like lines of giant frisbees. For weeks
afterwards analysts scratched their heads in bewilderment as
they tried to fathom what the aerial photographs of the
bombed facility had uncovered.

The answer emerged only by accident when John Gogain, a
retired atomic scientist in his seventies, glimpsed the grainy
black and white pictures. 'My God, that's Oak Ridge, Tennessee, where I worked all my life.'

A much younger colleague chided him. 'Don't be stupid.
These pictures were taken over Iraq earlier this month. How
can it be where you worked when we have just bombed it?'

Gogain looked at the prints again. He explained that the
'frisbees' that had been puzzling the intelligence agencies were
the vast calutron magnets used to separate out weapons-grade
uranium. Jaffar's decade-long secret was uncovered.

That same night in February 1991, Iraq's most brilliant
physicist locked himself away and slowly sipped his way

through most of a bottle of whisky, reflecting on his troubled journey from happier days as a student in London to endless nights now spent cowering in bomb shelters.

He wondered if absent friends, like Hussein Shahristani, had survived the weeks of bombing raids. Jaffar couldn't know that one attack had knocked out the power at Abu Ghraib prison and that Shahristani and others had taken their chance to escape.

The remorseless bombing had left Baghdad without food, water, electricity and telephones. Water trucks toured the streets for those few residents who dared emerge from the shelters. Many had to use the foul smelling River Tigris as their only lavatory.

Each morning as people crept from their hiding places they would notice how many more buildings had been disfigured or just disappeared from the city's skyline. The 14 July suspension bridge had split in two and lay half submerged in the Tigris. The Palace of Congress looked as though it had melted and elegant arches in front of Saddam's palace lay in heaps of rubble.

Hospitals were running short of bandages and medicines, and in street markets the traders were asking extortionate prices for rice and bread. Saddam showed little interest in the daily bulletins of how his people were suffering. He was more concerned at what the carpet-bombing by the B52s was doing to his Republican Guard, cowering on Kuwait's border. He could only hope that many of his chemical and nuclear plants still remained intact. The damage would have been worse but for the Allies' obsession over Scuds.

In a dozen briefing rooms at air strips across the regions pilots began arguing with commanders about why they seemed to be doing little else but hunting mobile Scud launchers. One exasperated flight lieutenant paced the floor, waving a damage assessment report of his success the previous evening when the heat-seeking imagery in his cockpit picked up what he was sure was the crew of a Scud launcher, turning over its engines to keep warm.

'I got too close to having my hair singed from their triple-A last night and look what I hit,' he said, flipping the report at his wing commander. 'It was a goatherd.'

Schwarzkopf sided with his air crews. Never a man to court popularity, he hardly endeared himself to the Israelis by complaining in front of the television cameras.

'There is more chance of me being struck by lightning in the street than being hit by a Scud. So why am I risking my pilots' lives?'

General Powell was required to admonish his field commander over the telephone – and not for the first time. He knew there were some in the White House who wondered out loud if the strain was not getting too much for Schwarzkopf and if he should be relieved of command. Powell argued vehemently against this. He also warned Schwarzkopf to temper his behaviour after complaints from senior officers about the general's foul-mouthed tantrums.

Schwarzkopf's humour was not improved when he was ordered to send British and American special forces – at the Israelis' prompting – on what were often suicide missions to take out the Scud launchers.

Asked by Powell in another telephone call why he was dragging his feet over the start of the ground war, Schwarzkopf railed at the 'armchair generals'.

'I will move when I'm damn well ready,' he told them.

After that conversation Powell, too, worried that his field commander was cracking up.

Schwarzkopf was ready at 4 AM on Sunday 24 February. Sitting at his desk with his arms folded, he showed no emotion as he unleashed his forces to evict Saddam. It had taken six months of planning. The general painstakingly ticked off each unit as it crossed into Iraq. They met surprisingly little resistance. Demoralised Iraqi conscripts had been dug in so long that those who survived the carpet-bombing by the B52s had used up all the fuel and the battery power in their tanks trying to survive the freezing winter.

Infantry units effortlessly bulldozed their way through the sand berms that Saddam had built to trap them. The main obstacle to this perfectly executed advance was the endless stream of bedraggled Iraqi troops walking towards the tank crews waving white flags and begging for food and water.

Morale had all but collapsed in Saddam's army. To disguise the losses, wounded soldiers were forbidden to return to their own villages. Families who lost loved ones were told they could not mourn. To try to stop deserters, Saddam ordered that one man from every battalion from the front line was to be hanged and left hanging for five hours in front of his comrades. Anyone suspected of trying to run away was shot on sight.

The televised war was too much for the squeamish. Watching in the Oval Office, President Bush winced as he listened to his jubilant pilots describe 'the turkey shoot' as they picked off the procession of Iraqis fleeing Kuwait along Mutla Ridge.

In a final, spiteful stab at his neighbour, Saddam ordered his retreating armies to set fire to Kuwait's oil wells. Allied tank crews had to manoeuvre their way through suffocating clouds of acrid black smoke to liberate the gutted capital.

After reading that morning's situation reports, Bush wanted to halt the ground war after just four days. What stopped him was a plea from his air force chiefs that they had devised a new bomb powerful enough to slice through the concrete defences of the bunker where they were sure Saddam was holed up.

Bush was pensive as he chewed the end of his pen. He turned to Powell and said, 'You've got another twenty-four hours.'

A transport plane slipped unnoticed into Taif airport in Saudi Arabia that same afternoon, ferrying two 2,000-kilogram bombs which the air force had barely had time to test. Within hours the massive cylinders had been slung underneath a pair of F111 jets for the short flight to Taji, northwest of Baghdad, where intelligence chiefs believed Saddam had a shelter twelve-and-a-half metres underground.

Both pilots hit their target, and fire belched from ventilation shafts as the bombs crashed through the roof and exploded deep inside the bunker. In the Oval Office they waited for news of their quarry. When it arrived Bush read it impassively, then crushed it into a ball and tossed it into a wastepaper basket. Saddam had not been inside the bunker.

He was safely in Baghdad staying in a cousin's villa. The few officers who were with him thought he looked to have lost twelve kilograms in weight since the war began, but as Bush appeared on CNN to announce the ceasefire Saddam smiled. The sun was dropping over Washington as the president's aides polished his statement. It first ran through what Saddam had to do now – hand back the downed Allied pilots and other prisoners of war. He had to disclose where his minefields were, and to stop all Scud launches. Saddam was required to repay Kuwait and rescind all claims against his neighbour.

The US president insisted he didn't want to gloat about the victory.

'Over 500 of our Allied forces have died,' he had reminded his aides. 'Three hundred and ninety of them were Americans. No war is ever completely won.'

He scribbled a note to himself in the margin to remember the dead from both sides. Bush ended the speech simply.

'Kuwait is liberated. Iraq's army is defeated. Our military objectives are met.'

Saddam knew better. He had feared Baghdad would be overrun. He was sure coalition forces would be camped out in his country for years to come, occupying the towns where his nuclear installations were hidden and where his arsenal of chemical and biological weapons was buried.

He wondered what he had left and could not quite believe his good fortune when General Powell appeared on the television screen showing on a map of Iraq where the Allied advance had stopped.

'Look where they are,' Saddam said to those gathered at

the back of his chair. 'Look what is still in our hands,' he added, pointing to where the coalition's front line stopped – well short of the cluster of nuclear facilities radiating out from Baghdad. As far as he was concerned, the heart of his nuclear programme was still beating.

There was a line of lobbyists from the CIA, the Defence Department and others trying to badger President Bush about what to include in the ceasefire deal. Bush remained enigmatic while General Powell spent hours on the telephone with his field commanders. To Schwarzkopf it was simple.

'I just want to get my soldiers home as fast as possible. I want to finish this now. Don't load me with clauses the Iraqis can haggle over,' Schwarzkopf snapped. He got his way.

The rotors of his Blackhawk helicopter spat dust over the honour guard as Schwarzkopf arrived at the desert air strip at Safwan to sign the formal ceasefire. He had massive tents erected alongside the runway, cooled by portable air conditioners. The general tore aside the tent flaps to inspect the plain wooden table he had insisted on as the only furniture.

'I want no ceremonies, no handshakes. I'm going to give these guys nothing. Repeat nothing. I'm here to tell them what they have to do.'

Just after eleven in the morning, the Iraqi delegation arrived at the agreed rendezvous. They were told to abandon their own vehicles and were pointed in the direction of the four American Humvee jeeps that would drive them the rest of the way to Schwarzkopf's tent.

General Schwarzkopf stood waiting for them outside. Through his interpreter, he told the two Iraqi officers they would have to submit to a full body search. As they began to protest, Schwarzkopf held his arms above his head and motioned for the young American captain to start searching him first.

Schwarzkopf strode into the tent. The Iraqis were unsure whether they should follow. Their olive green uniforms were impeccably laundered, prompting the general to turn to his aide and say, 'I don't think these guys have been anywhere near their front line throughout this war.'

Schwarzkopf began by lecturing the stern-faced Iraqis that he was a soldier and was not there to waste his time discussing politics. 'That's the United Nations' job, not mine.'

For the next two hours, Schwarzkopf told the two Iraqis what they could and couldn't do. As they parted, the senior Iraqi held out his hand. Schwarzkopf had told his staff that morning there would be no handshakes. Now he changed his mind and slowly offered his enemy his hand.

When Saddam was shown the formal ceasefire later that night he turned the pages quickly, scanning each one with his thumb. As he skimmed through the last page he smiled. There was no mention of the word 'nuclear' in this deal.

14

HIDE AND SEEK

Hussein Shahristani learned that his country had gone to war when the walls of his cell began to vibrate as the first Tomahawk missiles thumped into Baghdad.

Showers of dust fell from the ceiling. Lumps of concrete split from the wall during the bombardment. The nuclear chemist, who had spent the past eleven years in Abu Ghraib prison, cringed in the darkness and wondered if Saddam was as scared as he was.

He could hear the distant rumble of explosions and tried to picture what it was doing to the city he had last seen in November 1982, on the day when Mukhabarat guards burst into the villa where he was under house arrest.

That day in 1982, Shahristani had been in bed. The two men roughly tied his hands behind his back and forced a blindfold over his eyes. They refused to answer his questions about where they were taking him. He remembered banging his head as he was pushed into the back of a car, and the silence of the long drive. He was fearful he was about to be hanged.

Shahristani found himself back in Abu Ghraib. In silence, he was pushed along a stone corridor and thrown into a cell two metres by two metres. Only when the door was locked was he allowed to remove his blindfold. The only furniture was the thin army blanket on the floor and a bucket of water in the corner. As the cell door slammed, Shahristani was certain he must be on Death Row.

There were no windows so he could not tell when dawn broke. He was a scientist and was torturing himself about how he could mark time. His food, when it came, was passed through a hatch. For months he lived like this. He was never allowed out of the cell, not even to wash or use a toilet, and he only ever saw the same Mukhabarat officer, who never exchanged a word with him.

This mental torture continued for years. His captors would permit him no books, no radio and no conversation. Shahristani tried to create a routine to his day to sustain himself and his sanity. Much of his time he would spend praying, trying to remember as many verses of the Koran as he could.

He would try to meditate but found his concentration would lapse and he slipped into thinking about the man responsible for all this, Saddam Hussein. He would whisper imaginary conversations with Saddam.

'I do not feel bitter towards you, I feel disgust. You are a creature that has lost all contact with reality, and nothing, not torture, not killing people can give you sleepless nights. You feel nothing.

'All those you use, Barzan who tried to bully me, Fadel Barak my torturer when I was first in prison, and the others, they are all people of no education. You have moulded them, and you never let them forget that without you, they are nothing. You have involved them in your blood lust and they know there is no escape for them now. You have turned your own children into killers. If you go then they all know they are dead.'

Often his mind would drift towards the fate of his friend, Jaffar, who had succumbed to the pressures to build Saddam his bomb. In his imagination Barzan Tikriti gloated about how highly regarded and well rewarded Jaffar was.

Shahristani pictured the two of them back in the laboratories of Tuwaitha. He pitied Jaffar. He rehearsed over and over what he would say if they ever got the chance to meet again. 'How could you do it, Jaffar? None of us are brave when it comes to threats and torture. But you were a man of integrity as well as competence and wisdom and should never have been blackmailed.'

After four years, Shahristani was allowed to set foot outside that cell, but only for fifteen-minute periods every other day. The guards would first clear the prison yard, and he would be allowed a few moments to warm his face in the sun. His hair was matted and he had lost twelve kilograms in weight. The silence in which he was condemned to live was still maintained. Nobody spoke to him.

Without warning he was pulled from his cell one morning and taken, protesting, into an empty room. The guards escorting him insisted he wrap his head in a towel so nobody could recognise him. Shahristani felt he was hallucinating when he watched Berniece walk through the door.

Two Mukhabarat officers sat on either side of him and put their hands on his shoulders to stop him from standing to embrace his wife. Berniece sat a metre from him. They were not allowed to touch, and he was given ten minutes to absorb as much news as he could about what she and their children had been doing for the past four years. He steeled himself in order not to cry, not to show Berniece how much he was suffering. As a guard ushered her outside Shahristani found it impossible to speak, wondering when, and if, they would ever be a family again.

His captors soon tired of him, and enlisted one of their favoured inmates in Abu Ghraib to pass Shahristani his meals and empty his bucket. The man was intrigued by why the chemist was still suffering in this jail. He had heard the guards talking about how stupid this man must be and how he could have been a minister if he had only done as he was told. After two weeks, the prisoner dared to whisper a few words to Shahristani as he passed him his bowl of soup and rice.

'My name is Ali Oryan,' he said.

Shahristani was so startled he couldn't reply.

Over the next four years, Ali was the only man he ever spoke to and Shahristani relished his brief appearances each day. When Ali told him he had a plan of escape, as he was trusted with the master key for that cell block, the scientist presumed it was a trick.

'If I escape they know where my wife and children are and they will kill them,' Shahristani said. He used this as his excuse for not taking up the offer.

Ali shrugged and told him the invitation remained open.

Just over eight years after he returned to Abu Ghraib, Shahristani was without reason or explanation moved out of solitary confinement. He was still alone in a room of the jail's closed section, but he was allowed out for several hours a day when he could mix freely with hundreds of other prisoners.

He was desperate to know what had become of scores of his colleagues from Tuwaitha, as well as the fellow prisoners from whom he had been separated in May 1980. Many had high academic degrees and the guards had rounded up almost a thousand of them. The inmates he now met didn't want to speak of such things. Most were fearful of being overheard.

One old man, though, a former professor at Baghdad University, muttered to him how many of the scientists had been executed. Others had just vanished. The professor described how guards had rounded up a group called the High Qualifiers because each had a string of the highest university qualifications. None were ever seen again.

When Shahristani finally did escape from prison, he was to discover that 30,000 men had disappeared from Abu Ghraib during his time there.

When the bombing started, Ali, who by now had convinced Shahristani of his sincerity, persuaded the chemist that they should use the confusion of the repeated raids to escape. Their jailers were so terrified, they no longer bothered about the prisoners and how they were surviving. Ali had managed to get word to Shahristani's family that they should move to a safe house on the outskirts of Baghdad and wait.

By chance the Mukhabarat had given Ali the keys of one of their land cruisers so he could clean it and change the oil. Ironically, Shahristani and his friend hijacked the car the secret police were hoping to use for their own getaway. During that night's bombardment around Abu Ghraib, Ali used his master key to free Shahristani. The two men blundered through the darkness to where Ali had parked the land cruiser along with a change of clothes.

'No one will dare stop us; this is a Mukhabarat car,' Ali assured Shahristani as they passed through the first of four sets of steel gates. At the last checkpoint, the guards insisted Ali roll down the smoked glass window. Shahristani pretended to be a senior Mukhabarat officer and barked out a stream of orders. All the guards wanted was a lift to safety, but Ali brushed them aside and, ignoring the air raid, drove the car through the blacked-out streets to the safe house.

Berniece had arranged for another car. She barely had a chance to speak to her husband as they bundled their three children, Zahra, Maryam and Muhammad, into the vehicle. They drove for hundreds of kilometres towards Suleimaniya in the north along the prearranged escape route. There in the mountains of Kurdistan they were given refuge for the rest of the war. In the few weeks when Saddam's hold on power slipped and spontaneous rebellions erupted across the country in March and April, the Shahristani family joined the procession of thousands seizing their chance to escape Iraq's borders.

Shahristani headed for Iran, intent on spending his next years trying to discover what had happened to all his missing colleagues from Tuwaitha and his fellow inmates from 1980.

Others from the bomb programme also took their chance to escape.

Many of the scientists were just brushed aside in this chaos on the borders. The first of these defectors was greeted with suspicion from the CIA agents. The scepticism at CIA headquarters at Langley changed by the time the fifth and sixth defectors arrived with similar stories about the huge construction works and heavy equipment that Saddam had hidden.

One man was forceful enough to persuade a British officer to drive him all the way to the border town of Zakho, where he spilled out a torrent of secrets to startled intelligence experts. Realising the importance of the man, they put him on a helicopter to a Turkish air base operated by the North Atlantic Treaty Organisation (NATO). It was the start of a much longer journey that would end in Washington, where America's incredulous nuclear fraternity heard firsthand what Saddam had managed to achieve without their knowledge.

When the director of the CIA telephoned Bush that morning to arrange an appointment, he asked the president if they could meet alone. Bush soon understood why. The colour drained from his face when he read the testimony from Saddam's scientists. The president could not believe what he was reading.

'How did we miss this?'

The director just raised his eyebrows.

'We can't tell anyone for the moment,' the president said.

Bush, who was savouring the accolades of victory, was in no mood to admit to anyone what the Allies had missed in their six-week bombardment. This was supposed to have been the 'perfect war'. Schwarzkopf and the other triumphant generals were being fêted with ticker-tape parades and banquets in a dozen cities where the speeches trumpeted how Saddam's military machine had been smashed beyond repair.

The sobering reality Bush was learning that morning was that a third of Iraq's troops had gotten away and that the elite Republican Guard had escaped with half its tanks intact. The air raids had somehow missed over a hundred Scuds, at least nineteen mobile launchers, seventy tonnes of nerve agents, and 400 tonnes of mustard gas. More alarming were the scientists' revelations about Saddam's nuclear programme.

One of the defectors, an engineer at Tuwaitha, chilled his CIA handlers when he told them that Saddam had actually tested a small nuclear device. The two agents questioning him at the American embassy in Ankara rushed from the room to contact Langley on a secure telephone line. Careful not to reveal their source, the CIA agents asked their Turkish counterparts whether they had ever picked up any evidence of a major blast in Iraq.

It took several days for the answer to come back, during which time the defector was flown to Washington on an unmarked Lear jet and moved to a variety of safe houses where he was interrogated by the finest minds from America's nuclear fraternity.

The Turkish authorities sent back word that their seismographs had picked up some disturbance but they correctly calculated it a minor earthquake, which was not uncommon in those parts. The Turks' subsequent enquiries about why the CIA was so bothered about some tremor in the Iraqi desert were met by a polite silence. The Americans were not ready to share this information with any of their allies.

The CIA was ordered to do all it could to tempt more scientists to leave Iraq. What these defectors had to say was rewriting what US intelligence knew about Saddam's weapons of mass destruction.

Little was seen of Saddam after the war ended. His family complained to his private secretary that they had heard nothing from him as he remained holed up in one of the fortified bunkers the bombers had missed. For days he studied reports of the extent of the damage to his armies and, more important, his nuclear ambitions.

Those closest to him worried about him. He was not his usual fastidious self, often sitting for hours in the same crumpled uniform. He seldom ventured out, except after dark and only then wearing some ridiculous disguises. After the punishment Iraq took from the B52s, there were rumbles of discontent from the Republican Guard unit at Basra. Saddam was persuaded to visit the barracks, driving there in the cab of a trucking rig carrying emergency food supplies.

His aides fostered the myth that the president was out daily amongst his people, listening to their stories of suffering and courage. They used two of Saddam's 'doubles', who would show up at market stalls and cafés where they would be filmed by the state-run television network.

The Iraqi ambassador to Hungary had found one of these stand-ins by accident in Budapest only a few months before. The diplomat was walking to his favourite restaurant when he stopped in his tracks. His companions joked that he must have seen a ghost as a heavy-set Hungarian labourer walked past in his work clothes. The man was an absolute ringer for Saddam Hussein – the same build, the same style of moustache – and the ambassador was suddenly troubled that his president had arrived unannounced.

He had his chauffeur chase after the baffled workman, who was offered a holiday to Baghdad and more money than he could dream about. The man was too simple to ask what the catch was. He would soon learn he could never leave Iraq.

The double was a little shorter, but otherwise the physical likeness was so uncanny the plastic surgeons' skills were not required. The only trouble was that after months of coaching, the stand-in still could not properly imitate Saddam's lumbering walk. Television producers had to carefully edit out the double's jerky movements as they faked him chatting to newspaper sellers and market traders.

The CIA and other agencies mischievously planted stories that Saddam had been assassinated. Their idea was to foment even more unrest and goad the president into showing himself, so that psychiatrists working for the Pentagon could study how he looked, how he spoke and how he behaved.

Saddam learned of Shahristani's escape at the same time

that the scientist and his family reached the safety of the Kurdish mountains. When he was told that Shahristani was not the only scientist who couldn't be found, Saddam's knuckles went white as he gripped the edge of the desk.

There was near anarchy on both his northern and southern borders, but Saddam ordered the Mukhabarat to scour the columns of refugees for the defectors. If they could not recapture them, they must kill them. To encourage his security forces, Saddam offered a $100,000 bounty for each of the missing nuclear scientists.

He then turned to his son-in-law Hussein Kamil, who had produced a preliminary report that morning describing how much of the nuclear project was unscathed. Kamil's satisfied mood turned sour as Saddam hectored him about how their years of subterfuge were now wasted.

'These traitors will give away all our secrets. They must be found before they can betray us, or all will be lost.'

The scientists, including Jaffar, who remained at Tuwaitha and the other sites found themselves under even closer scrutiny. Security agents forbade them to leave the compounds where they lived and followed them around their laboratories. Once more there were rumours that some scientists were disappearing. Most were abducted at nights by security agents. A handful escaped before they could be rounded up.

One of them was an electrical engineer in his thirties who faked his own death in a car crash on the road to the Turkish border. He set fire to the car, and the wreckage was so fused and mangled that it was impossible to match the scorched identity documents with the charred remains in the driving seat. Saddam learned of this particular deception and, unable to reach the engineer, had his wife, children and other close relatives executed as a warning to others. The engineer had his revenge by tipping off the Americans about the set-up of Jaffar's laboratory, where the heavy calutron magnets were starting to produce weapons-grade uranium.

Many others died. Among them was Musa Al Janabi, a

gifted chemist who was always haunted by the work he was made to do for Hussein Kamil's Military Industrialisation Organisation, which was still in charge of the remaining weapons for mass destruction. Janabi was a sensitive man who claimed he would have preferred to make his living by writing poetry. Such an ambition attracted the suspicions of the Mukhabarat and he was jailed. After a few months at Abu Ghraib he was freed, but was found to be suffering from an unknown disease which caused him to lose weight rapidly. He died in a matter of weeks. A spate of young engineers suffered similar symptoms with the same fatal results.

Others could not escape. Dr Qadamah Al Malla, the head of Baghdad University's Nuclear Engineering Department, disappeared after he was caught near the border with a fake passport that described him as a merchant. A security guard at the last checkpoint recognised the doctor because he used to present a popular science programme on Baghdad Television called *The World in the Year 2000*.

Frightened of trying to cross the border, where the Mukhabarat were waiting, some scientists settled for hiding out in the Kurdish strongholds of northern Iraq. Five years later, in August 1996, Saddam used the pretext of a security operation around the city of Irbil to send his hit squads to murder every last one of them.

The assassination squads were also sent abroad to hunt down the defectors. The one Saddam wanted most, Hussein Shahristani, was in Tehran. Several times hit teams got within metres of him, but Shahristani's luck held and he was able to elude them.

Border guards reported back to Baghdad how a fifty-two-year-old nuclear engineer, Muayad Al Janabi, had managed to cross into Jordan. The engineer had told his colleagues he was going on holiday with his wife and children. He paid $4,000 for a fake passport which disguised his real occupation. In Amman, Al Janabi toured Western embassies begging for asylum, though none took seriously what he had to offer. Al

Janabi had worked at Osirak and been part of the nuclear programme from its infancy. All he could fix up for himself was a
teaching job in Libya.

Iraqi spies spotted him coming out of the embassy of
Libya, where he was making arrangements to emigrate. The
Iraqi agents forced a taxi driver who lived next door to Al
Janabi in Baghdad to telephone him to say that he was bring-
ing some money from his brother to help pay for his journey.
Excited at the news, Al Janabi told the taxi driver to meet him
outside the Tunisian embassy, where he had to pick up a tran-
sit visa for his trip to Libya.

He was talking to his wife, Wafa, and holding hands with
their four-year-old son, Omar, and six-year-old daughter, Ala,
when they saw the taxi driver. As they waved to him, a man
standing beside the driver, dressed all in black with a scarf
hiding his face, walked swiftly over to Al Janabi, put a gun to
his head and without saying anything pulled the trigger.

Wafa screamed as her husband tried to reach out to her. As
he fell, he said to the gunman, 'Why are you killing me?' The
gunman stood over him and fired three more times at point-
blank range. The assassin turned and ran down the street,
tearing off his bloodstained clothes as he did so, and climbed
into a jeep with Iraqi number plates that was waiting a few
hundred metres away.

Back in Baghdad officials mourned Al Janabi's murder and
publicly blamed Mossad for the killing. King Hussein ordered
his own investigation into the assassination. When he discovered Iraq's hand, he expelled several of its diplomats from
Amman and offered the scientist's wife a safe haven and a
pension. Mindful of the repercussions, Saddam sent his
regrets to the king that blood was spilled on the streets of
Amman. But he did not apologise.

What worried Saddam was the continuing trickle of highly
qualified nuclear specialists who refused to be cowed. Khidr
Hamza was troubled by the way Saddam was hunting down
his colleagues. In 1994, when a close friend and colleague in

the nuclear programme was murdered and his body dumped near Hamza's farm, he decided he could take no more. The director of weaponisation fled across the border through Kurdistan, taking with him precious secrets of how Saddam intended to detonate his nuclear bomb.

Most of the defectors were given new identities by the CIA and moved to obscure suburbs around America. They were found jobs in schools and universities where their real talents were deliberately hidden. The names of all of them are on a file in Saddam's private office. He has sworn that however long it takes, he will find them all and make them pay with their lives.

When the Americans passed on only some of what they had learned from the defectors, the United Nations did not hesitate to adopt a ceasefire resolution that banned Iraq from any nuclear activity. Saddam was told to hand over all that he had, along with his chemical and biological stockpiles and missiles that could reach beyond his borders.

The Security Council said that until he did, Iraq would face unprecedented sanctions. George Bush went further, warning Saddam that if he didn't comply the American jets would return. After all, Bush knew more than any other leader what Saddam really had.

President Bush flew to Camp David for a weekend with his security advisers. As they walked through the spring sunshine, the group was supposed to be discussing how quickly they could bring home the American forces from the Arabian desert. Bush had his hands stuffed deep into his pockets as he asked Dick Cheney and his national security adviser, Brent Scowcroft, how they were going to disarm Saddam once and for all.

They decided the United Nations represented their best hope. Washington was seen as the enemy in Baghdad, so why not send in an inspection team under the blue flag of the UN to prise open Saddam's secrets?

Strolling across the damp grass back to the presidential

lodge, Bush told his advisers that if Saddam didn't come clean with what America knew already from the defectors he would order air strikes. He wanted squads of inspectors to have a free hand to search wherever and whenever they wanted. After the abysmal record of the International Atomic Energy Agency in tracking Saddam's nuclear progress, Bush was taking no more chances.

His diplomats persuaded the Security Council to set up what became known as UNSCOM, the United Nations Special Commission for Iraq, but in its early days the White House could not decide how much help it would give these inspectors in their mission to disarm Saddam.

15

THE SMOKING GUN

The half-dozen weapons inspectors led by a bespectacled American, David Kay, had spent a restless night in the Palestine Hotel. The antiquated air conditioning was not up to coping with the cloying summer heat in Baghdad that June. As they gathered in the lobby at dawn, the team was careful not to say too much, knowing the hotel was bugged. Packing their water bottles, they prepared to head back to Al Faluja, near Babylon, where they were sure Saddam had hidden much of his nuclear paraphernalia.

The previous evening Iraqi troops had frustrated their attempts to enter the barbed-wire compound. The garrulous Dr Kay had stood toe to toe with an Iraqi officer in an hour-long screaming match.

'If you deny me entry to this site, I will report you to the Security Council!' Kay said as his face reddened.

The officer moved even closer to Kay and replied, 'We haven't denied you anything. We have to get permission and it's difficult because you bombed our telephone lines and they're not working properly.'

The team was forced to retreat. Back in the hotel Kay

suggested to his key advisers that they take a walk in the souk. By now, all of them knew what that meant. Every corner of the hotel was under surveillance. The only chance the men had to discuss their tactics for the following day was to wander about in a crowded marketplace where their conversation would be drowned out by the jumble of noise.

That first morning they had already sprung one surprise on their military minders, who when leading them to Al Faluja had deliberately tried to take the inspectors down the wrong road to an innocent housing estate for Iraqi officials. Kay swung his land rover off the road and doubled back, pursued by his confused Iraqi shadows. They didn't know the inspectors were carrying hand-held electronic displays that linked them to global positioning satellites that would direct them to precisely what they were looking for.

As Kay and his team arrived for their second visit, the Iraqis found a new excuse to delay them. An officer walked from the guardhouse to the main gate and explained it was a religious holiday so he had to get special permission for them to enter.

Kay could see through the wire mesh dozens of cranes and bulldozers tearing at the earth and loading equipment on to tank transporters. They needed to see more and Kay noticed a dirt track running around the perimeter. To distract the Iraqis, he told the rest of his team to continue haranguing the guards while he climbed into his land rover and raced to the opposite side of the compound.

There his view was obscured by clumps of bamboo planted alongside the electrified fence. Kay climbed on to the roof of his vehicle and began to take photographs. On his walkie-talkie he called to the others, 'They're moving a lot of stuff around. But I can't see exactly what it is. Bring our bus. It's higher and we can get a better view.'

Looking down, he suddenly realised he was surrounded by Iraqi soldiers pointing guns at him and motioning for him to get down. One of the Iraqis said in broken English, 'This is a military site. Move or I shoot.'

Once again, Kay and the others were forced to limp home to their hotel. That night, using a prearranged code on their satellite telephones, they were told that the Iraqis had moved the equipment to the opposite side of the main desert highway, next to a training school for military drivers.

Armed with a fresh set of satellite coordinates they returned to the Faluja area for the third morning running, but this time with a ploy to out-manoeuvre their minders. As they passed through a road block, Kay ordered his New Zealand driver to overtake their startled Iraqi escorts, who tried to chase them on the highway. One hundred metres past their turn-off, the inspectors swung their land rover across the central reservation and into the path of oncoming traffic. By the time the Iraqis caught up with them, Kay had bullied his way inside the base where the nuclear equipment was being stored.

From where he was standing and listening to the roar of truck engines and heavy machinery, Kay noticed a water tower just inside the perimeter gate. He ordered two of his fellow inspectors to climb to the top. Within seconds Mike Baker shouted down to him, 'There are loads of tank transporters starting to move and kicking up dust. They look like dinosaurs in heat. They are heading for the back exit.'

Surveillance pictures had missed that rear exit because it was buried at the bottom of a deep gully that the heavy transporters could barely negotiate.

By now the Iraqis were trying to physically eject the UNSCOM inspectors from the compound. Kay brushed past them and climbed back into his land rover. He tailed the convoy of eighty heavy trucks. One of his team was taking photographs as the battered UNSCOM vehicle tried to overtake the military convoy on the wrong side of the road. Kay realised the minders had also joined the chase and were shooting at his land rover. He had no option but to pull over.

The enraged Iraqis tried to grab the camera from Kay's American colleague, Rick Lally, who hid the digital disc film between his buttocks. He held out his hands to his guards, saying, 'I don't have a camera. These are my wife's binoculars and I can't give them to you because I promised to return them safely to her.'

Incredibly, the guards let him leave with the camera and the hidden film.

While the minders tried to contact their superiors in Baghdad to find out what to do next with the troublesome inspectors, Kay set up his cumbersome satellite telephone by the side of the road. For the next twenty minutes he talked to his two bosses – Hans Blix, the director-general of the IAEA in Vienna, and Rolf Ekeus, who was leading the UNSCOM team in New York – about his latest violent confrontation.

Both men insisted they would immediately fly to Baghdad to defuse the row. Kay found that suggestion risible since the two men could rarely agree about much. Kay was never sure why this operation needed the two of them but the tetchy Blix insisted on having the monopoly on nuclear inspections. The Americans were never going to rely upon the IAEA and wanted Ekeus's team to lead the search. Kay learned there was personal animosity between the two Swedes. They were from rival political parties at home and their already strained relationship was not eased when Ekeus's wife went to work for Blix.

Kay was certain that he had stumbled upon the Iraqis' efforts to move Dr Jaffar's calutrons. Some of these soft iron magnets measured nearly eight metres across, prompting the American inspector to describe them to his colleagues as 'giants' frisbees'.

The fiasco at Al Faluja continued when the Iraqis invited Kay and the others back for a fourth day, promising they could inspect the trucks that had aroused their suspicions. When the team turned up in the desert there were eighty vehicles lined up, but they were filled with industrial waste, and these were clearly not the same trucks. Even so the inspectors rolled up their sleeves and, in temperatures touching 100 degrees, they sifted through this rubbish for the next ten hours, searching for any clues about what was hidden in that compound. Kay complained these were not the vehicles he had expected to see.

A smiling Iraqi officer put his hand to his forehead and said, 'Oh, the trucks from yesterday. You should have said. We will take you to them now.'

Exhausted and longing for a bath to wash away the stinking grime, Kay was about to tell the grinning Iraqi what to do with his offer when his two bosses stepped from their air-conditioned limousine and told him to complete his inspection.

This meant a gruelling drive out towards Habaniya airport, where the UN planes were based. There the Iraqis produced some of the missing trucks, which, predictably, had been stripped of any clues. The UN team was introduced to a well-dressed Iraqi scientist who spoke colloquial English. Within minutes of meeting them, the scientist suddenly burst into tears, moaning that his life's work had been destroyed by the bombing.

Gulping for air between huge sobs, the scientist pointed to what was left of his mass spectrometer that lay broken in the desert. Kay walked over to examine it, and shook his head. He realised this harmless piece of equipment had clearly been snatched from some lab that afternoon and dumped in this wasteland for the inspectors' benefit. He was astounded to see Blix put his arm around the scientist and offer him a lift back to Baghdad. Kay sat morosely in the front seat with an AK-47 resting between him and their Iraqi driver.

In his perfect English accent the scientist turned to Blix and said, 'I know the CIA has told you they have detected radiation which would indicate we are working with enriched uranium, but I can tell you that scientifically it's impossible to detect at that level.'

Kay swivelled around in his seat to correct the man but Blix butted in testily, 'Don't you ever contradict a government official again.'

The weary inspector thought this not the moment to

recount the dozen lies the Iraqis had told him in the past week alone.

Blix had brought his legal adviser, Mohammed El Baradei, with him. The Egyptian lawyer travelled back to Baghdad in the UN bus with the other inspectors in their foul-smelling clothes, not realising the team all carried voice-activated tape recorders which were to capture his breathtaking naivety.

'I know you haven't seen what you think you've seen,' he told them in all sincerity, 'because the Iraqis have told me they never had a nuclear weapons programme. I'm an Arab and one Arab would not lie to another.' Nobody on the bus bothered to reply.

The inspectors' suspicions were vindicated twenty-four hours later when the film Rick Lally had secreted away was flown to London and developed.

After he had seen it the director of MI6 had, in his usual understated manner, telephoned the prime minister, John Major, and asked if he might have a word. An hour later he was standing in the ground floor cabinet office in Downing Street showing John Major and a select group of invited ministers a photo montage. It stood one and a quarter metres high and stretched three metres across the room and provided the first irrefutable proof that Saddam was lying about his nuclear programme.

That night the same pictures were shown to the UN Security Council, who immediately sent instructions to Baghdad to produce these calutrons for the inspectors or risk another bombardment. Caught out, the Iraqis adopted a more conciliatory tone. When the next UN inspection team arrived in September, they were shown the mangled remains of twenty calutrons being bulldozed into the sand. Kay was not alone in protesting that there must be many more still hidden somewhere in Iraq.

Kay and the others were still indignant that the Americans had refused to give UNSCOM photographs taken by the U2 spy planes which clearly showed Iraqi engineers moving equipment from Tuwaitha and burying it just beyond the perimeter fences on the eve of the inspection team's first visit.

Ekeus argued for hours with senior American officials from the Pentagon that, armed with such evidence, his inspectors could confront the Iraqis with proof of their duplicity. The diplomats, bred in a tradition of secrecy, were unmoved.

'We are not about to let Saddam see what our satellites and planes are capable of photographing,' they told Ekeus.

As a consequence, ten weeks after the ceasefire that ended the Gulf War, UNSCOM could do little more than ask Iraq to produce an inventory of its nuclear stock, knowing it would be told lies.

The original Security Council ultimatum – called Resolution 687 – had given Saddam only fifteen weeks to reveal everything about his chemical, biological and nuclear operations. Already Saddam had managed to change the rules. He was supposed to volunteer all the information and let the UN verify it. The Iraqis were able to tell the inspectors, 'We've got nothing, but if you think otherwise then you find it.'

The successful interception at Al Faluja had won the inspectors the grudging approval of the Security Council, which was beginning to doubt UNSCOM could do the job. Kay was the first to admit their early days hardly inspired confidence. One of his fellow inspectors was an Italian, Maurizio Zifferero, who before he joined the IAEA had made a considerable living selling vital nuclear equipment to Iraq. And Kay had to spend the first day of his new appointment hunting around the Vienna headquarters of the IAEA where he worked looking for a filing cabinet he could purloin along with a fax machine and a telephone. Without asking, he seconded a secretary to work for the team.

The team was disorganised, but the advantage UNSCOM would have was that as there were no precedents for what they were about to do, members of this disarmament commission could improvise the rules as they went along.

The first practical difficulty was how to get to Baghdad.

There were no commercial flights allowed into Iraq, so the inspectors had to lease an aging Romanian BAC111 that had gaffer tape strapped to a wing and rattled alarmingly on take-off. They had to fly to Bahrain first and then on through the blackened skies above the burning Kuwaiti oil fields before they touched down at the old British air base at Habaniya with its manmade lake and gardens. From there it was nearly 100 kilometres over potholed roads to Baghdad.

The only way the team had of passing confidential messages was laborious. Each of them was issued with the same romantic novel, which would only confuse the Iraqis if they discovered the book in any of the luggage. The inspectors could then communicate by passing each other a series of digits that correlated to letters on a page. The trouble was a five-word message could take twenty minutes to decode.

They also carried two sets of radios, persuading the Iraqis to eavesdrop on one channel while they kept the other secret for emergency calls. They were also issued with digital cameras. They could transmit by computer pictures of anything they couldn't identify back to their New York headquarters, where experts could interpret them and send back the answers.

From the beginning, the Iraqis were shameless in their attempts to frustrate the UN inspectors. They were hours late for the inaugural meeting. Foreign Ministry officials apologised but explained they had to find a temporary home because their office had been flattened in the bombing. The general who chaired that initial meeting turned up after everyone else, complained that he had been dragged from his daughter's wedding reception and chastised the inspectors for not appreciating that this was a religious holiday. The general then left in a foul mood without agreeing to anything.

Kay told his staff they had better get used to being yanked around. Once when they asked to be taken to Tarmiya they were driven around for hours and ended up in a hospital for amputees and a women's dormitory. The UNSCOM team kept asking to meet the Iraqi scientists who devised the PC3 programme, but it was months before Jaffar appeared.

He hadn't intended to reveal himself at all, but his arrogance got the better of him. Jaffar had been standing at the back of a meeting at Tuwaitha where some of his junior staff were making a fist of explaining his calutron programme. Proud of his own inventiveness, Jaffar shouted, 'I will take over and explain.'

He refused to identify himself and wouldn't let one of the inspectors take his photograph, but he gave a lucid account of the calutron programme. Kay's tactic with the boastful Dr Jaffar was to compliment him on the scale and sophistication of his operation. In return, Jaffar would invite the team to his spartan wood-panelled office on the upper floors of the MIO building, which the Allies had never gotten around to bombing. These meetings would always be held around midnight. Kay noticed how Jaffar always wore the same style of white shirt, slightly too big for him, and the same blue, polka-dot tie with a food stain down the front. Jaffar would generously offer his guests copious amounts of smuggled whisky but would drink only tea himself and would, of course, deny everything.

One night as Kay was packing up his papers at the end of another frustrating session, Jaffar suddenly blurted out, 'Of course if we had wanted to build a nuclear bomb we're smart enough to do it.'

Jaffar sat down, pulled out a sheet of paper and started to show Kay how to build a bomb. First Jaffar listed the steps in the design and manufacture and then described the technical hurdles and how he would conquer them. For two hours he didn't stop. He drew sketches of explosive lenses, of how to shape the nuclear core and how to get the enriched uranium. At the end Jaffar just smiled and walked out.

Kay was speechless, as was the rest of his team.

'Why did Jaffar as good as tell us that he has built a damn bomb?' one team member asked when they were back at their hotel.

'Because he doesn't want us to think he is just some dumb desert Arab,' Kay replied. 'He wants to show us he is technically as good as us. Better, in fact. He is telling us, "Don't waltz in here with your smug Western thinking that we don't know how to do things".'

As they got to know each other better, Jaffar invited Kay and a few others to a restaurant for a late-night dinner. Once again the Iraqi scientist made sure his UN guests' glasses were brimming with wine while he sipped water.

'Why did you bother with calutrons when we abandoned them over forty years ago?' Kay asked.

Jaffar drew his knife across the tablecloth in symmetrical patterns and smiled.

'Because I knew they would still work, and I knew that you would never think we would invest in something so old-fashioned when we could afford the latest centrifuge technology. I think you call it bluffing.'

Most of Jaffar's senior staff were just as arrogant. The inspectors found out that the Iraqis were producing the feed-stock for the calutrons at a site near Mosul only because one sulky technician pointed out how they had problems because Jaffar had stupidly told them to use galvanised iron pipes, which corrode.

'We told him we had to have stainless steel, but he said, "No, be satisfied. We would have to import the steel, so just get on with it."'

Looking around to make sure Jaffar wasn't in earshot, the technician said, 'That decision has cost us years of wasted time.'

Jaffar may have made mistakes, but both American and British intelligence agents spent weeks devising an escape plan to get him out of Iraq. They knew he was the architect of PC3 and if they could tempt him to defect it would save years of work by the weapons inspectors.

Jaffar carried most of Saddam's nuclear secrets in his head. If he would share them, it would blight Saddam's ambitions for years. He knew where much of the equipment and designs were hidden. He was close to all the key figures in PC3 and the agents reasoned that if they could get Jaffar to leave then others might follow.

The Americans were willing to offer him any amount of money, and protection. But Jaffar was never going to risk escape. That one brief period of incarceration was enough for him. He resolved then never to give the regime an excuse to jail him again. He knew the penalties for trying to defect and how Saddam's hit teams had murdered many who thought they were safe abroad. He was aware how valuable he was to the pro- gramme and that Saddam would spare no effort to get him or his new family. He had remarried and, while most Iraqis were suffering deprivations after the war, the Jaffars enjoyed a privileged life.

'What would I do in the West?' he said to his wife. 'Work in some American high school teaching sixth-grade physics to teenagers?' He reasoned that if he could survive Saddam, then as a scientist he would be valued by any successor. Jaffar enjoyed his intellectual sparring with Kay and the rest of the inspectors. What he seemed to let slip was always a deliberate exercise in self-aggrandisement.

The plausible excuse the Iraqis offered for not surrendering all their weaponry was that Baghdad feared America was shap- ing up for another war and that traditionally hostile neigh- bours like Iran would take advantage of their weakness. When they felt confident they weren't going to be attacked again, the Iraqis realised they couldn't suddenly produce this hidden arsenal because they would be accused of lying. Their only option, they told the UN inspectors, was to destroy these weapons themselves.

While Kay had expected Jaffar and everyone else in Iraq to be awkward, he was irritated by the refusal of intelligence experts in London and Washington to help the teams. The likes of the CIA were quick enough to seize on what UNSCOM uncovered but they still refused to share their satellite surveillance.

From the start of UNSCOM, American intelligence chiefs had realised this was a unique opportunity to infiltrate spies into a country they had singularly failed to penetrate. The shocking lesson of the Gulf War was that the most powerful country had no idea of what was going on in an Arab nation that was building a nuclear bomb.

UNSCOM officials insist that they were never told how the CIA slipped its own agents into the inspection teams going to Iraq. The intelligence agents not only needed to discover the whereabouts of nuclear and chemical arms dumps, they wanted to track Saddam's whereabouts and set up a spy network inside Iraq. On both counts they failed.

The CIA was careful not to let UNSCOM know who the spy was in their midst and would not share what little it discovered with Kay and his nuclear investigators. The Agency was equally obstructive to the inspectors trying to uncover Saddam's chemical and biological arsenals.

U2 spy planes lent to UNSCOM were busy taking high-quality pictures of Iraqi weapons sites. But the Americans delayed handing over the photographs. When they arrived, they were fuzzy and showed precious little detail. Not only that, but the precise locations, showing the latitude and longitude of the sites, had been erased.

Ekeus had enough experts on his staff to know that he was being played along. He called several senior air force commanders and America's UN ambassador, Thomas Pickering, to his office and thundered at them that he didn't know where the U2s were flying until the Iraqis told him.

'These planes carry the United Nations flag. The pilots wear UN insignia, and they belong to us. And what do they do for us?'

Scooping up a handful of the latest photographs, Ekeus said, 'These are no good to anyone.' Waving them in front of the ambassador, he added, 'May I remind you that this is what America and the Security Council are ready to go to war over again?' With that he threw the blurred photographs into his wastepaper basket.

Pickering got the message. The service improved and the next slide show provided by the Americans included the U2's flight path over Iraq. It had the time, the place and the name of the facility clearly stamped on the high-resolution photos.

It was Bob Galluci, the deputy head of UNSCOM, who persuaded the American intelligence community to be more helpful. The White House wanted the IAEA rowed out of this operation and in return was willing to share some of its secrets.

Kay was given a tip-off that the Iraqis had stashed most of their sensitive documents in the New Design Centre just across the road from the Al Rashid Hotel. Kay went back to Baghdad with his largest ever team, forty-four inspectors. The usual Iraqi minders met him at the airport with an enthusiastic welcome. When Kay asked why the effusive greeting when the usual form was for their hosts to berate UNSCOM for being CIA spies, the senior Iraqi officer embraced him.

'While you are here, Bush will not bomb us. We hope you stay for many years,' the officer told him.

The civility did not last. When Kay told the officer they wanted to begin an inspection at five-thirty the following morning, but would not say where, the Iraqi replied that was impossible.

Kay told him, 'If you are not there, I will just go without you.'

Walking through the bustling souk that night, he explained to his key lieutenants that he didn't want to go into an office full of staff because it would be easy for them to pick up bundles of sensitive information and walk out. He began his ambush just as dawn was breaking, ordering some inspectors to use the stairs to reach the top storey. That way no one could pass them coming down with secret files. Kay himself made for the L-shaped basement in the Design Centre, where his informer told him the most valuable files were stashed in metal lockers. He stopped as he read one document that was an order from a senior Iraqi security official warning Kay would be coming to the site that morning.

'How did they know that when the majority of my own staff didn't know until a couple of hours ago?' he said to one of his aides. 'We must have a leak, so let's find it – quick!'

One of his staff burst in waving a file that was obviously the bi-annual report on Baghdad's entire programme. It also revealed the intended size of Saddam's first bomb. Kay whistled through his teeth. This was a progress report compiled just before the Iraqis invaded Kuwait.

The dossier listed the vast number of European contractors that had supplied the Iraqis with everything they needed. There were more than anyone had ever imagined. Foreign governments would spend years investigating how Saddam managed to put together such an elaborate operation without attracting attention. Thumbing through the pages, Kay knew he had found Saddam's smoking gun.

'Now let Saddam Hussein tell us he wasn't trying to build a nuclear bomb,' he said to his staff.

Kay realised from a cursory glance that he had to get this document back to Washington. The trouble was that his Iraqi minder was now trying to wrestle the file out of his hand.

'You can't touch any of these or remove them! They are Iraq's national heritage and culture.'

'I can take any document I want!' Kay shouted while trying to slip the file to another member of staff.

The agitated Iraqi ran out of the basement looking for his superior officer. Kay had already organised with the Iraqis that he could fly one of his staff, who was sick, out of Habaniya that afternoon. He stuffed the file down the trousers of one of his aides who was going with that flight.

This dossier was so important that Kay risked using his satellite phone to contact UNSCOM's German pilot, warning him to delay the flight until the emissary arrived with the file.

An hour later, it was the diminutive figure of Jaffar himself who arrived in the basement. Flicking through the pile of documents, photographs and blueprints that the UNSCOM inspectors had collected, Jaffar tipped them on to the floor.

'This is Iraq's national patrimony,' he insisted. 'So they stay here.' Looking directly at Kay, he went on, 'The blood, treasure and wealth of Iraq have gone into these activities and they are not going anywhere.'

Kay had an open line to New York on his satellite phone and held up the receiver so they could hear Jaffar's patriotic rant. The team had already loaded over 100,000 pages in metal trunks into the fleet of UN land rovers. Kay stood squabbling with Jaffar about whether the team could leave as Iraqi troops ripped open the lockers on the land rovers to retrieve the documents. Kay pointed a video camera at the troops but when he noticed several of them pulling pistols from their holsters he ordered his team not to resist.

Once again Kay and his inspectors had to retreat to their hotel. He shouted to Jaffar that he would describe his part in this incident to the Security Council, which was meeting that night. One of the inspectors was heard to mutter that the quicker the Tomahawk missiles started slamming into Baghdad again the better.

Kay had insisted his team would be in the hotel lobby at 5:30 AM the following day for another visit, though he didn't say where. At 3 AM he was awoken by a telephone call telling him the documents he wanted were downstairs waiting for him. When he got to the lobby he soon realised the files he was being offered were not the ones he had marked the previous day.

Kay was not bothered, as it was no more than he expected. Besides, he had been given another tip-off about a building to raid. His intended destination that morning was an apartment complex directly across the road from the team's hotel. The flats there had never been lived in, as immediately after they were built the six towers in the complex were taken over by the Internal Security Ministry.

Only a handful of Kay's staff knew of his plan. Obviously,

the team could have walked to the complex in two minutes but Kay had his inspectors load up their land rovers as their Iraqi minders ran around demanding to know where they were going. Kay wouldn't say and ordered the UN convoy to set off. It turned left out of the Palestine Hotel and swept around the block before pulling into the car park of the high-rise block.

By now the Iraqis had drafted in ten soldiers for each of the forty-four inspectors who that morning just ignored the minders and tore through every office, sifting documents and copying the discs in the banks of computers. It was clear the Iraqis shadowing them did not know what this building was used for. The security team was led by a scientist and chief minder, Sami Araji, who had a PhD in nuclear engineering from an American university. His job was to stop UNSCOM from getting to the nuclear sites.

What Kay had stumbled on were the records of everyone who ever worked in PC3. He had his translators read out some of these security records where Mukhabarat officers had questioned neighbours, friends and colleagues about each individual's loyalty. Kay teased Sami, asking if he should try to find out what his private file said.

Sami was not amused, telling them to leave and take nothing with them. Kay refused.

'We're not going this time. We will stay here as long as it takes.'

The security team obviously thought the inspectors meant it this time, as they brought chairs for them and arranged them in the car park alongside the UN land rovers that had again been loaded with files.

This stand-off was to last for four days.

Kay, who as always had his satellite telephone with him, called the UN in New York to report how his team was marooned in a car park. Television networks and newspapers knew Kay's phone number and so for the next four days he kept up a running commentary on their siege.

Members of the team took it in turns to telephone their

families to assure them they were safe, if hot, dirty and uncomfortable. On the third night Kay was awakened by the telephone. He wondered if it was the Iraqis finally offering to back down. Instead, a clipped English voice came on to say that in the past forty-eight hours he had used that telephone for forty-three hours and demanded his credit card number. Kay explained who he was and eventually a senior supervisor appeared on the line offering to shift the communications satellite if it would help them.

Hundreds of troops now surrounded the apartment complex. Kay confided to Bob Galluci that he was afraid the Iraqis would start shooting, or that one of his inspectors might lose his temper and hit one of the soldiers. Kay decided he had to try to reason with Sami, who looked as though he had not slept since this siege started.

When he went to look for Sami he noticed that a large motor home had slipped through the security cordon and was parked on a curb fifty metres away. The curtains were drawn across the windows. Kay noticed that all the senior Iraqi officers had immediately rushed over to the vehicle. They waited outside, and occasionally the door would open and one would be invited in.

Kay knew the rumours that Saddam had taken to touring Baghdad in such a vehicle. He wondered if the president himself had decided to take a hand in resolving this siege. Three hours later the mobile home pulled away as the security cordon parted to let it pass.

Kay eventually found Sami and told him, 'Understand we are not crazy and we're not going to stop you from seizing anything you want by force. If you want to overrun this camp, someone will get hurt.'

Sami looked confused as Kay continued, 'If you just want to take me and Bob Galluci and threaten to use force on us, we're not going to stand up against you. We'll take the blows and then you can go and get the documents.'

The Iraqi scampered away, saying he had to ask Dr Jaffar

what to do, while Kay telephoned his bosses to relay his offer
to volunteer himself as a human shield. The following morning Sami returned and told a startled Kay that he and the rest
of the UN team could leave with what documents they
wanted.

As they walked to their land rover, Sami pulled Kay aside.
He asked, 'Did you mean it that we can still take you, and beat
you and take back the documents?'

Kay just smiled and ordered his team to drive back across
the road for a welcome bath.

That night over dinner at the Palestine Hotel Kay sat
amused as the other UNSCOM teams investigating Iraq's
chemical and biological stockpiles relayed how they were
being obstructed by the same delays and excuses. The only
difference was that while Kay had to deal with the cunning
Jaffar, the other teams had come up against a formidable
woman they nicknamed 'Doctor Germ'.

A dowdy, humourless creature, Dr Rihab Taha al-Azawi
was presented as the architect of the biological programme,
though the inspectors had their doubts when at their first
meeting she protested Iraq didn't have any such weapons. For
weeks she tried to confuse the team searching the huge complex at Salman Pak. She pretended not to know why tons of
fresh earth had been spread over sites where buildings had
clearly stood until a few weeks before. She feigned surprise
when inspectors stumbled over animal cages where Iraqi scientists had tested their toxins on apes and chimps. Iraqi
defectors claimed Saddam had also experimented with human
guinea pigs. The inspectors combed the cages for any evidence, examining hair and scraping faeces from the bloodstained cages. The inspectors found scratches on a wall, close
to one of the cages, where a hand had clearly tried to reach a
lightswitch. No one could say for certain whether humans had
been used.

Dr Taha's stock response to any question was to insist
Salman Pak was a scientific research centre. This did not

explain why it was the size of a small town, with its own air strip, anti-terrorist training school and tank traps all around. The compound had been built so that it was defended on three sides by the banks of the Tigris.

When she was caught out lying Dr Taha, who had studied at the University of East Anglia, would burst into tears. The inspectors were not fooled by her act. The feisty doctor was married to one of Saddam's most brilliant technocrats, the British-trained General Amer Rashid, who was directing Iraq's relations with UNSCOM. He also had a seat on the board of Hussein Kamil's MIO committee.

As they sorted through the mass of paperwork they had retrieved, Kay and the rest were sure they still hadn't put together Saddam's jigsaw. Too many pieces were missing.

It wasn't until Hussein Kamil escaped across the border to Jordan four years later that they could complete the picture. Among the secret documents he stashed in the trunk of his Mercedes were plans for a crude radiation bomb. This was the evidence of how shards of radioactive chaff had been packed in warheads and dropped on the waves of Iranian troops charging across the marshlands of the Fao Peninsula. Saddam hoped they would die of radiation sickness. It didn't work because when the bomb hit the ground the chaff didn't disperse widely enough.

But this was not the only surprise Kamil had brought with him.

16

HEIRS APPARENT

Jealousy was eating into Uday.

The front page of his own newspaper, *Babel*, was carrying a front-page story of Hussein Kamil's 'heroic efforts' in stamping out a rebellion by Kurds in his customary brutal fashion.

'Why did you print this nonsense without first checking with me?' Uday screeched, screwing the paper into a tight ball and hurling it at his editor. The trembling figure fended the missile off with his hands, praying that worse was not to follow.

'But, sir, the order came directly from the palace. The president insisted he wanted this on the front page,' the editor replied as he watched for what Uday was going to throw at him next.

The offending front page showed a grinning Lieutenant-General Hussein Kamil shaking hands with Saddam. The president also appeared to have his arm around his son-in-law, who was increasingly being talked of as the heir apparent in Baghdad.

For months Uday had been seething at Kamil's increasing influence in the Jadriya presidential compound. Uday had beaten up a servant whom he overheard gossiping about the favouritism Saddam was showing his son-in-law by moving his office closer to his own private quarters.

It irked him that while Kamil appeared to visit the president whenever he wanted, Uday had to make an appointment to see his own father and was nowadays subjected to the indignity of a body search. Saddam wouldn't see his son until Uday first handed over his shoulder holster.

Kamil was familiar with Uday's violent reputation and was careful to keep out of his way as much as he could. He knew that Uday had infiltrated people inside his MIO department to spy on him, not so much to find out about the progress of the nuclear programme but to calculate the money Kamil was making in business commissions and bribes.

If there was a corrupt scheme, then Uday wanted his cut and he hurt those who denied him. When a distant cousin refused to hand over a Ferrari he coveted, Uday shot the boy and drove off in the car. Recently, he had become obsessed with the money his uncle, Watban, was reputedly making on currency deals which Uday thought were his preserve. The two had argued in public, with Watban refusing to humour his nephew or pay him any money.

The last time they clashed, Uday pulled his gold-plated Makarov pistol on Watban in a nightclub, screaming he was going to kill him. Mindful of the trouble he was in before with Saddam, some of Uday's cronies bundled him away. Honour was not satisfied for Uday. The following night he was in his usual drunken state when an associate walked into the restaurant and told him that Watban was boasting at a nearby club how he was thwarting Uday. The provocation was too much to bear.

Uday turned over a table in his haste to reach the nightclub. Pushing aside Watban's bodyguards, he marched up to his uncle, put his hands around his throat, screamed abuse at him and wrestled him to the floor. As they rolled around, scattering the partygoers, Uday groped for his gun and fired at his uncle. Watban cried out and lay still. Uday believed he had killed him, though in fact he had only wounded his uncle in the left leg. Both Uday's and Watban's guards drew their weapons and started shooting, killing several Gypsy musicians who had crowded into a frightened huddle.

Straightening his clothes and smoothing down his hair, Uday went back to the restaurant to celebrate, pledging to those around him that Hussein Kamil would be next. Word of this threat soon reached Kamil. He woke his wife, Raghad, saying, 'It's not safe for us to stay in Baghdad. We should go abroad for a while until your brother, Uday, calms down.'

Raghad had never seen her husband so nervous. She wiped the sleep from her eyes and suggested he approach her father to rein in Uday. Kamil did not reply. He was distracted, thinking about how they were going to escape. He telephoned his brother, Saddam Kamil, who was the commander of the palace guard and Saddam's other son-in-law. Kamil's phone was bugged, so they arranged to meet at the VIP guest house in the Habaniya gardens. As they walked by the artificial lake the brothers thrashed out their plan for a joint escape. Saddam Kamil was reluctant and kept asking if there was no alternative. Kamil put a protective arm around his younger brother and said, 'There is no other way. Only we can save ourselves.'

The Kamils arranged for a family party and let it be known that Saddam Hussein would be attending. If the president was going, then Uday and his younger brother, Qusay, had no option but to accept the invitation. Besides, their mother, Sajidah, would be there and Uday rarely misbehaved in front of her. Hussein Kamil made sure that Uday and Qusay were drunk and distracted by the young secretaries he had invited from his ministry before he slipped away. He had told some of his staff that he had to go to Bulgaria on an official trip. Others had been informed that he needed post-operative care after surgery for a suspected brain tumour six months earlier.

By the time Kamil reached his sister's home, a line of six Mercedes were packed ready for the ten-hour drive to the

Jordanian border. His wife and children thought they were going to Sofia. Only his brother knew otherwise.

Shared out among the cars were suitcases full of dollars and gold, as well as a sealed trunk of documents. Kamil had used his security apparatus to stash most of the nuclear secrets and knew the most sensitive ones to copy for his own safe-keeping.

At the border crossing the Iraqi guards snapped to attention, immediately recognising the minister. His convoy was waved through on to the winding tarmac road that crosses no man's land to the checkpoint on the Jordanian side. Unprepared for the arrival of this Iraqi VIP, Jordanian security officers telephoned the palace in Amman. Hussein Kamil grabbed the receiver and spoke to the head of the royal court, asking for an urgent appointment with King Hussein.

The stream of Mercedes headed for the Raghadan Palace, where the king was waiting for them. His Majesty was intrigued. He knew how powerful Kamil was in Baghdad and was anxious to find out what was so important. As the two men walked towards each other, the king was holding his left hand behind his back. Hidden in the folds of his jacket was a pistol. The two men shook hands. Kamil proferred his apologies for the interruption and whispered his reasons for coming. The king relaxed and tucked the gun into the waistband of his trousers so that it couldn't be seen.

King Hussein arranged for the party to stay in one of his residences and called first the American and then the British ambassador. He wasn't entirely convinced by Kamil's story of defection, but the king knew that both embassies would be keen to speak to Saddam's son-in-law to discover what it was he was after.

Inside the sumptuously decorated apartment Raghad turned on her husband, demanding to know what was going on. When he explained, she angrily paced the room, threatening to telephone her father to get her and their children back to Baghdad. When that tactic failed she tried pleading with him.

'If he finds out he will kill you. We still have time to go back.'
Kamil was unmoved.

Kamil was alone when the American ambassador called at
the Raghadan Palace later that afternoon.

'Saddam is destroying our country, Mr Ambassador, and
the people of Iraq deserve better. I am ready to take on the
responsibility of saving the Motherland.'

The ambassador blanched, took another sip of his tea and
asked, 'What do you expect from us?'

By the time the two men parted forty-five minutes later, it
was agreed that Kamil would meet a high-powered team that
Washington would fly out to Jordan that same night. In
Baghdad, Saddam was still in the dark about his son-in-law's
defection. When foreign stations like Radio Monte Carlo
started broadcasting the news, those who were with him at
the time said Saddam went purple with rage.

His first response was to telephone King Hussein to demand
Kamil's extradition. When the king politely demurred, Saddam
began to shout that he wanted his daughters and grandchildren
returned. All the king was prepared to promise was that
Saddam's family would be 'looked after'. What the king was
really saying was that the women would not be allowed to leave
Jordan.

Baghdad Radio put out Saddam's version of Kamil's disappearance. The official line was that Kamil had been drugged by
the CIA and smuggled across the border against his will. This
did not explain why his brother, cousin, their wives and all
their families had vanished as well.

By morning, nineteen CIA, State Department and Pentagon
officials had flown into a military airport in Amman. After a
brief stop at the sprawling US embassy complex, they were
taken to the Raghadan Palace and shown into a cavernous
room where Kamil was sitting in the tallest chair, almost like
a throne. He did not get up and simply motioned for the
Americans to sit around him. He was already behaving like a
president in waiting.

Deferring to him through one of their translators, the Americans humoured his obvious ambition while anxiously firing off a series of questions about Saddam, his health, his state of mind, who his most trusted lieutenants were and what his plans now were regarding his neighbours. They wanted to know what morale was like in the army, how many tanks were still operational, what had happened to his fighter jets which had been moved to Iran during the war. They asked about the true state of the Iraqi economy and the strength of the opposition.

Deliberately, they left till last their questions about the work Iraq was still doing on its missile technology and on the development of chemical and biological weapons. When they asked about the nuclear programme, Kamil smiled and tapped his highly polished shoe against the metal trunk resting by his chair.

'The answers you want are in here,' he told them. But for the moment, he added, he wished to know what help he could expect from Washington to install him in Saddam's place. For the next three months Kamil kept the Americans' interest with a steady drip of information, while the CIA helped the Jordanian security police hunt for the Iraqi assassination squads known to be lurking in Amman. The king had to field calls from Saddam's tearful wife, Sajidah, who begged to be allowed to come and see her daughters. For the moment the king refused.

Every few days, Kamil would part with a morsel of information, delighting in the occasions when he would shock his audience. One morning, he suddenly blurted out how Saddam had intended to retake Kuwait in the late summer of 1993 and would have tried it had the Americans not flown in thousands of troops from their Rapid Response Force to counter the threat.

'Of course, what Saddam can't have he destroys,' Kamil went on as he explained about detonating the 'beach ball' bomb in Kuwait.

The American team sat open-mouthed as he described the plan, line by line, with all the blueprints and supporting documents laid out on the desk beside him. It was a skilful performance designed to finally shock the Americans into giving him the unqualified support he desired. But his arrogance blinded him to the fact that Washington could never support a man with so much blood on his hands. The truth was, nobody wanted to see him take over as president of Iraq and neither did they want to reward him with sanctuary.

The spoilt Raghad was canny enough to recognise the weakness of her husband's position and behind his back she was negotiating with her mother for safe passage back to Baghdad. Sajidah was finally allowed into the kingdom and came with a message from Saddam that he missed his daughters and was prepared to forgive them. She brought no such promises for her sons-in-law.

After waiting for months for his reward, Kamil became a frustrated and despondent figure. Palace staff would regularly hear him in screaming matches with his wife. Between their arguments, he would lie slumped on a settee, flicking through the television channels in the vain hope that commentators were still talking about him as the next president.

King Hussein had tired of his unwanted guest and told him he had to move to more modest lodgings in an unfashionable quarter of Amman. Kamil drew the obvious conclusion. When his wife told him that Saddam had now sworn not to harm him, Kamil was reluctantly persuaded that he was left with no other choice but to risk a return to Baghdad.

When Rana heard about this plan she pleaded with her husband, Saddam Kamil, not to join them: 'We don't have to go with them. We have enough money here and we will be safe in Jordan.' Saddam fatally refused to listen.

The Jordanians sealed the border the morning that Kamil's cavalcade left for home. He sat sullenly in the back seat, saying nothing. When the Mercedes crossed over into Iraq, Kamil noticed that his brother-in-law Uday was waiting for them.

Kamil rested his chin on his chest and reached across the seat for his wife's hand.

Uday immediately ushered his two sisters and their children to a couple of waiting army helicopters that sat with their rotor blades slowly turning at the desert crossing. The women were put in one helicopter, the youngsters in another. The aircraft tossed up clouds of dust and grit as they took off, making it impossible for the two women to see what was happening to their husbands.

As the helicopters banked away Uday walked across to Kamil and, without exchanging a word, slapped him. The former minister was delivered straight to the Jadriya complex, where his father-in-law paced the floor in vengeful anticipation. Two bodyguards stood with their backs to the door as Saddam spat vitriol at the traitor.

'You illegitimate son of a whore. You betrayed me and you betrayed the Motherland I have fought to protect. You and your brother will divorce your wives now. I never want to see your faces again. It is up to others to decide your fate.'

Kamil was stripped of his military rank and forbidden to see his wife. When he got to his villa he found it surrounded by troops and so sneaked out of a back entrance to his sister's house.

Saddam wouldn't dirty his hands by killing Kamil himself. Besides, that morning Sajidah had reminded him of his promise of safe conduct for his errant sons-in-law if they came home. All Saddam had said in reply was, 'I won't do anything to them.'

This did not prevent him two hours later from summoning the head of the Al Majeed clan to which the Kamil brothers belonged. Looking sternly at the clan chief, Saddam said, 'I thought I could always count on the loyalty of the Al Majeeds. I cannot believe you will tolerate traitors among you.' He didn't need to say any more.

That night Uday arrived at the house where Kamil was hiding, flanked by scores of armed Al Majeed clansmen backed up by Iraqi Special Forces. Uday shouted to Kamil to come outside and meet his fate like a man. Inside Saddam Kamil told his brother to hide. Kamil shook his head and opened the front door. He couldn't make out Uday in the glare of headlights pouring on to the house and asked if he could let the children leave. He recognised Uday's voice screaming back that nobody would walk out of that house.

Uday ordered the clansmen to open fire.

Kamil ducked as the first volley of automatic gunfire ricocheted above his head and he rolled inside the door. The ensuing gun battle reduced the villa to rubble and at the end of it the man whom Saddam had briefly considered as his heir lay dead. So too did Kamil's brother, his elderly father, his sister and her three children.

After watching the three-hour siege, Uday walked through the smoking ruins until he found the dead body of his brother-in-law. He dragged it out into the street and threw the bullet-riddled corpse on to a trash heap.

Saddam preempted Sajidah's reaction by telephoning her. 'Kamil is dead. His family took matters into their own hands. They say it was a question of honour.'

His two daughters never forgave either him or Uday for the murders. Saddam had them sent to a palace and held them under virtual house arrest on the outskirts of Tikrit. He refused to see either of them. Dressed all in black, the young widows share their bleak existence with Sajidah, who mourns the decimation of her family. The only visitor the women receive is a spiritualist who consoles them with stories about their slain husbands in Paradise.

Rana tried to embarrass her father by instructing lawyers to force a Jordanian bank to hand back money left by her husband. She claims to be destitute, and insists that she needs the money to support her children. The sum she is after is only $450,000, held in an account under the name of the South Asia Organisation. It is a fraction of the nearly $40 million that Hussein Kamil took with him when he fled Iraq.

Hundreds of millions more, creamed off in commissions he made from the nuclear programme, are buried in offshore banks. Rana insists she knows nothing about this buried treasure. Her sister says the same.

Saddam does not believe them and has murdered to try to retrieve these larger sums. He instructed Uday to find those who helped Kamil salt away his money. It was a task his son relished. One target was Namir Ochi, a millionaire businessman. He was staying with a wealthy Iraqi, Sami George, whose two-storey home in the wealthy Rabia suburb of Amman was a popular meeting place for his fellow countrymen.

One night when George was hosting a dinner party in Ochi's honour, five men knocked on the door and were invited to join them. After a few drinks the visitors began arguing with Ochi about money. All of a sudden the five stood up and pulled knives from under their jackets. They easily overpowered those sitting around the table. One of the gang produced lengths of twine and tied up the host and his guests.

The assassins went to each man in turn and stabbed them, ripping out their insides. The only woman there, Sami's girlfriend, was gagged and forced to watch as the gang wiped their knives on the shirts of their victims, after stabbing them for a final time through the neck. Three servants who witnessed the carnage were also killed.

As the hit team walked out of the house they bumped into the Iraqi chargé d'affaires, Hikmet Al Hajou, who had come to join the dinner party. He was dragged into the house and killed. His wife, Leila, was still in the car and one of the assassins went out and told her that her husband needed to speak to her. As she walked in she too had her throat cut.

The Jordanian authorities closed the airports and sealed their land borders, but never caught the killers.

A few weeks earlier an influential Jordanian lawyer and his son were gunned down as they visited their doctor. Saddam was told the lawyer had advised Kamil on his investments.

These included a cigarette factory in Jordan, a pharmaceutical plant in France and interests in a dozen other countries.

One man whom Saddam still hasn't reached is Major Izzedine Majeed, a cousin of the Kamils, who wisely scorned Saddam's promise of amnesty and refused to return to Baghdad. He is cushioned by the near $40 million that Kamil left with him for safekeeping.

Following the murder of his son-in-law, Saddam at first assumed total control of the nuclear programme, chairing the all-important MIO committee in charge of protecting what remained of his weapons of mass destruction. Unsure of how much information Kamil had divulged, Saddam's personal instructions were that the most sensitive components of his nuclear programme must be moved every thirty days to prevent them from falling into enemy hands.

Worried that the files Kamil had passed on would reveal how he had been deceiving the United Nations weapons teams, Saddam decided to retaliate first. Only a few days after Kamil's defection in August 1995, the telephone rang at the Palestine Hotel. The senior UNSCOM official who took the call was told by a breathless Iraqi official that they must come immediately to the Haidar Farm on the outskirts of Baghdad.

The UN team drove to a battery chicken farm and were pointed in the direction of a prefabricated barn. Iraqi troops swung open the doors to reveal a room, three metres high, packed with metal crates. Some of the trunks had their locks broken. Spilling out of them were mounds of scientific documents, procurement lists, catalogues of suppliers and designs for warheads. Most dealt with Iraq's biological programme, which up until then the regime was denying ever existed.

The Iraqis explained to bemused UN officials that these files had belonged to Hussein Kamil, who hid them from his own government. An army general told the inspectors, 'We are shocked at what this man was doing in his private capacity and without the approval of the authorities.' It was, said the general, proof of Kamil's megalomania. It was also proof of the scale of Iraq's deception since the end of the Gulf War.

Saddam had been persuaded by his scientific advisers, like General Amer Rashid, to yield more than he wanted to blunt the impact of his son-in-law's disclosures. Iraqi scientists agonised for days about what to leave at the Haidar Farm. The haul had to look convincing. The trouble was that this cache of documents proved their chemical, biological and nuclear programmes were way past the experimental stage.

For years, the Iraqis had protested they had no interest in germ warfare. Now they were obliged to explain to a sceptical UN why they had acquired so much killer biology. They had produced over 400 litres of a pungent gas that causes gangrene. They had over 9,000 litres of anthrax – enough to kill four million people – and nearly fourteen litres of a pesticide called ricin that causes death in two days.

Saddam had also amassed 23,300 litres of botulinum toxin, which first paralyses and then strangles its victims. This was enough to kill the entire world's population three times over. The Iraqis were also forced to reveal some of the chemical arsenal scientists had been working on, including the infamous VX nerve agent. One drop kills. They had stockpiled over 400 tonnes of the chemicals needed to make it. There was even evidence of experiments with a virus that would strike only infants, whose immune system was not strong enough to resist.

But Saddam was still keeping many secrets from UNSCOM. He did not reveal how some nuclear parts were buried under his own palace, and hidden in bunkers beneath the gift shop at the Ba'ath Party headquarters and in bomb-proof cellars below his children's homes.

Kamil's defection provoked the most serious family rift Saddam had known. With two of his daughters refusing to speak to him and his wife, Sajidah, blaming him for the bloodletting, Uday saw his chance to reestablish himself in his father's affections.

Uday had already redeemed himself by helping to lure back the defectors and then personally taking part in their murder. He took command of Iraq's oil-smuggling operation, which was providing his father with money to secretly rebuild his armoury and his weapons programmes. Uday, of course, took his own generous commission from these deals.

Saddam still wouldn't allow his son anywhere near the nuclear operation. Angered by this rebuff, Uday was soon in trouble again. His father had put him in charge of a phantom army called the Fedayeen. Saddam did not trust Uday with any position of power in the military, fearing he might launch a coup. To indulge his son, the president created this Fedayeen force of a few hundred paramilitary commandos. Most of the time, Uday used them as his personal enforcers.

The position also meant he could strut around in a military uniform as the head of this force. Uday soon set about increasing its number by finding new recruits from prisons and state orphanages. But as usual he overreached, and when he was caught diverting sophisticated weaponry meant for the Republican Guard to his own Fedayeen force, Saddam relieved Uday of his command.

The Fedayeen was handed to his younger brother, Qusay, who was already in charge of national security. He also commanded the Amn Al Khass, the presidential bodyguard that had been under Saddam Kamil's control. Qusay preferred to enjoy his pleasures in private, unlike the volatile Uday. He was obsessively secretive and therefore ideal for the running of the Mukhabarat intelligence agency.

Uday hated the increasing influence of his brother. Qusay, along with General Abed Hamid Mahmoud, Saddam's brother-in-law and longtime private secretary, were now the only two men in Iraq who knew the president's whereabouts at all times.

Qusay was also one of the few told about his father's third marriage in 1996 to a young engineering graduate, Nidal Hamdani. Her family were from Mosul and Saddam first met her by chance in the corridors of the presidential palace. Nidal was in charge of the team maintaining the solar-heating unit in the Jadriya compound. She was supervising some workmen and hadn't heard the president approaching. He was amused and impressed by the young woman and later that night invited her to a small reception he was hosting for some of his scientists.

Saddam remembered what had happened when Uday had discovered that his father had transferred his affections from Sajidah to the glamorous Samira Shabander. The new bride was given her own bodyguards to protect her from Uday, as was Samira, who retired from Baghdad's social scene on Saddam's orders. By that time, Samira was seldom seen at the few official functions the president bothered to attend. Wisely, she keeps her counsel about the appearance of a younger wife and her own seclusion.

Like his father, Uday was always on the prowl for young women. On the evening of 12 December 1996 some of his friends arranged a 'girl party', as they liked to call it, in a fashionable corner of west Baghdad. His cousin accidentally let slip details of the rendezvous to a junior Iraqi army officer who had waited years for a chance to avenge the murder of his uncle, a respected general. The uncle's mistake was to get drunk in an officers' club and criticise Saddam's handling of the war against Iran. For this he was tortured and had his tongue sliced off and was then shot. Eight years later his nephew saw his opportunity.

The officer tipped off an underground student group, Al Nahdah. Knowing the time of the party and the house where Uday was heading, they decided to ambush him at a crossroads where Mansour Street meets Baghdad International Street.

Four gunmen with AK-47s and four clips of ammunition hid themselves in doorways, ready to attack Uday's car whichever road he took. Dusk was falling as the first gunman standing outside a sports club spotted a white Mercedes hurtling down Mansour Street. He signalled to two other gunmen waiting opposite at the entrance of the Ruwad restaurant. The last of the group moved nearer their getaway cars, ready to fire at the other two identical Mercedes that Uday's bodyguards drive.

For once Uday had decided not to drive himself and was slouched in the passenger seat listening to his tape deck. As the Mercedes slowed at the crossroads, the first gunman ran to the driver's window and fired. One of the men standing on the other side of the road, realising Uday was not driving, screamed a warning to his colleagues and sprinted to the far side of the car, spraying bullets as he ran.

Many of the bullets bounced off the armour-plated doors, but Uday was hit eight times in the abdomen and legs. He was bleeding heavily and his driver was dead when the last assassin poked his gun through the shattered window. Uday was at his mercy but the weapon jammed.

The four gunmen, certain that Uday was dead, fled in their getaway cars across the desert towards the border with Iran. Bystanders, terrified they would be implicated in the shooting, ran for any shelter they could find. Mukhabarat agents sealed off the area within minutes. But the streets were already deserted. The Mukhabarat began house-to-house searches.

Families who did not want any suspicion to fall on them feigned distress at news of the shooting. Old women tore at their black shrouds and slaughtered sheep, smearing the blood on the pavements as a sign that death had been cheated. Television announcers interrupted programmes and solemnly broke the news that Uday had been shot, stressing he was only slightly wounded.

In fact Uday had been rushed to the Ibn Sina hospital inside the presidential compound. One of the first to reach him was his father. When Saddam saw Uday unconscious and covered in blood, he pulled at Uday's shirt and shouted, 'Get up! Get up! We the family of Saddam never die.'

Surgeons operated for hours on Uday's shattered legs. He

had lost six pints of blood and, though they saved his life, the doctors doubted he would ever walk again. When he recovered consciousness days later and was told he was paralysed from the waist down, Uday picked up his gun and began firing wildly, killing one of his own guards.

It was weeks before doctors dared tell him that his injuries meant that he was impotent. Uday cursed them and to prove them wrong he ordered his guards to bring him a nurse who had attracted his interest. The frightened young woman was ordered to strip and forced on top of Uday. When he couldn't perform he lashed out at the nurse and tried to strangle her. Bodyguards pulled her away and she fled crying from the room.

Doctors were flown in from abroad to try to cure Uday's condition, and, as rumours of his impotence spread through the souks, he went through a bizarre wedding ceremony in his hospital room to a fifteen-year-old cousin. She was the daughter of General Ali Hasan Al Majeed, better known as 'Chemical Ali', because he was responsible for gassing 200,000 Kurds. He was also Saddam's choice as governor of Kuwait after the invasion.

Uday decided to prove the doctors wrong about his potency. He had become obsessed by Asil Salman Mansour, a young woman he had noticed shopping near her home in Dora on the outskirts of Baghdad. She was abducted by Uday's guards and brought to the palace. When he again failed to get an erection, Uday beat and then shot her. His guards were sent to tell her family that Asil had been in an accident and gave them $700 and an Oldsmobile car. They also promised the family $50 a month to keep their mouths shut.

Exasperated by the increasingly corrupt and violent behaviour of his closest relatives, Saddam ordered a family summit. Family members were told to go to Uday's bedside. They presumed the summons was to lift Uday's morale. None of them knew what lay in store. Sajidah turned up wearing a headscarf and dark glasses and looked surprised to see so many there. It was at that moment that Saddam made his appearance.

Without saying a word to his stricken son, he shouted at the astounded family group, 'Your craving for other people's property is the talk of Iraq. It has got to stop.'

Nobody made a murmur.

Saddam turned first on his cousin, Ali Hasan Al Majeed. 'You made me invade Kuwait and when you were there you looted half the valuables that went missing from that country.'

The general said nothing.

Poking a finger at him Saddam said, 'Remember you used to be my driver.'

His next target was his half-brother, Sabawi. 'You call yourself the director of security services, and yet you're drunk half the time. You're never in your office before 11 AM, and when you are there you're always half asleep.'

Another half-brother and former interior minister, Watban, was castigated for smuggling much-needed grain across the border to Iran. Saddam thundered at him, 'You ruined the ministry when you were in charge.'

One by one Saddam berated them. Finally, turning to his crippled son, he asked him, 'Are you a politician, a trader, a people's leader or a playboy?'

By the end only one figure had escaped his tirade, Qusay. As Saddam barged out of the room Uday eased himself back on his pillows and glowered at his brother. Qusay was now the heir apparent.

17

END OF THE ROAD

Ambling around the United Nations headquarters, the CIA agent looked up at the digital clock in the foyer. He had seven minutes to make his rendezvous.

Quickening his pace, the agent bounded the stairs two at a time, the small brown suitcase knocking against his leg. He thought this a stupid idea, but had said nothing when he was briefed that morning. The agent had been shown a photograph of the man he was supposed to meet. Glancing up at the line of faces streaming down the stairs, he wondered if anyone thought his behaviour suspicious. He had never felt more self-conscious on a mission.

He noticed surveillance cameras on every landing, and he reckoned UN security staff outnumbered the visitors to the building that afternoon. The agent was fearful he had missed his man and was about to turn around when he spotted his contact trying to ease past a delegation of UN bureaucrats who had stopped to argue about something on the stairs.

The CIA agent slowed, moved closer to the wall, set down the suitcase and kept walking, not bothering to see if his contact had retrieved it.

Charles Duelfer, deputy executive chairman of UNSCOM,

scooped up the case and headed straight for his office, where he locked the door. Duelfer picked up the telephone and said, 'We have it.'

The previous week Duelfer, along with his boss, Rolf Ekeus, and UNSCOM's most aggressive inspector, the former US Marine Scott Ritter, had met a senior CIA officer for lunch in the Princeton Club. All four men picked at their Caesar salads and drank only mineral water as the UNSCOM team put its proposal to the intelligence agent.

The inspectors wanted the CIA to let UNSCOM show the surveillance pictures taken by the U2 spy planes to the Israeli Secret Service. If the CIA agent was disturbed by that idea, he didn't show it. Waving his fork at Rolf Ekeus, he asked the white-haired Swede to explain some more. The CIA knew that the weapons inspectors had already been in touch with the Israelis, asking for help in discovering where Saddam had hidden his nuclear parts.

A few months before, in November 1994, Scott Ritter and two other UNSCOM officers had flown to Tel Aviv for a meeting with Uri Saguy, the chief of Israeli military intelligence, and some of his senior staff.

Ritter bluntly told his Israeli hosts, 'Saddam is making fools of the UN. We know it and you know it. So, can you show us your intelligence on what he has done with his weapons of mass destruction?'

Saguy was not impressed. 'And why should we do that? Understand we have our own security interests that prevent us from simply throwing open our files to you, no matter how valuable your work.'

Saguy's mood changed when Ritter offered him a trade.

'What if we were to bring you the films from the U2 planes and let you process those pictures and identify for us what sites we are looking at and which places we should target for inspection?'

The Israeli general paused, rubbed his fingers across his forehead and replied, 'That we can help you with.'

The problem now for UNSCOM was getting the Americans to let them barter with the U2 pictures. From the start the Pentagon had made it clear that the photographs were their property. UNSCOM could look at them, but they couldn't remove them and certainly couldn't tell anybody else about what the photographs showed.

Over lunch in the Princeton Club, the CIA officer listened patiently as Ekeus tried to change those rules. The Agency had anticipated this request and the CIA man listed Langley's demands for a deal. The CIA was desperate to find out what the Israelis knew about Saddam.

For the moment the CIA was willing to trust Ritter as the go-between. But the agent insisted the U2 films had to be kept in a safe, inside a locked room, that could be opened only by a dual key. Ritter would keep one of the keys and the Israelis the other.

The CIA agent pointed his fork at the crop-haired former Marine. 'You are never to let those photographs out of your sight,' he said. 'And everything the Israelis tell you, you pass on to us.'

The suitcase Duelfer had picked up on the staircase was the first consignment Ritter took with him to Tel Aviv.

UNSCOM chiefs impressed on Ritter the need for secrecy because of the diplomatic fallout if it were discovered that the UN's first-ever intelligence-gathering agency was swapping information with spies from Saddam's two most hated enemies, Israel and the United States. Ekeus had agonised over the morality of this deal but decided there was no other way. He recognised his UNSCOM teams could waste years searching Iraq's desert for nuclear plans and parts. Why not take a short-cut and employ the information the Americans and others had been collecting ever since Saddam had invaded Kuwait?

Some of the details of what Hussein Kamil would tell his CIA interrogators about Saddam's military hardware were passed on to UNSCOM. In return the Pentagon, the CIA and others were seeing the reports UNSCOM sent to the UN secretary-general every six months, about what the weapons inspectors were uncovering in Iraq and the games Saddam was playing to hide his nuclear secrets.

Ekeus preferred not to dwell on whether any of his inspectors were telling intelligence agencies any more than they had submitted in their reports. What worried him more was that he could foresee the day when the CIA, Mossad or some other friendly agency would ask UNSCOM to spy for them.

Scott Ritter disregarded the CIA and on his first trip he did let those U2 photographs out of his sight. Worse, the Israelis made copies of them, but in return they passed on revealing information about the sites captured on film by the aerial surveillance.

Neither Ritter, UNSCOM nor the CIA ever asked how it was that the Israelis – whose intelligence on Iraq was woefully short at the start of the Gulf War – now knew so much about how Saddam's security service was operating and where he was hiding his hardware. All of them were aware, though, that the films the Israelis now possessed would be vital if the order was ever given in Tel Aviv to attack Iraqi targets.

No one in the UN high command was told about this swap deal and Ritter flew back to New York with the films safely locked in the same suitcase the CIA agent had dumped on the stairs.

He put the original films in a locked safe in the UNSCOM offices and then took the first flight down to Washington with a bag of negatives, which had come from the Israelis' making their copies. He tried to hand them over to the same CIA agent, but nobody at Langley seemed to know what he was talking about. They hadn't planned for this eventuality. When another CIA officer was sent to reception to see him, Ritter asked what he should do with these negatives.

The agent replied only, 'Do the right thing.'

Ritter went home and stuffed the bag of negatives under his bed.

His colleagues nicknamed him 'Darth Ritter' because of

his size and his dark moods. Square built and standing over six foot four inches, he presented an intimidating figure to the Iraqis and he had the personality to match. Ritter had delayed his resignation from the Marines when Operation Desert Shield began in August 1991. He was desperate to be involved in the action.

He was sent to General Schwarzkopf's intelligence head-quarters in Riyadh, where his job was to spot the Scud launchers. He shared the general's doubts about the dangers the Scuds posed, compared to the rest of what Saddam possessed, but fell foul of Schwarzkopf for questioning the coalition's success in bombing Iraq's missile launchers.

Ritter's daily reports pointed out that the Allied bombers were claiming to have knocked out more Scuds than Saddam possessed. If they were so successful, how was it that the Iraqis were still firing missiles? Ritter was dumbfounded when during a televised briefing Schwarzkopf showed video footage from an F15's gun camera of how seven launchers were taken out in one strike.

The following morning, when he had assessed all the battle reports, Ritter recorded the confirmed 'Scud kills' as zero. When his superiors argued that the Allied commander had just told a global television audience of several million that seven Scuds were destroyed – and so who was he to call the general a liar – Ritter refused to back down. He was soon moved to another post.

When he learned of the UNSCOM mission, Ritter badg-ered friends in New York to get him on the team. On his first mission to Iraq in 1995, Ritter was quickly angered by the Iraqis' intransigence. In an early confrontation with a smug Iraqi officer who wouldn't let the inspectors inside an office block, even though they already had written permission to enter, Ritter pulled down the peak of his light blue UNSCOM baseball cap and muttered an insult.

His interpreter turned to Ritter and said, 'Welcome to Baghdad – Saddam's Never Never Land.'

Ritter turned and gathered his inspectors around him, like a football huddle, and told their Iraqi minders to move away. Bowing his head so he couldn't easily be overheard, he said, 'Things have got to change. We have got to be more aggressive. The Iraqis are like sharks. Fear is like blood. They smell it and they'll come at you, and they'll intimidate you. Once that game of intimidation starts, you're never going to win.

'So in the future when we go to a site we're going to be polite. We're going to shake hands and if they growl at us then we growl at them. I'm going to let them know who is boss here. They report to me. From now on they do what I say.'

Ritter called it 'shaking the tree'. The Iraqis weren't so lyrical in their description of his tactics. Like Kay, Ritter wondered how it was the Iraqis always seemed to be one step ahead. It hadn't entered his mind that Saddam had created a new security apparatus whose sole purpose was to thwart UNSCOM.

It was after a meeting with an Israeli agent in a Manhattan bar that Ritter was told where to look for this new unit. His guest mentioned that Saddam's Special Security Organisation (SSO) was now under the personal direction of the president's faithful secretary, General Hamid Mahmoud.

The Israeli agent told him, 'Find them, you find the weapons.'

Mahmoud's plan was brilliant in its simplicity. His SSO units commandeered a fleet of new Mercedes trucks and piled them high with all the sensitive nuclear material that UNSCOM had been searching for since the Gulf War had ended. Components were excavated from their burial sites and loaded on to the convoys.

Saddam kept himself safe nowadays by staying on the move in his mobile homes. These never stopped long enough in any one place to be targeted. In exactly the same way the vital elements of his nuclear programme were shunted around so they could not be detected, targeted and destroyed.

The SSO was ordered to keep five bases around Baghdad

where they would temporarily hide the nuclear material. These bases were changed on Saddam's personal instructions every thirty days.

Israeli agents and Iraqi defectors told UNSCOM how the SSO teams operated on a tight cell structure to avoid detection. No one group would be told by the other where it was heading. Informers described how the SSO vehicles were given a variety of disguises to look like refrigerated container trucks. The vehicle registration plates were swapped daily, but spies managed to tip off UNSCOM about some of the Arabic brand names painted on the sides of these trucks.

The SSO drivers did not know precisely what they were carrying and no communication was permitted between the five convoys. The only allowed contact was through General Mahmoud's SSO central command. The convoys were never told their final destinations until they were on the road.

What they had on board were the remnants of the 'beach ball' crash programme.

Saddam's main nuclear centres, like Tuwaitha and Tarmiya, that produced weapons-grade uranium had been destroyed. But the components manufactured for the 'beach ball' operation had been salvaged and hidden by the SSO. Saddam's scientists assured their president that when the dust settled and the likes of UNSCOM had given up, he could buy plutonium or weapons-grade uranium from the black market and slot it into place. Jaffar had recently explained to him the terrible beauty of their salvage operation.

'Saidi, we still have the chassis safely hidden. Give us the engine and we can be back on the road. If you buy weapons-grade material, I promise that your scientists can build three nuclear bombs in three months.'

Jaffar listed what Iraq had managed to save: three sets of explosive lenses, neutron generators, the uranium casings for the bomb (called the tampers), the firing sets and the electronic gadgetry that had been tried and tested at Al Atheer before the start of Desert Storm.

It was this that had been packed on to trucks. Over thirty tonnes of nuclear material were constantly on the move around Iraq.

Once, while an UNSCOM team was investigating a weapons site the size of New York's Kennedy airport, a line of SSO trucks was trundling 200 metres in front of the inspectors without their realising it. When the inspectors left, the Iraqis buried the components again in the same place, knowing UNSCOM would not be back there in a hurry.

Even when they were caught, the Iraqis tried to bluff their way out. One inspector asked an Iraqi general for a document he knew was hidden in a safe. The general told him that particular file had been burned. Looking around the office that clearly showed no signs of a fire, the inspector enquired why nothing else seemed to have been touched. The general said the inferno had been confined to a single drawer in a metal filing cabinet.

When the UN team found a pile of documents later that morning which the Iraqis claimed they had never seen before, the inspector asked the general from where they had suddenly appeared. The general looked momentarily flustered and said he would find out.

As he left the room, the inspector turned to a colleague and said cynically, 'No doubt he will claim they fell off a truck.'

The UN team laughed.

Minutes later the general reappeared and said, 'I gather these documents fell off the back of a truck, but we can't say where.'

Frustrated by these games, UNSCOM decided to retaliate.

Rather than hunting for buried Scuds and digging up nuclear parts in the desert, Ritter was told to just find proof that the Iraqis were deceiving them and hanging on to equipment the Security Council had ordered Baghdad to destroy. The thinking was that when the Security Council was shown this evidence, it would lose patience with Saddam's continued defiance and agree to send back the bombers. This was the new kind of warfare being fought by the UN. But for reasons

Ritter couldn't fathom at the time, President Clinton refused to sanction new bombing raids.

The UNSCOM inspectors in Baghdad were demoralised. They kept providing the UN with proof that Saddam was violating his obligations and New York just told them to go back and find out some more. They did.

An Iraqi army doctor defected, bringing with him evidence of hideous experiments that Saddam had carried out in his western desert in 1995 to test new strains of biological toxins on prisoners. The doctor described how ninety-five political prisoners were taken from Abu Ghraib and bussed to the test site. There they were blindfolded and chained. For weeks they were injected and sprayed with a variety of germs.

Saddam chaired the meeting that sanctioned using these prisoners. His scientists showed him videos of what their inventions had done to animals. Saddam demanded film of what these toxins would do to humans.

Some of the prisoners died in seconds from the doses they were given. For others, death took longer and was more painful. By the experiment's end, all the prisoners had perished. The defector told UNSCOM the addresses where they could find proof of these human guinea pigs. He said there were prison records showing that the men were moved from Abu Ghraib. An ironic aspect of Saddam's regime was that while it claimed to be hiding nothing, it couldn't help listing every banned item it ever bought or built.

Ritter ordered simultaneous raids on the prison and the General Security Directorate – the secret police headquarters. The former Marine was the first through the door of the police building. He shouted at the senior officer who tried to block his path.

'I'm telling you right up front that you guys tested biological agents on humans. This is the organisation that did it and I want those responsible.'

Once again the Iraqis seemed to have known that the UNSCOM team was coming.

The officer explained that of course the inspectors could search the building but not now. Unfortunately, he said, this was the eve of an Islamic holiday and his staff were expected home for the traditional celebrations. Sensitive to the growing criticism of UNSCOM's heavy-handed approach, Ritter agreed to wait until the following morning.

On the drive back to his headquarters, Ritter wondered out loud how the Iraqis had yet again anticipated what was supposed to be a surprise inspection. He also sensed he had made a dreadful error by agreeing to the delay. His instincts proved right. By the time he got back to UNSCOM's offices at the Baghdad Monitoring and Verification Centre, his staff were running around in panic. The Iraqis had just announced that all inspections were suspended. Their justification was that UNSCOM was stuffed so full of British and American intelligence agents that it could no longer be described as impartial.

Saddam also complained that the inspectors were intruding into his private life by demanding to search every one of his palaces and those of his children.

It was Qusay who advised his father that this was the excuse he needed to finally get UNSCOM expelled. While the inspections were suspended in the first weeks of 1998, Qusay and General Mahmoud used the time to shift tons of equipment and documents to safer sites.

A resurgent Saddam was suddenly more visible. He was personally chairing meetings, addressing public gatherings and taking the salute at military parades rather than sending one of his many doubles to pose for the photo call.

Hussein Kamil's defection and the assassination attempt on Uday had wounded him. But six months on, he had wreaked his revenge on Kamil, Uday was recovering and, most important, Qusay was proving to be a worthy lieutenant. Indeed, Qusay had reorganised the country's security apparatus, was making key military decisions and was the new scourge of UNSCOM.

what dribbles of intelligence information he could glean to figure out how to pounce on the SSO operation and seize at least some of the five convoys as they made their monthly move to a new base. To do this Ritter would need hundreds of American Special Forces and blanket air cover.

The Pentagon was doubtful such a plan could work. The White House was concerned at the reaction in the Arab world, and beyond, to what amounted to another invasion of Iraq, so the proposal for a smash and grab raid was shelved.

The Iraqi press celebrated Ritter's removal by accusing him of being a CIA spy. A buoyant Saddam could not resist baiting the UN still further and after a summer of blocking inspections on various sites he once again threw out the remaining inspectors. In November, Clinton lost his patience and authorised air strikes.

Targets like the eight palaces that UNSCOM was never allowed to fully search were locked in to the computers on board the USS *Gettysburg* and the rest of the battle fleet in the Gulf. Crews donned their white-hooded, flash-proof suits as the Tomahawks were loaded. At their bases in Kuwait and Saudi Arabia, the British and American pilots were briefed on their missions. Some were strapped into their cockpits and the engines of their fighter aircraft had started to whine in their hardened shelters as they went through their final checklists. On that clear desert night of 14 November, the crews were less than fifteen minutes from take-off when Saddam backed down and invited UNSCOM back. The truce lasted less than a month.

Ritter had gone and his deputy, a former British army major, Chris Cobb Smith, also resigned. Smith told his UN bosses, 'We were getting closer, but when we needed support for the final push, it wasn't there.

'The British and American governments could not face the world seeing that their approach to Iraq was a farce. There is a belief that we can go anywhere and see anything according to our UN mandate. The implication was that a credible effort was being made to disarm Iraq. Well, that perception is just wrong. Before the war Saddam was a bully and was feared. Now, we've made a martyr in the Arab world and he won't be happy to stay at home. There's no easy solution. I fear the price we'll have to pay is a huge and horrible one.'

The Iraqis were now flagrantly mocking the UN. Vehicles which the French car-maker Renault had supplied as ambulances had been hijacked by Iraqi troops the minute they were in the country, painted khaki and used by the army.

Weary inspectors who made another dawn raid on a suspected weapons establishment found to their astonishment that the Iraqis were once again waiting for them. A handful of senior staff concluded there had to be a leak inside their operation. To unmask the mole they set a trap. At the next top-secret security meeting, attended only by senior team leaders, the mole hunters planted a false trail. Within hours this fake information went straight to the Iraqi high command and UNSCOM discovered its leak. A Russian inspector was regularly briefing his own country's diplomats and secretly recording some of UNSCOM's meetings. What he was telling Moscow, the Kremlin was passing on to Saddam.

The UNSCOM chief, Richard Butler, was instructed by the Security Council to evaluate whether the Iraqis had any intention of ever complying with their promises to disarm. On 9 December 1998 the Iraqis answered the question by refusing the inspectors access to a suspect site in Baghdad.

Within a week, Butler's damning report was completed. He detailed how Saddam was still deceiving the UN about his armoury, and how in UNSCOM's view that wouldn't change. When he read it, Kofi Annan threw up his hands in frustration, recognising how Saddam had lied to him as well as everybody else.

The suspicion was that an advance copy of the Butler report found its way to the White House, because within hours of the final draft President Clinton alerted his chiefs of staff that this time there would be no reprieve for Saddam.

New York ordered the weapons inspectors to pack up their belongings and leave Iraq on 16 December. Twelve hours after they flew out of Habaniya on their UN plane, cruise missiles landed on Baghdad in what Clinton called Operation Desert Fox.

In the half light of the operations room on the carrier USS *Enterprise*, Captain Marty Chanik watched the bank of computer screens tracking the missiles on their path to Iraq. The Americans had decided not to target any of Saddam's chemical and biological sites, fearing what would happen to ordinary Iraqis if a bomb split open a bunker hiding lethal toxins. Instead, US warships launched 325 Tomahawk missiles at military and security targets, including the Republican Guard barracks. From the skies, B52 bombers fired their cruise missiles into government buildings in the capital. Try as they might, they failed to hit the SSO convoys carrying the components for the 'beach ball'.

Strikes were launched at Saddam's many homes, like his palace at Jabal Makhul, north of Baghdad, which sprawls across sixteen square kilometres on the banks of the Tigris. UNSCOM thought Saddam might have been hiding a small nuclear reactor somewhere under the ninety buildings in the compound. There were bombing raids on his hometown of Tikrit, and jets targeted the palace where his favourite daughter, Hala, lived. She had no idea that nuclear components had been buried under her ornamental gardens and fountains.

In the White House Rose Garden, the president refused to say how long Operation Desert Fox would last. Nor would he say if Saddam Hussein was a target. His critics at home accused him of ordering the raids to distract attention away from efforts in Congress to impeach him and from accusations that the president had lied about his sexual dalliance with Monica Lewinsky.

Four RAF Tornadoes were in a holding pattern over the Iraqi border. They could see the lights of Baghdad ahead of them as they paused momentarily before commencing their bombing run. The crews were anxious. The first quartet of Tornado crews who completed their mission radioed back that the anti-aircraft fire was the heaviest they had yet encountered in four days of bombing. It was about this time that the politicians in London and Washington decided for their own reasons that Saddam's military machine had been punished enough.

A message was flashed to the four Tornado crews to abort their mission in mid-flight and immediately head for home. The squadron leader was confused. He asked for the message to be repeated, convinced he had misheard it the first time. His commanders at the Ali Al Salem base in Kuwait confirmed the order.

Outside the front door of 10 Downing Street, British Prime Minister Tony Blair stood by a Christmas tree and announced that Desert Fox was over. Minutes earlier, Bill Clinton had suddenly appeared on television in Washington to do the same. Both leaders insisted the operation was always meant to last only four days. The air crews knew differently. They had dozens more targets on their hit list, but the White House decided to end the raids. To present this as a victory, their generals were wheeled out to show video footage of laser-guided smart bombs destroying aircraft hangars where Saddam hid pilotless drones that could deliver deadly bacteria. The jets had flown 500 sorties against ninety-three targets.

Thirty sites connected to Saddam's weapons programme were hit time and again. Ten of the Republican Guard's head-quarters were pummelled every night of the campaign. More Tomahawk missiles were fired in three days than during the entire Gulf War. And, just as at the end of Desert Storm, no one could be sure what had been achieved.

Suddenly the politicians were talking about 'degrading' Saddam's weapons of mass destruction, not destroying them. Iraq's response was that UNSCOM would never be allowed back again. To prove that he had escaped again, Saddam appeared on television three times in as many days. He had no way of knowing that the CIA had been engaged in a new covert operation to hunt him down. For, earlier that year, in March 1998, the CIA had sent a secret mission into Iraq. In a desperate bid to find Saddam and the remnants of the 'beach ball', a CIA operative slipped into the country posing as a UN weapons inspector. While he was there the agent installed a highly sophisticated electronic eavesdropping device which would allow the agency to monitor the mobile telephones and the walkie-talkies used by the SSO. They could also listen in to Saddam's calls to trusted lieutenants like the SSO's General Mahmoud.

The excuse was that UNSCOM had some months before asked for technical assistance from the Pentagon to help inspectors listen in to the Iraqi security networks that operated on frequencies that they couldn't pick up. The CIA needed more than that. They wanted to track both Saddam and his SSO entourage.

This listening device picked up the Iraqi traffic, beaming it to a computer in Bahrain which filtered the conversations for trigger words like 'missile' or 'nuclear'. Even this didn't work. Saddam was guarded about what he said concerning the 'beach ball' and his own whereabouts. But the consolation for US intelligence was that its bug helped them locate a number of targets that they hit in Operation Desert Fox, including the homes of General Mahmoud and others in the SSO.

The revelation that the CIA had used UNSCOM as a cover further undermined the special commission's reputation. Richard Butler and the rest of his staff angrily denied that any of them had knowingly worked with any intelligence agency, the CIA included, but the damage had been done.

Despite eight years of intrusive inspections and repeated bombings, Saddam managed to retain more nuclear secrets than the West dare imagine.

Epilogue:

THE LAST SECRET

Squatting on his haunches under a palm tree, the spy could see the dust trails thrown up by the fast-moving convoy as it poured out of the hospital in Saddam City. The man, who was in his late thirties, had fought with the Republican Guard in the Gulf War and detested Saddam for the needless sacrifice of so many of his comrades. Now he watched the squad of police cars seal off both ends of the street minutes before a line of refrigerated trucks emerged at ridiculous speeds from the narrow entrance to the hospital.

A fellow officer had recruited him to an opposition group that had its headquarters in London. That morning the disaffected soldier was tipped off that units of the SSO would be on the move again with their cargo of crucial remnants of the 'beach ball' nuclear programme.

Casually dressed, the man stuffed his hands in his pockets and strolled slowly towards the road, memorising the number and size of the trucks in the procession. He didn't bother with the registration plates, knowing they changed daily. The information about the convoy had come from his cousin, who worked as a nuclear scientist. When the two had met at a street café earlier that day, the scientist had passed on details that nuclear components were being shifted from a basement room under the hospital canteen.

The spy was careful not to attract attention as he walked on to the post office to make a telephone call, ostensibly to a relative abroad. The coded conversation took less than three minutes. Within an hour his information was passed to the CIA.

The convoy was the proof that after eight years of UN inspections and Allied bombing raids, Saddam's nuclear operation was still alive. It was also a rebuke to those Western politicians who insisted that Saddam's most dangerous project had been shut down.

At Langley in Virginia and at MI6's new headquarters by London's Vauxhall Bridge, the intelligence services' desk officers responsible for Iraq are all too aware that the 'beach ball' can easily be resurrected. Secrets like this the CIA and MI6 do not wish to share with the public. They know Iraq's nuclear army of scientists has not been disbanded and that five separate sets of blueprints for the bomb are still missing. The spy from Baghdad also reminded them that vital components are still being shunted around Iraq.

All that Saddam is missing is the uranium explosive. The Gulf War wrecked his plans to convert the nuclear fuel stockpiled at the Tuwaitha complex. That uranium had been sent back to its suppliers, Russia and France. Even so, surveillance planes regularly scan the country, taking air and water samples, to make sure that Saddam has not managed to hide or acquire other weapons-grade material.

The intelligence agencies are convinced it will not be long before Saddam tries to buy what he covets most on the international black market. More than 2,000 tonnes of weapons-grade plutonium and uranium are stockpiled in military stores around the world. They are surplus to requirements and in many cases poorly protected. Impoverished scientists, soldiers and site managers at power plants, military barracks and dockyards in the former Soviet Union face the daily temptation of making millions by selling just a few kilograms of this material.

Some have tried. Ten officers at a former nuclear base in Belarus, including a general and two colonels, faced court martial in April 1998 for stealing. Six months later police in Turkey seized more than four kilograms of unprocessed uranium and six grams of plutonium smuggled from a military base in Kazakhstan. A group of eight men, including a colonel from the Kazakh army, tried to sell the material to undercover agents for $1 million cash.

Special nuclear tracking units have been set up in the major Western capitals to hunt down every gram of plutonium and highly enriched uranium. Even by their own accounting, the experts admit there is scope for pilferage and loss. They call it the 'MUF' factor – Material Unaccounted For. There is more of it than anyone is prepared to admit.

When technicians from Moscow were helping Iran revive its nuclear power plant at Bushehr on the Gulf, a truckload of critical parts and other 'unspecified materials' went missing. An indignant Russian minister insisted the truck had not been stolen from his government, but could not be so sure about what had happened to sensitive consignments handled by private companies involved in the same contract.

In an effort to police the black market, German security agents posing as wealthy middlemen staged a series of sting operations to see who was willing to sell nuclear material. Some Russian scientists took the bait. After months of secret meetings, the scientists smuggled slivers of both plutonium and enriched uranium for the Germans to test. The scientists promised they could get hold of enough material to make a bomb. Before they could make good on their boast, they were arrested and jailed with as little fuss as possible by their embarrassed government.

Such operations are seldom reported.

One that was involved a successful ambush by undercover MI6 agents to prevent a consignment of more than six kilograms of plutonium from falling into the hands of the Iraqis. The shipment was being smuggled through Eastern Europe and across the Bosporus into Turkey, from where it could be slipped across the border into Iraq. The agents tracked the nuclear pirates as they crossed into Bulgaria, where on a deserted stretch of road they boxed in the truck with a half-dozen vehicles in an operation that lasted a matter of seconds. The plutonium was recovered and no mention was made of what became of the smugglers.

Ever since Hussein Kamil defected and revealed the details of the 'beach ball', elaborate traps have been set to try to lure Saddam into buying the nuclear hardware he needs. One of these operations involved an Iraqi middleman who helped run Saddam's sanctions-busting. The businessman, who had addresses in Paris and Bonn, was negotiating to buy millions of dollars' worth of spare parts for Iraq's military helicopters.

He met his Russian contact in a hotel coffee shop in Amman. The former Soviet general was as good as his word in providing all the machinery needed for the helicopters. For several minutes, the two went through the details of how they would smuggle the spare parts across the border with Iran. Satisfied with his day's work, the Iraqi handed over the banker's draft drawn on an account in Switzerland. As the Russian slipped the paper into his attaché case and shook hands, he surprised the businessman by whispering that he also had access to enough uranium for one bomb. The Iraqi middleman was a skilled negotiator and showed no emotion as he listened to what the Russian had to offer.

As he drove back across the desert to Baghdad he wondered what to tell Saddam. That night the Iraqi president studied the proposal, looking up at the scientist and then back to the document. His son Qusay was the only other person in the room. As Saddam flicked the file to Qusay, he asked the businessman to describe again how an ex-Red Army soldier could get hold of so much uranium without anyone noticing it was missing. He sensed it was a trap and told his emissary to tell the Russian that Iraq had no interest in such matters.

This was not the first time Saddam believed his enemies had tried to tempt him.

Another offer came from a prominent Pakistani scientist who approached an Iraqi diplomat he knew. While they were walking through a park, the scientist offered to hand over the finished designs of a nuclear bomb. He also volunteered to work in Iraqi laboratories to show Saddam's scientists the quickest way to obtain weapons-grade uranium.

The Pakistani said he could buy the materials needed from Western Europe without attracting suspicion by using his own offshore company set up in Dubai. Suspecting it was another trick, the diplomat politely declined.

Saddam has no option but to use the black market or to steal, so such sting operations will continue. His own nuclear facilities have been destroyed or dismantled, and he is so closely watched there is little chance of his rebuilding enough to produce the weapons-grade uranium himself. The advanced warhead design centre of Al Atheer is flattened. The huge calutron magnets were stripped from Tarmiya and Al Faluja, buckled, buried deep in the desert and covered in concrete by weapons inspectors. All that remains of the $18 billion infra-structures that took nearly twenty years to build are a few harmless laboratories at the original nuclear research head-quarters at Tuwaitha.

The one priceless asset Saddam can still draw upon is his nuclear army. There remain 7,000 scientists of every disci-pline dispersed throughout Iraq. To keep their identities a secret from UN inspectors, Saddam sent them to work in schools, hospitals and anonymous factories. Many of them were employed restoring Iraq's electricity network, decimated during the Gulf War. Saddam made sure they continued to receive their generous salaries even though other Iraqis, including some in the government, were suffering.

Those in this nuclear army rash enough to desert risked execution. A handful did get away. What they took with them were the secrets that led the inspection teams to the core of Saddam's nuclear enterprise. They were the first to identify the hidden laboratories and sites like Al Atheer and Tarmiya and explain what was going on inside. They marked the burial sites in obscure government ministries where Saddam had concealed the documents naming his suppliers and all the scientists working on the bomb.

The CIA and other beneficiaries never asked what these defectors had done for Saddam, or how they escaped. The engineer who faked his own death by leaving a charred corpse inside his burnt-out car was not asked who the dead man was.

Western agencies cared only about preventing rogue governments from recruiting these scientists. The first six defectors embraced by the Americans were generously rewarded to tempt other colleagues to follow them. The one man they wanted above all was Dr Jaffar Dhia Jaffar. CIA agents who masqueraded as UN inspectors were told their priority was to contact Jaffar and offer him anything he wanted.

Relatives living abroad were courted. His half-English sons were approached, and colleagues who had worked with him in the West were contacted to persuade him to leave Iraq. Nothing worked.

Jaffar is so closely watched he knows it would be suicide to try to make a run for it. He is not even sure he wants to. No other job will ever match what he has now. Where else will he have the opportunity to play with the most powerful forces of nature? Jaffar sees himself as the father of the Iraqi bomb. Saddam may have paid for the nuclear programme, but Jaffar has made it work.

He justifies staying on by wrapping himself in the flag. As a born-again patriot, he believes Iraq cannot be denied what its enemies already possess. He has told close friends that he has spent too long and sacrificed too much to give up now. Many of his colleagues think the same and will not be lured away by any amount of money or other temptations. Fear also plays a part.

There has been only one nuclear refusenik. Hussein Shahristani alone suffered twelve years of torture and solitary confinement for refusing to collaborate on the bomb. At any time he could have been like Jaffar, exchanging his prison cell for a villa in the presidential compound and all the privileges that go with it. Since his escape he has continued to defy Saddam. From his sparsely furnished apartment in Tehran he searches for the hundreds of colleagues who have gone missing.

Jaffar and the others who have stayed behind know Saddam is playing the long game. He has seen off the international leaders who went to war with him and has outlasted their successors. All he cares about is his personal survival. He knows that if he stays in power the time will come when he can resurrect Tuwaitha and the dozens of other installations. Until then whatever money he has at his disposal is spent on preserving his security apparatus and the avaricious relatives who protect him.

Sanctions are estimated to have cut the state revenue by between $10 billion and $15 billion. But the deprivations of ordinary Iraqis who go hungry don't concern him. Hospitals kept short of vital supplies never dare point out that Uday Hussein smuggles pharmaceuticals back across the border to Jordan to be sold by street traders in Amman. Uday spends some of the profits on expensive medical equipment to help him recover from the injuries inflicted by his would-be assassins. Half his left calf was torn away and he wears an expensive body brace so he can stand unaided. He cannot bear to be seen as an invalid. He experiments with expensive treatments to cure his impotence, though intelligence reports from foreign doctors who have treated him suggest that none seems to work.

Uday is sufficiently recovered to take personal control of Iraq's extensive smuggling networks. He gets a handsome cut from everything sent across the border, from humanitarian aid to the smuggled luxuries that appear in the new boutiques opened in Mansour Street. He stole milk powder sent from Japan for Iraq's infants and sold it. When King Hussein of Jordan sent schoolbooks, Uday refused to distribute them simply because they carried the monarch's picture. His remedy was to tear out the offending photographs and then sell the texts.

Saddam has never cared if his son embezzles millions so long as there has been enough money for him to reshape his nuclear operation and his military machine.

Uday chose the old enemy, Iran, to help thwart the oil embargo by filling barges with diesel fuel at Basra and ordering the crews to hug the coastline so they were out of reach of the British and American warships. His contacts in Iran have been getting $100 a barrel and all they have had to do is switch the flags on the barges and doctor the paperwork before sailing into international waters.

Still Uday wanted more.

His teams of investigators in Jordan and European capitals still search for the millions of dollars that Hussein Kamil buried in offshore accounts and foreign businesses. When he finds those who helped Kamil, he has them murdered.

No one is immune. His own private secretary had his front teeth pulled out with pliers as punishment for negotiating a new cigarette-smuggling route. The next victim was the front man his father had chosen to run a network of dummy companies in Europe to handle Iraq's contraband. Sami Salih was making Saddam more than $1 million a day, but Uday accused him of being a spy so he could take over the lucrative syndicate himself.

After being jailed and tortured, both Uday's secretary and Salih managed to escape. Their defections provided the intelligence services with information about the sanctions-busting operations and, more important, how the regime was holding together.

Saddam has become ever more estranged from his clan. But he still has time for the young men he calls his 'two cubs', Uday and Qusay.

Uday is so obsessed with money that he has converted private rooms at his Baghdad high-rise headquarters into sealed vaults piled from floor to ceiling with bundles of banknotes. But no matter what he does, Uday remains convinced that he is still his father's choice to inherit the mantle of power. Saddam has always been intent on establishing a dynasty in Iraq and envisaged his eldest son as his natural successor. But Uday's erratic behaviour reluctantly persuaded Saddam to groom Qusay for this role.

A shorter, slightly hunched figure, Qusay is closer in looks to his father, with the hooded eyes, the same hairline and the neatly clipped moustache. Unlike his older brother, Qusay cultivated his father's approval with a shameless exhibition of flattery. When he was due to meet Saddam, Qusay made a point of discovering what his father was wearing that day. If Saddam chose to outfit himself in one of his military uniforms, Qusay would don his olive green fatigues. If the president appeared in one of his hand-stitched suits, his son would do the same.

At meetings it was Qusay who would wait for the moment to lead the choreographed applause for some utterance by the president.

He was careful to avoid his brother's mistakes. Not for him nights spent roaring around Baghdad in expensive cars and abducting any girl who took his fancy. He eschewed Uday's thirst for publicity and was unconcerned about how his brother was using his television stations and newspapers to promote his cause.

Qusay's increasing prominence owes much to his brother's infirmity as well as to Saddam's belief that Qusay is the more trustworthy of the cubs. Whatever his personal ambitions, Qusay has been careful not to presume too much. Even amongst his small circle of confidants he shuns any talk of succession, knowing his father does not appreciate shows of naked ambition, even from his sons.

Ever since they were children the younger cub has been wary of Uday. Qusay has seen his brother dispatch other rivals for his father's affections and anyone who threatens his world. Once when Qusay stopped his brother from entering his father's study the two stood toe to toe screaming at each other. The confrontation ended when Uday warned his brother that he would suffer the same fate as Hussein Kamil. It is a threat Qusay does not take lightly and he now does all he can to keep his distance from Uday.

Qusay earned sufficient trust to be given the job of protecting his father's secrets and his life. Saddam increasingly came to rely upon his younger son's political judgement, particularly about how to handle the weapons inspectors. It was Qusay who manoeuvred the last showdown that ended with UNSCOM's expulsion.

Father and son share the same concerns about how their enemies in the international community intend to police their weapons programmes, but they are confident these outsiders will never uncover all their secrets.

They have never taken seriously the International Atomic Energy Agency. They never had to, since, as one leading defector revealed, for a decade before the Gulf War Iraq had two IAEA inspectors on its payroll who gave Baghdad advance warning of the Agency's every move.

Having duped the IAEA and outwitted the UN weapons inspectors, Saddam and his son remain confident they can see off any investigators, whenever they choose.

The Iraqi president was contemptuous of America's floundering efforts to create a new monitoring agency. Clinton was nervous that for over a year after UNSCOM was thrown out, nobody had been inside Iraq to check on Saddam's clandestine efforts at rebuilding his weapons of mass destruction. Clinton lobbied friend and foe to find a substitute for UNSCOM. After months of wrangling the best the UN Security Council could come up with was a new name for an old idea, the even more clumsy sounding UNMOVIC – the United Nations Monitoring, Verification and Inspection Commission.

To get that far Clinton had to concede that as few as possible of the new inspectors would be recruited from America and that there would be a new 'College of Commissioners' to oversee the work to ensure the CIA could not infiltrate the commission as it had with UNSCOM. Critics pointed out that UNMOVIC would have even fewer powers to search for hidden weapons than its predecessor. How, they asked, could such an emasculated commission persuade Saddam to reveal his nuclear secrets?

Some in the White House urged the president to live with the impasse rather than sanction another sham inspection regime.

The thinking is that if Saddam refuses to cooperate then America can insist he remains an international pariah. Should the Iraqi leader manage to dupe another UN team and sanctions are lifted as part of the deal then the message to other rogue states is that cheats can prosper.

The uncomfortable truth for Clinton is that inspections cannot work unless they are backed by military muscle, and America's commander-in-chief is as reluctant as ever to give the order for more punitive air strikes or for US troops to move into Iraq.

Neighbouring powers, including Israel, concede it is impossible to stop Saddam from eventually acquiring the bomb so the strategy should be how to live with a nuclear Iraq on their doorstep.

Saddam was only too well aware that Clinton's lack of leadership meant even America's closest allies were losing heart for the continuing blockade against Iraq, with the French in particular anxious to lift sanctions so Paris could be the first to secure lucrative business contracts.

It was obvious as 1999 drew to a close that the UN sanctions regime was not working.

As oil prices rose to their highest level since the end of the Gulf War, Iraq was managing to illegally sell 70,000 barrels of refined crude a day. Satellites showed Iranian tankers loading the contraband from barges brought from the Basra refinery in southern Iraq. The West's naval blockade, by operating too far away, near the mouth of the Gulf, was powerless to stop Saddam from raking in $21 million in one month alone from this smuggling operation.

The State Department in Washington was forced to admit in December 1999 that Saddam was getting ever richer and to explain how the money was being spent to 'develop weapons of mass destruction and to line his family's pockets to build palaces and vacation villages for regime supporters. Yet again it demonstrates that Saddam Hussein puts his own interests ahead of those of the Iraqi people.'

Saddam no longer bothers to contradict such accusations.

Instead the state-controlled media are ordered to record elaborate stunts to bolster their leader's monstrous ego. Television cameras were there when thousands of stage-managed supporters gathered at a former airfield on the outskirts of Baghdad to cheer on construction workers, too many to count, who were working day and night to complete what would be the world's biggest mosque. The message was meant for his enemies in Washington – you claim Iraq is on its knees and yet I, Saddam Hussein, can still build something like this. It is a monument to Saddam's vanity, planned as the enduring symbol of his success in defying a decade of sanctions.

The CIA noticed that after years of hiding in bunkers to avoid US hit teams, Saddam was suddenly far more visible. It was a measure of the Iraqi dictator's confidence that he was willing to be seen more often in public. CIA agents studied video footage of cabinet meetings, public appearances and receptions for visiting dignitaries in Baghdad and were sure this was no stand-in.

Boastful as ever, he commissioned Iraq's most celebrated filmmakers to produce an 'epic' about his life. This would have a budget that Steven Spielberg would envy. Locations were carefully selected throughout Iraq. Lavish sets were built and every man in the country was invited to audition for the impossible role of playing Saddam. For some obscure reason it was to be entitled *Count Down . . . Count Up*.

No one was allowed to mention an earlier film hagiography called *The Long Days*, as the man who played Saddam in that eminently forgettable epic was his son-in-law who was later executed for treason.

Predictably, the president had the final say in casting the three who would play 'the young Saddam, the dashing teenage revolutionary and the beloved father of the Iraqi people'. He chose his own relatives for all three roles.

At the age of sixty-two Saddam reappeared for the annual race across the swollen waters of the Tigris. This event commemorates his version of his dramatic escape in 1959 after his involvement in the failed assassination plot against the then prime minister, when he claims to have swum the river despite a bullet in his thigh. He was shown on television in a black swimsuit and white cap emerging from the river after supposedly beating men half his age and defying anyone to claim that he had used a double to do the job for him.

To foster his image of invincibility among the Iraqi masses, Saddam changed the style of his attacks against America. Instead of railing against the evils of Washington, the tirades were directed more and more against Bill Clinton personally. There were endless editorials in the state-run press pillorying Clinton for his conduct over the Lewinsky affair and the troubles he was having with political opponents at home.

Saddam used the last months of the twentieth century to enhance his prestige at the expense of the American president by telling his people that the rest of the international community would take its cue from Baghdad and soon get rid of Clinton. He of course did not explain to his untutored masses that the American constitution required Clinton to step down at the end of his second term, in January 2001.

What mattered to Saddam was to survive yet another American president, not to mention every other foreign leader who had fought him in the Gulf War and who had predicted his downfall by the end of 1991. So contemptuous was he of Clinton that Saddam delivered a Christmas message on 25 December 1999 instructing 'All believers in Jesus Christ to face up to the criminal enemy of God', which is how he caricatured the American president.

By comparison the White House spin doctors had little to offer in the continuing propaganda war.

Any notion that America was intensifying support for the would-be leaders of a Baghdad coup seemed foolish when it was revealed that this ran to a handful of pointless military stunts. For example, in 1999 the Clinton administration invited four Iraqis – including what the White House boasted were two of Saddam's most valued army commanders – to visit the air force headquarters in Florida to be taught 'how to organise armed forces in an emerging state'. The Iraqi defectors did not bother to point out they knew how to do that. They had come to the Florida sunshine really to find out how the Clinton government was going to help them oust Saddam. They left without getting an answer.

Clinton has made much of how he persuaded Congress to sanction $97 million for the Iraqi opposition. But, critics have pointed out, this was a fraction of what the CIA and others had wasted on the Central American Sandinistas and the Afghan mujahedeen. And besides, the Clinton administration had yet to spend all but a few million of the allotted funds. One Iraqi dissident group who had set up a political base in south London complained that while they petitioned the White House for military hardware and aerial support for another planned coup, all they got was a delivery of second-hand filing cabinets, desks and fax machines plundered from a disused American army base.

The White House was less inclined to publicise the $1 billion a year that was being spent to garrison the Gulf. This did not include the cost of the almost daily air strikes against Iraqi defence installations. The Pentagon admitted that more than a thousand bombs had been dropped on Iraq in the year since Operation Desert Fox. Clinton claimed at the end of that flawed operation that Saddam was now 'contained in his box'. If that was the case then the Pentagon did not explain how it was that Iraq had challenged Allied warplanes more than 500 times since December 1998 with surface-to-air missiles, artillery fire and its own fighters.

Senior figures in the Pentagon also conceded they had little idea how Saddam was rebuilding his nuclear empire, since the satellites that once smothered Iraq were switched for much of the spring and summer of 1999 to spy on America's other bogeyman, Slobodan Milosevic. Clinton was so engrossed in the campaign to liberate Kosovo that he took his eye off what was happening in Baghdad.

If Clinton failed to stick to his agenda, Saddam kept to his. Aware he had slipped out of the headlines for a while, the Iraqi president took the opportunity to restock his arsenal.

His scientists had perfected designs for a much smaller nuclear device. This new version of the bomb was light enough to be carried by a Scud missile, and Saddam was believed to have nine of those rockets hidden in the desert.

His prototype bomb had weighed a tonne. This smaller, more efficient design was only about 1,300 pounds and measured just over two feet in diameter. The weapons inspectors were agreed this bomb would work. Chilling improvements had been made in creating the shock wave needed to squeeze the bomb's nuclear material enough to trigger the chain reaction. Intelligence agents believed that he had to have bought or stolen this technology from abroad.

The CIA and others also received a stream of evidence of how Saddam was continually trying to cheat the sanctions embargo to smuggle in vital components. Agents were puzzled at one order the Iraqis placed in Germany for some medical equipment that was exempt from the UN blockade. Baghdad wanted to buy a half-dozen lithotripters, which use shock waves to disintegrate kidney stones. These machines need high-precision electronic switches to trigger a huge burst of electricity. The puzzle was why Iraq ordered 120 of these switches, which experts agreed was about a hundred more than the kidney machines needed. The terrible beauty for Saddam was that these switches can also trigger the bomb.

Gary Milhollin of the Washington, DC–based think tank the Wisconsin Project revealed that the order was placed with the German electronics firm Siemens, which had worked with Saddam in the past. Siemens apparently passed the order onto its French supplier, Thomson-C.S.F. Unfortunately for Saddam, the French government was suspicious and stopped the sale. None of the companies involved would say if they knew whether Saddam has managed to get hold of these switches.

There was further disturbing evidence that ever more weapons-grade uranium was seeping onto the black market. The combined efforts of a number of intelligence agencies helped authorities retrieve a third of an ounce of the material at Bulgaria's borders in May 1999. Russian documents found in the cargo suggested where this material had originated. The smugglers had concealed the uranium sample in a lead container tucked inside a pump in a family sedan. What Western agents couldn't prove was that Saddam was the intended customer.

At home Saddam felt strong enough to engage in a new round of bloodletting against his enemies. Opposition groups reported mass executions of their followers. Saddam ordered the victims' bodies sent back to their families with a warning that they were not to hold funerals. He had his troops burn down the houses of jailed opponents. Their families were thrown onto the street. Relatives were advised not to offer them shelter.

There were the inevitable purges of his high command. A new army chief of staff was appointed in December 1999 –

General Ibrahim Abdul Sattar, who had commanded the Republican Guard and, equally important, was from Saddam's hometown of Tikrit. Most of the governors of Iraq's eighteen provinces were army commanders who had taken part in the Gulf War. This was, he announced, reward for their 'victory' in that conflict.

What was noticeable in the various changes among his military and party faithful was that the main beneficiary was almost always the younger of the cubs, Qusay.

Reports that Qusay had been appointed deputy commander of Iraq's armed forces, after his father, and given control of the troublesome north of the country, infuriated his older brother, Uday.

The crippled Uday's response was to insist various Iraqi ministers contact foreign newspapers, and those he ran himself, to deny such promotions for Qusay and stress how there was no power struggle between the brothers.

In truth, Qusay made sure the pair seldom met, concerned his jealous brother would make good the threat to kill him. Qusay refused to court publicity the way his brother did, as those closest to Saddam recognised there was no dispute over who was heir apparent.

Two days before Christmas 1999, Uday was furious to see the state-run news agency report how Saddam had honoured his most cherished lieutenants. First in line to be decorated with yet more medals was 'Fighter Qusay Hussein, supervisor of the Republican Guard', who was praised by Saddam for his 'heroic role in defending the honour of the great Iraq'. Uday was conspicuous by his absence at this ceremony; he was pointedly not among the seventeen in the receiving line for a medal.

Some that were present included officers whose job was protecting Saddam's nuclear cargoes on their endless journeys to new hiding places around Iraq.

UNSCOM's intrusion had meant that more of the regime were now aware of the nuclear programme that Saddam had treasured in secret for years.

While the inspectors had roamed across Iraq's deserts Saddam would spend hours with his younger son explaining to him why the bomb is so fundamental to their grip on power.

Qusay understands his father's thirst for power. If he succeeds, the pursuit of the bomb will continue with just as much vigour. This is true for the rest of those in the regime who now know the secrets of the 'beach ball'.

A measure of Qusay's eminence is the way senior ministers on the Revolutionary Command Council now defer to him, sensing that he might be the next Hussein to rule Iraq. He has already made his presence felt among the nuclear fraternity, and, sitting behind Hussein Kamil's former desk, he is the one whom Dr Jaffar Dhia Jaffar and the other key scientists see every morning.

The question Qusay asked at their first meeting, and has repeated ever since, faithfully reflects his father's obsession: 'Tell me, Dr Jaffar, when can you give us the beach ball?'

Iraq's Position in the Middle East

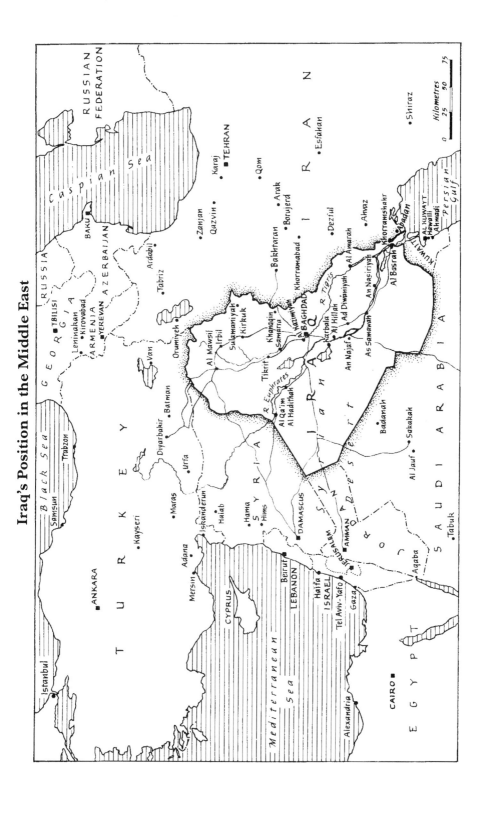

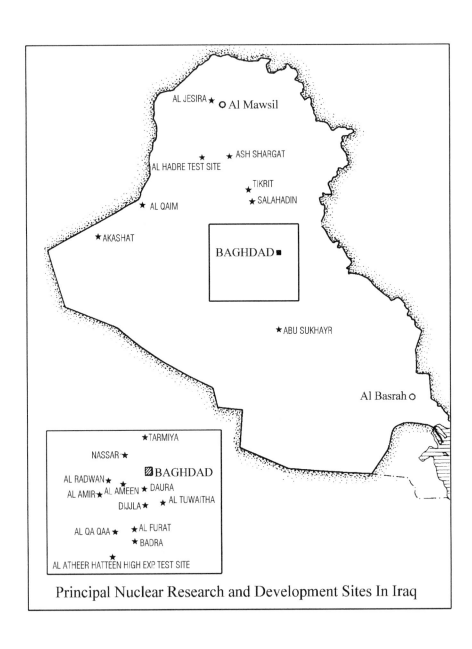

AL JESIRA ★ ○ Al Mawsil

★ ★ ASH SHARGAT
AL HADRE TEST SITE

TIKRIT
★
★ SALAHADIN

★ AL QAIM

★ AKASHAT

BAGHDAD ■

★ ABU SUKHAYR

Al Basrah ○

★ TARMIYA
NASSAR ★
AL RADWAN ★ ▨ BAGHDAD
AL AMIR ★ ★ AL AMEEN ★ DAURA
DIJJLA ★ ★ AL TUWAITHA
AL QA QAA ★ ★ AL FURAT
★ BADRA
★
AL ATHEER HATTEEN HIGH EXP. TEST SITE

Principal Nuclear Research and Development Sites In Iraq

INDEX